Falcon's Cry

Falcon's Cry

A Desert Storm Memoir

Major Michael Donnelly
USAF, Retired

With Denise Donnelly

Westport, Connecticut
London

Library of Congress Cataloging-in-Publication Data

Donnelly, Michael (Michael William)
　　Falcon's cry : a Desert Storm memoir / Michael Donnelly : with
　Denise Donnelly.
　　　p. cm.
　　ISBN 0–275–96462–0 (alk. paper)
　　　1. Donnelly, Michael (Michael William) 2. Persian Gulf War, 1991–
　Veterans–Medical care–United States. 3. Persian Gulf syndrome–
　Political aspects. 4. Persian Gulf War, 1991–Personal narratives,
　American. I. Donnelly, Denise. II. Title.
　DS79.744.M44D66　　1998
　956.7044′27–dc21　　　98–19471

British Library Cataloguing in Publication Data is available.

Library of Congress Catalog Card Number: 98–19471
ISBN: 0–275–96462–0

First published in 1998

Praeger Publishers, 88 Post Road West, Westport, CT 06881
An imprint of Greenwood Publishing Group, Inc.

Printed in the United States of America

∞™

The paper used in this book complies with the
Permanent Paper Standard issued by the National
Information Standards Organization (Z39.48–1984).

10 9 8 7 6 5 4 3 2 1

Copyright Acknowledgment

The authors and publisher wish to thank the following for excerpts from W. B. Yeats, "The
Second Coming ," reprinted with the permission of Scribner, a Division of Simon & Schus-
ter from *The Collected Works of W. B. Yeats*, Volume 1: *The Poems*, Revised and edited by
Richard J. Finneran. Copyright © 1924 by Macmillan Publishing Company, renewed
1952 by Bertha Georgie Yeats; and by permission of A. P. Watt Ltd., London, England.

for Erin, for Sean

that you may never go to war
that you may live lives blessed with peace
that you may never let the bitterness sting or the anger fester,
at least not forever
that truth may guide you
that you may learn that only love matters, in the end

Acknowledgments

Many people have helped us along this journey, some with their time, others with their constant prayers, and still others with quiet but unfailing solace at moments when we feared that we had forever lost our bearing on life's moral compass. We thank all of you. You know who you are.

We are most grateful to John DelVecchio, our guardian angel who always believed. Without his support, faith, and guidance, this book might never have found a publisher. We thank Father Charlie McCarthy, through whom we came to know Blessed Teresia de Benedicta; Dr. Ana-Maria Lobo; Pat and Ed Allen; Andrew Cederstrom, who found a title when no one else could; Lisa and Mike Hayes; Tim and Ana Donnelly; Jay and Steven Donnelly; Elizabeth Ellis, Keith Burris and Thane Grauel of the *Journal Inquirer*; Father Jerome Massimino; Barbara Kiernan for her beautiful, dignified article in *Fairfield Now*; Thomas Dennie Williams of *The Hartford Courant* for his tireless dedication to the cause of Gulf War veterans; Karen Gilson; Robert Adelman; William North, M.D.; Chuck and Nancy Schad; Joanna Duda; Speer Morgan; Charlotte Jerace; the pilots of the 10th Tactical Fighter Wing, whose history of the war proved invaluable; and all the great Air Force buddies Michael flew with over the years.

We are grateful to Congressmen Bernie Sanders and Christopher Shays for their diligent efforts to bring the truth to light, and to Laurie Bigelow, Susan Mancuso, Kathleen Terhune and Terry Wilson for their gentle care.

Special thanks to Charlie, Edie and Linda Regulbuto whose love and constancy have nourished us all; Ed Tyler and the heavenly music he created with the Manchester High School Roundtable Singers; Carol and Dick Kelley and all the fine members of the South Windsor Rotary Club, including Ralph Alexander, Andre Charbonneau, Fred DeFeo, Joel Gordon, Ralph Lawrence, John Mitchell, Larry Murphy, Roy Norman, Frank Pierce, Dan Seypura and Steve Wisneski; and all the wonderful people who donated time and materials in renovating Michael's house, including Ed and Jimmy Armstrong, Bob Balbi, Pete Black, John Chamberlain, Harold Condon, Steve Dalene, Mr. and Mrs. Davis, Tom Dzikiewicz, Joe Fradiani, Gordon Graham, Ed Haberbern, Hank Heath, Jimmy Heldmann, Mr. Paquett, Frank Payne, Martial Pelletier, Mike Salvator, Jay Wilson, David Wisneski and Mark Woodcock. We also would like to thank our editor Lynn Taylor for her grace and courage and the wonderful people at Greenwood Publishing.

Most of all, we thank our parents, Rae and Tom Donnelly. You have been fountains of strength and courage. At a time when most people are looking forward to a few years of well-deserved rest and pleasure, you looked back and saw a wasteland where once had bloomed the harvest of a lifetime's hard work. But you persevered, and your adamantine faith in the power of love sustains us all.

Some of the names and places have been changed for privacy reasons. Photo essay follows p. 110.

Preface

From Hahn Air Base in Germany, where he had been stationed since late 1989, Captain Michael Donnelly, an F-16 fighter pilot, deployed to Operation Desert Shield on December 28, 1990. His wife Susan, pregnant with their second child, had left Germany for the United States the day before, taking with her their three-year-old daughter, Erin.

At that same time, Michael's brother, Timothy, a lieutenant in the Marine Corps, was aboard the USS *Inchon* in the Mediterranean, awaiting the start of the land war, in which his battalion was scheduled to participate.

Michael Donnelly flew 44 successful combat missions during the Persian Gulf War. He and his brother, along with 700,000 other troops, returned to the United States as war heroes. When they came home, we festooned them in patriotic bunting. We welcomed them as the saviors of our bruised self-esteem. Politicians embraced them. Journalists celebrated them. Generals retired and launched lucrative careers from the honorable debris of the war they fought. They made us proud to be Americans again. Not since the end of World War II had we enjoyed such a powerful tide of national self-confidence.

We had won a war. We had got it right this time.

Today, Timothy Donnelly is healthy. Released from the Marines, he is newly married. His first child, a healthy baby girl, was born in August 1997.

Michael Donnelly, 39, is confined to a wheelchair. He suffers from ALS—amyotrophic lateral sclerosis—more commonly known as Lou Gehrig's disease. This in itself might be sad but unremarkable, if it weren't for the fact that at least 18 other Gulf War veterans, all men younger than 40, are also suffering from this same rare disease. Any neurologist worth his clinical independence from federal funding will tell you that 18 cases of ALS among a healthy population of 700,000 people under the age of 40 places this incidence at *more than 18 times the norm*. And these are only the cases we know about.

More than 110,000 Gulf War veterans are sick. Many are dying of rare and ravaging cancers, heart conditions, and neurological diseases of mysterious and unknown etiology. Their children are born with birth defects at a rate of two to ten times the norm, depending on whom you ask.

The media occasionally report on what seem to be the minor but life-altering conditions they say plague Gulf War veterans: skin disorders, digestive problems, persistent insomnia. The retired generals, once so concerned with claiming credit for the success of their perfect war, are suddenly invisible. And those who sent them into battle, the Pentagon, the White House and the CIA, pretend to help these brave young men and women. But George Orwell himself would be awed by the scale of deception and misinformation issuing from these bastions of prevarication in streams of stunning, institutionalized denial.

While the media dissemble, while the retired generals strut, while the bureaucrats buzz, real men and women suffer and die, their war wounds unacknowledged, their sacrifice ignored. Real families are devastated, left isolated, abandoned, betrayed.

The Gulf War never ended. We did not learn the true lessons of Vietnam. We did not get it right this time. We are getting it wrong—again.

This is Michael's story. Let us hope that, together with other truths, with other stories told in spite of all the forces that conspire to silence us, we can begin to reconstruct a house of truth that will shelter our children, so that they might someday get it right.

Part I

Air Warrior

A Prophecy Against Babylon

An oracle concerning the Desert by the Sea:
Like whirlwinds sweeping through the southland,
an invader comes from the desert,
from a land of terror.

A dire vision has been shown to me:
the traitor betrays, the looter takes loot.

At this my body is racked with pain,
pangs seize me, like those of a woman in labor;
I am staggered by what I hear,
I am bewildered by what I see.
My heart falters,
fear makes me tremble;
the twilight I longed for has become a horror to me.

Isaiah 21:1

Needle, Ball and Air Speed

November 1997

I taxi my P-51 Mustang up to the runway and line up for take-off. I push the power to 100% and accelerate down the runway. I'm 100 knots and I'm airborne. Gear and flaps up. I set my course at 178 degrees, 1,000 feet. Waypoint 1 at 1:15.

HQ reports a JU88 in sector 17,17.

Watch it! JU88 bandits at 12:00 low.

I'm in! Line up the pipper and let the bullets fly.

I fire. Got him!

I watch him go down in flames off my right wing, the black smoke of death spiraling through the heavy air.

Waypoint 2 course 388 degrees at 2,000 feet. ETA :023.

See ya!

Tally ho!

Enemy contact: JU88 at 10:00 low.

There are more bad guys. Longnose FW-190 at 1:00 low.

I roll in behind him. He turns hard right and I follow him into the turn. I'm in pursuit and he knows it. I got him on the run. Watch it, he's jinking left. Reverse course. He goes straight up and I pull lead in the vertical. Put the pipper out in front of his aircraft and pull the trigger. He flies through a storm of bullets, and they splash through the metal like it was water. Streaks of fire shoot out his engine. He flames down the long alley of sky and hits the earth in a tremendous explosion of red and black.

Splash one more! Whew!

Bombs burst on the flat green expanse that stretches out below me. The sky is a flat empty blue rimmed by a white horizon that opens endlessly in the distance. The sun hangs flaccid and yellow in my loud, echoing universe.

I reset the pipper range at 500 yards. There goes another P-51 and he's after a JU88. I watch as his bullets transform the JU88 into a fireball of molten metal. I swing out low and wide to the right.

HQ: Longnose FW-190 reported in sector 16,17.

I keep my altitude steady and low between 1,000 and 2,000 feet. I hang in the sky. The world swings beneath me, as if suspended from the underbelly of my P-51.

Up ahead, the air is peppered with enemy aircraft. I approach through a black cloud as anti-aircraft artillery rockets up to greet me. I barrel roll to avoid the incoming fire. It thunders around me, the thuds like the sound of a giant marching over the landscape, crushing everything under his boots. Now it echoes into the distance as I veer off to the west toward Waypoint 3.

I'm hit! I'm leaking oil! I gotta take her in! I take a look back off the tail at the plume of white smoke filming off behind me into the sky. Oil pressure is down to 50. I spot the runway and drop the gear. Climb up to take a look and get some altitude in case I flame out. I radio in.

"My crate's blowing smoke! This will be an emergency landing!"

I slow her down and so she won't use up the oil too fast, I shut the engine down. Now I'm flying without instruments. I'm on just needle, ball and air speed. Pressure still sinking. The cockpit is silent, but for the wind whistling through the canopy. If I close my eyes, I could be standing alone on a remote mountaintop surrounded by a winter wind and billows of innocent white clouds.

I'm at 500 feet, oil pressure at 30 and still falling. 200 feet. I take her in gently. The chirp of the tires on the tarmac tells me I'm in. I make it. This time. I roll her over to the hangar that ground control directs me to as the smoke still belches off my tail.

The engine is clacking at me now, complaining. She got me in, that's enough. I glide her in under the brown arch of the hangar and the smoke fills the space. I emergency egress. She shudders. As I run out of the hangar I look back at my plane. She's smoking like a cigar from hell. I'm outta here.

<Esc> <E> <Enter>

I'm back in the operations room for debriefing. Up on the board my results are posted. I'm getting pretty good at this.

Mission status: An outstanding victory!
Score: 10,190 points
Fjock1@aol.com logging off.

*   *   *

"Sue!" I call. I've been sitting here so long I forgot how badly I need to go. I wheel into the bathroom. Finally.

"Let's go, Michael," Sue says. "It's late. I'm tired." She helps me pee and then crawls back into bed. I wheel back out to my study. I'm not done tonight. Not yet.

The last few months I've been spending more time flying than maybe I should. Sitting here in my quiet suburban home, the night hums outside my windows as I skim over France and Germany, glide in on runways on distant Pacific islands, fire at North Koreans in air battles over the Yalu River. Outside, crickets creak in the weeds, the traffic on I-84 rushes to a million urgent destinations. Here in the house everyone is asleep but me. The kids are tucked in upstairs. Sue is in the bedroom next door, curled up against the light edging under our bedroom door.

I am surrounded by mementos of some other man's life, one that seems so distant and unreal to me now it's hard to believe I lived it. To my left hangs the framed lithograph of an F-16 in profile, signed by all the members of the 10th Tactical Fighter Squadron who flew during Desert Storm. Over the plane this title is printed: "Capt. Mike 'Big D' Donnelly. East of the Lakes Team Member. Fightin' Tenth Sabres." Their signatures form a kind of outline around the jet, each pilot signing with his given name and his call sign.

Next to that is a framed photograph of an OA-37 and an A-10 in mid-flight over Arizona. The chrome plaque reads: "Mike Donnelly, Nail 75, April 86–April 89."

Did I really live that life? Who remembers anymore? Now I realize that nothing is real but the present. This late night flying on America Online. It's what I have left.

On my computer, though, I fly all day and all night, my hand resting on the joystick, guiding the planes left and right over battlefields from Amiens to Guadalcanal, from Dresden to Midway. I fly online, with other anonymous air jocks. I fly alone, with my CD-ROM version of the game. But I fly. These days I can't really type fast enough to talk to the other pilots online, so I fly in cyberspace, as silent as outer space now. Just the simulated sound of a P-51, a Spitfire, or sometimes an ME109.

But I fly.

Some of the guys online are really good, but I can't keep up anymore. Now that I've lost the use of my fingers, I can't hit the keys. If only they knew who they were flying with. I was the real thing, not some online wannabe. A real air jock. Until I got sick.

*   *   *

January 1996

Another clear day in Wichita Falls, Texas. The air is cold and crisp, but not biting cold, not Texas cold, which can be awful when the wind blows down from the plains, and the wind blows a lot in this part of the world, squeezed up on the far shoulder of the state, just south of Oklahoma, just northwest of Dallas. Today it's calm. No winds. Good flying weather, if you were going to be flying.

For me, 2 January is not a flying day. It's the day I take the first step on a journey through medical nightmares I could not begin to imagine on this winter morning. It's my first visit to the flight surgeon. I'm here to tell him about the strange symptoms I've been experiencing for months, a trip I've postponed for as long as I could.

Any professional pilot will tell you that when you're sick, you don't tell and you surely don't show. The last thing you want is for someone to suspect you of being unhealthy. If you're unhealthy, you don't fly. And if you're a pilot, you want to fly. More than anything else, you want to fly.

Reluctantly, I make my way to the flight surgeon's office. I can no longer put this off, and I know the time has come to get this problem checked out.

For months I've been hiding my symptoms from my family, from my fellow pilots, from my commander, from myself. I just have the flu, I tell my wife. I'm a little under the weather, I tell myself. I'm getting old. At work I say nothing.

The truth is, I haven't felt like myself since the war. Ever since we got home, I've felt sluggish, not quite up to full strength. Not sick, but not really healthy. I've had three bouts of strep throat in a row. For months I felt as if was getting the flu, but it never blossomed. Then suddenly all the symptoms started to pick up speed and severity.

If I had to put a date on when things got really bad, I'd say all hell seemed to break loose last August, late summer of 1995. I'd just finished up my 50 pages of reading: that night's assignment—SALT II. I was studying for Air Command and Staff College, which I needed to pass if I wanted to get promoted. After 15 years in the Air Force, and since they'd promoted me to major, I figured I had myself a career. The next day, I was scheduled to teach my class all about nuclear missile treaties.

Running was my release from the stresses of studying just ahead of a class of ambitious pilots, from working full time and from all the joys of living on an air base in north central Texas. Late at night, when the Texas summer air cooled enough to make physical activity possible, I headed out around the base housing, pounding out my frustrations on the brown chert pavement.

It was in August, too, that mosquitoes invaded Wichita Falls like fighter pilots on a mission of vengeance. They descended in great black swarms, making it impossible to go outside at certain hours. Children came home covered in huge red welts, which they scratched bloody. Mothers painted their thin arms and legs with calamine lotion, so every time you saw a kid that summer, his limbs were thickened with a dried pinkish crust.

The base had started fogging against the invasion, a lonely orange tank truck circling the silent blocks of single story houses. Nights when I lay in bed, I watched the reflection of the yellow rotating light atop the truck as it circled the neighborhood, spraying. The odor seeped into our houses, an invisible invader, and permeated our clothes, our furniture, our lungs.

I remember clearly the first night I encountered the truck as I was out running. It passed me, exhaling its poison, and I tasted the malathion on my tongue, a sharp, bitter taste almost like citrus. I remember wondering vaguely, surely they wouldn't spray something poisonous or hazardous in the base housing area, where people live with their families, women and children, soldiers. But I dismissed the unformed thought, so certain was I that they would never do anything likely to harm us. We were the soldiers, the families that bred soldiers. We were theirs, after all.

Years later, the image of that truck, circling around me, wheezing into the darkness, would come to haunt me. In my head, I would relive that night over and over, turn off the road before the truck passed me, watch from the safety of my front step as its ghost drifted into inconsequence, allowing me and my life to follow a different arch, one that would have me babysitting my grandchildren.

But I did not turn away. Several nights I watched as the truck slowly swerved around me, my feet pounding out the message of disaster on that Texas pavement, my lungs taking in deep draughts of poison fog.

Immediately after, I began to have odd symptoms. I lay down at night to sleep, but could not for the strange rhythms that percussed my rib cage. Some nights I couldn't get to sleep for the pounding in my chest; some nights I awakened drenched in sweat, heart racing. When I ran, a blind spot blotted my vision, something I later learned is called a schetoma, and I got fatigued very quickly. I had to pee all the time and noticed that suddenly even one cup of coffee made me jittery and jumpy.

Within weeks, I started to have trouble concentrating on my work. I would read a paragraph and lose interest or look in wonderment at the page and not recall anything I had just read. It seemed like I constantly had the impulse to yawn, but couldn't complete the yawn, couldn't get my breath. I had to put my head down on my desk at work during the day, such was my fatigue. At night when I came home, I headed for the bedroom to lie down before dinner. Here I was, a former F-16 pilot, a flight instructor, in a profession that required only the healthiest of individuals, and I was taking naps at work and in the evening.

I also began to experience short-term memory lapses. I forgot simple checks in the airplane, if I had done them or should do them at all. Sitting in the cockpit with a student pilot up in front of me, my mind wandered, and I couldn't recall whether the student had completed his checklist or was just beginning. I went back on a physical fitness regime. I knew something was wrong, but what?

I try to explain this puzzling history to the flight surgeon.

"It was right after the fogging incidents," I explain, "that I started to notice the symptoms."

I can tell he doesn't make much of my fumbling efforts to piece this mystery together, to link events that to his mind must seem random, unconnected. But I continue all the same.

"So in November," I tell him, "I went on a hunting trip with my buddy Steve Kirik (call sign "Puck"), to his cabin in the Pennsylvania woods. I had no trouble hiking up and down those hills with a rifle and a backpack and my symptoms seemed to subside, to my great relief." I laugh and rub my thigh, which is twitching under my flight suit, the muscle still taut with the phantom of strength.

"Maybe it was the exercise and the clean air," I wonder aloud, not for the first time. "Maybe it was being away from work. I did notice, though, that I couldn't stand the cold very well, although I was well outfitted. Nobody else in our group had a problem with the cold, but for some reason I couldn't keep my feet warm. It wasn't until December that the weakness in my right leg started to give me problems."

As I tell him my story, the flight surgeon looks at me over his glasses. He's finished his examination by now, and we're sitting in his office.

"Well, Major Donnelly," he intones, mostly to the papers on his desk, "I'd say there's a good chance that what you're suffering from is a serious case of stress reaction. Stress can do funny things to the body. It can cause symptoms that you'd never think to relate to stress. Like heart palpitations and night sweats. Like fatigue and trouble concentrating."

He stops and glances up at me. Maybe he knows what I'm thinking.

In the Air Force, it's widely acknowledged that flight surgeons are low on the medical totem pole. No one expects much of them, either their superiors or the officers and staff they're assigned to treat. So his assessment so far doesn't impress me much. Mostly I'm wondering what stress he could be talking about.

I answer, trying to hide my skepticism.

"You know," I say, "I've been in situations a lot more stressful than teaching student pilots to barrel roll a T-38. I've been to war, for crying out loud, and I've never reacted like this. You're telling me my heart races at night from stress? Doesn't make much sense to me, doc."

"I know, I know," the doctor nods patiently, scratching his sparsely populated scalp. "But the thing about stress is that the reaction can be delayed. Maybe your body got you through the situation it had to deal with and saved its reaction for a time when it was safe to let down its guard. We see it in the military all the time. It's nothing new and nothing to be too worried about. We should get that leg checked, though."

I hesitate. Like almost everyone else, I have heard about the whole Gulf War illness situation, and I've been wondering if there is anything to it. I mean there we were, hundreds of thousands of us fighting a madman who promised to use the chemical and biological weapons we knew he had, and now lots of those people are sick and no one knows why. Seems like there might be something to it. I figure now is the time to ask if I am going to ask at all.

"I've been wondering, doc," I begin, deciding to take the chance, "I fought in the Gulf War."

As soon as I say these words, the man in front of me changes. His body stiffens, and I notice that he doesn't quite know where to put his eyes. He shifts in his leather chair. I continue, although I'm a little shaken.

"I've read about a lot of people who served in the war," I continue, "and now they're sick. I even know a few guys who are having problems, and they're not the types to make this kind of thing up. I'm just wondering if there might be any connection."

He glares at me as if he could stare me down. A flight surgeon stare down a fighter pilot? I don't think so, buddy. I stare back and hope he can't read the terror in my eyes.

"Major Donnelly," he says, his face a void, "study after study has been done and there is no conclusive evidence linking service in the Gulf to any illness."

He could be reading from a script, his delivery is so bad. It was a speech I was to hear so often that I began to wonder if there really isn't a script somewhere that they are all reading from. I can just picture the Air Force memo informing all Air Force hospitals, doctors and other providers to stress to anyone who asks that "there is no conclusive evidence linking service in the Gulf to any illness."

"I'm going to recommend that you see the base neurologist. He'll probably want to do some additional tests."

He stands. Conversation over.

*   *   *

February 1996

I didn't know it was my last flight.

It's Valentine's Day, and from the back seat of my T-38 I look out over the flat, bleak landscape of northern Texas. We're at 12,000 feet, and a hundred shades of brown define a grim terrain of mesquite and live oaks. The Red River (which is actually brown, like everything else out here) snakes through the countryside, carving out the border between Texas and Oklahoma. It also serves as the major navigating point for the student who sits up front, flying.

We've just finished trying out his contact maneuvers in protected airspace over deepest Texas. He's practiced barrel rolls and loops, Cuban eights and stalls, and we're on our way back to base to practice emergency landings and normal overhead landing patterns. Right now, he's following the river back. It's the easiest kind of flying he'll ever see, and I'm so far ahead of him in my mind that I don't really need to pay attention.

I allow my thoughts to drift as we sail through bursts of cumulonimbus. I peer out over the landscape, so relentlessly brown. In my mind, I am in Connecticut, in the green fields behind my parents' house, kicking up dust as I wander between rows of just ripe broadleaf tobacco. The Indians grew tobacco here, and because the Connecticut River floods these plains every spring, no one's been able to claim them for a shopping mall or condominium complex, like most of the rest of the town.

I check back in on my student. He's fine. Or fine enough. "Check six," I order, and watch as he peers around. "Carry on," I say, and then return to my thoughts.

Here I am, I tell myself, an instructor in a T-38, an expert pilot, and what am I doing? Daydreaming. But this is where I find myself spending a lot of my time these days—in my memories. I'm thinking about a day maybe twenty-five years ago, when I saw the world from the ground, not from the air, and dreamed some day of flying jets.

It was one of those long Sunday afternoons, and my Dad was looking for reasons to go visit the airplanes at the Bradley Air Museum. A former Marine helicopter pilot, he too had flying in his blood.

He took me to see the Thunderbirds, who happened to be flying T-38s, the same type of trainer plane in which I now sit. But at that demo, the idea of actually flying a T-38—or any other plane—was still a boyhood fantasy. I smile at the picture of myself that comes to me, as I stared up at the sky, spellbound.

Four jets soared in tight formation as they went through their maneuvers of loops and rolls, the drone loud, the smoke flaring out of their tails, scrolls of white writing their aerial twists and turns in the sky. Two solo aircraft flew upside down over the runway at low altitude and performed what seemed to me at the time death-defying acts. Now I know better, but to a boy of ten, it was magic.

After the air show, we went over to where the Thunderbirds had landed. The pilots were standing around, waiting to meet the audience, autographing whatever anybody could find to write on, so I had the chance to see the planes and the pilots up close. Leaning coolly against their jets in their form-fitting flight suits, aviator sunglasses cocked on their noses, silk scarves embroidered with the Thunderbird emblem looped around their necks, they were majestic, impressive, awesome, those pilots. I wanted to be one.

My student pulls a somewhat jerky imitation of a barrel roll, and I catch us and flatten us out, but flying isn't what's on my mind at the moment. I'm wondering what's wrong with my leg. It's been six weeks since I saw the flight surgeon, three weeks since I went to the base neurologist. My leg has gotten worse, and I know they're getting ready to send me to Wilford Hall, the Air Force medical center in San Antonio, for more tests.

The student finishes up his landing practice and takes her in. After debriefing, I'm sitting in my office shoveling the usual paperwork when the flight surgeon calls.

"Major Donnelly," he says in his best doctorly voice. He clears his throat like he's starting a speech.

"I'm calling to follow up on your visit to your flight surgeon. We've discussed your situation and agree that it's probably a good idea that you not fly until you've undergone further tests down at Wilford. I'm sure you'll agree this is for the best."

Of course I'll agree. What else can I do?

"Thanks, doc. I understand." I'm trying to keep my voice professional, to hide the fear that is welling up in my mouth and threatening to strangle my words. "When can I get down there?" I ask. I want it to be soon. I want it to be over. I want it to be never.

"We've set you up for some tests in early March. You'll be seeing Dr. Stevens. You'll be in good hands, Major Donnelly."

I'm not completely surprised by the call. After all, the week before, I had been heading off to fly with one of the guys who works for me in Standardization and Evaluation, where I'm chief. We were climbing up the ladder to get in the jet and all of a sudden my leg gave out. I fell down off the ladder and onto my back. Because I had my parachute pack on, I wasn't hurt. The guy I was with looked down at me and laughed. I laughed it off, too. But it scared me. It scared me bad.

I never flew again.

Part II

The Widening Gyre

Turning and turning in the widening gyre
The falcon cannot hear the falconer;
Things fall apart; the centre cannot hold;
Mere anarchy is loosed upon the world,
The blood-dimmed tide is loosed, and everywhere
The ceremony of innocence is drowned;
The best lack all conviction, while the worst
Are full of passionate intensity.

William Butler Yeats, *The Second Coming*

The Apple Wars

July 1970

"The Orchard Man!"

I grabbed my whoompy stick, plucked a green apple from the nearest branch and stuck it onto the end of my stick. It was a good six feet from my perch to the ground, but I leapt, bounced off the foot-high meadow grass, hit the ground running.

A whoompy stick is made by cutting the suckers off the bottom of an apple tree, suckers that grow long and straight and flexible. You shave off all the leaves, sharpen the skinny tip and impale an apple, preferably a green one because they're harder, on the end. By holding the thicker end of the stick and whipping it from behind your head, you can easily launch an apple for a hundred yards or more. There's no other sound in the world like an unripe Delicious whipping through the branches above your head as it strikes leaves and limbs, knocking down more fruit all around you.

"He's coming! He's coming! Run!"

Duane, the lookout, the youngest, had been caught off guard. He was streaking down the hill behind us, screaming, his black bangs flying. From his advance position, he was the closest to being caught by the dreaded Orchard Man. I saw the panic on his contorted face when I turned back to launch my apple, all the while running downhill, toward the woods.

Chris and Mike Coleman, Steven White, Barry Noonan and I crashed into the underbrush and slowed our pace. We felt safe here in the woods. The Orchard Man had never actually pursued anyone into the thicket beyond his trees, at least as far as we knew. Duane brought up the rear moments later, tears streaking down his blotchy cheeks.

"He had his gun! He had his gun! He almost shot me!" Duane cried. "I wanna go home!"

"Weenie, weenie," we ragged him. "Go ahead home, weenie." By now we were snorting that ugly kid laugh, the one that describes the pleasure a ten-year-old boy gets from someone else's suffering.

Head hanging, Duane moved off toward the sunlit street, dragging his sneakers through the dead leaves. We half-heartedly lobbed a few green apples after him, making sure not to hit him. We just wanted to scare him a little. He broke into a jog, his snotty sobs filtering back at us beneath the sound of crunching leaves.

The Orchard Man filled the role of bogeyman perfectly. A burly hulk with wide arms, an even wider stomach and grayish white hair that haloed his head like a spent Brillo pad. I only saw him up close when my mother took me to the Orchard Hill store to buy the apples, peaches or pears I stole from his trees.

The Orchard Man patrolled the orchard in his primer-grey Ford Econoline panel truck, its bumpers liberally decorated with peeling American flag stickers, a vehicle so miraculously decrepit it was a wonder it could still travel the bumpy, tree-laced hills. Despite its age, that Econoline was a stealth fighter, and it would appear out of nowhere with no advance warning.

Somehow, we always managed to escape, though, no matter how clever his approach. He didn't have the advantage we did: the sudden rush of adrenaline to a ten-year-old's heart. Or perhaps, I now think, he really didn't want to catch us, but only to scare us. Perhaps for him, as for us, it was sport. Or perhaps he was trying to protect us.

It was during a whoompy stick war in that orchard that I first experienced incoming fire. I never got hit, although I did hit Steven White in the balls one time. He let out an excruciating high-pitched wail that brought the battle temporarily to a halt. Together we rushed over to marvel with some detachment and a great deal of satisfying fascination at the fierce spasms on his crimson, tear-stained face.

I couldn't have known then how well the lessons of the apple wars would serve me years later, or how I would return to those memories as I sat in my wheelchair, just blocks from the same orchard, wondering what had happened to my life.

A wiry, blond-haired boy, I was all sinew, bangs and front teeth. The second of four, I was a child of the outdoors and the physical. I lived to run, to bike, to play Army and guns, and later, every sport imaginable. And from a young age, I was fascinated by the jets that streaked across our innocent suburban skies.

When I wasn't outside, whipping apples at my friends, or lying spread-eagle on the lawn watching the white contrails of jets line the sky, I spent hours holed away in our damp basement, gluing model airplanes, affixing the U.S. insignia just so. My bedroom ceiling was the site of a permanent mock dogfight—the air above my bed prickled with jet models and fighters of every description.

Our house had four bedrooms, two baths, a big backyard, redwood paneling inside and out, and a brand new flagpole from which my Dad daily unfurled the fabric of his twin allegiances: the flags of the United States and the United States Marine Corps. Just about every house in our neighborhood flew the U.S. flag, but no one else flew two flags, and no other kids were trained to salute the flag when their Dad got home each night.

Every evening when Dad climbed out of his green Rambler, weary from a long day at the office, we greeted him, my sisters and brother and I. Patriots in training, our small, thin bodies rigid, at attention, we lined the front steps and screamed the Marine Corps hymn, which we all knew by heart no later than age four.

"From the halls of Montezu-u-ma," we shouted, just a hint of the actual tune coloring our song, "To the shores of Tri-po-li. We will fight our country's ba-at-tles on the land, in the air and on the sea."

I don't know whether he really enjoyed these daily serenades, but he was the reason we felt so proud to be Americans, and he must have felt obliged to stand there and listen. After all, it was he who blared the song from the record player on weekends, who led us around the living room in our bare feet, marching out the beat of patriotism on the carpet.

Sing it through to the end we did, each evening, our hands raised to our foreheads in salute, our posture stiff and straight. Americans in training.

"First to fight for right and free-e-dom, and to keep our honor clean. We are proud to claim the ti-i-tle of United States Marine!"

The ending we screeched in a crescendo of pride and childish euphoria for the sheer thrill of shouting, knowing that Dad couldn't exactly tell us to shut up.

In those days, the woods behind Benson Drive were still woods, an unbroken 200 acres through which several weak streams threaded—half cousins of the Podunk River that curled through town. I actually grew up in Podunk, the real Podunk, named for the Indians who first inhabited these woods and riverbanks. A muddy swamp bordered the lower end of the woods, right where the neighborhood storm drain opened up—exactly kid size—from the hill above.

It was a perfect place to be a wild boy. Orchard on one side, woods on the other. Storm drains to crawl through and terrify yourself in the long deep echoes with stories your mother told you of kids drowning in flash floods because they climbed into storm drains after their mothers told them not to. Skunk cabbage to be pleasantly revulsed at. Adventure everywhere.

Chris Coleman was my best friend, and we did everything together, including everything our mothers feared but never really believed we did. Shorter and much stockier than I, Chris was the kind of friend every ten-year-old wants to have. A thrill-seeker, he was powerful for his age and afraid of nothing, not even the Orchard Man. Not even a storm drain in a flash flood. Our mothers would have been horrified to know half of the stunts we survived.

To our minds, the Krauts were everywhere, waiting to get us. In the K-Mart parking lot, or behind a tree when we played war. This may have been the '70s and World War II may have been receding quickly into the past, but that was the war that populated our imaginations. Maybe it was the constant television reminders—*Hogan's Heroes, The Great Escape, The Dirty Dozen*—or maybe it was simply a permanent cultural memory that we were acting out. Whatever the reason, the enemy was always the Krauts and the good guys were always the Americans, fighting for truth, justice and the American way.

*　　*　　*

Those were the days when sports were played in the season to which they belonged. Summer was baseball, fall was football and winter was basketball—indoors or out. Street hockey and bikes were summer, or any season, as long as the streets were passable.

Neighborhood team sports depended on the number of kids available to play. Every season saw its pick-up games, with the same players rearranging themselves in infinite combinations. When Sunday television had nothing to offer but pro football, when players like Joe Namath, Roman Gabriel, Roger Staubach and Bart Starr were famous, we were sliding in heroic tackles on icy streets, diving into snowbanks to make dramatic sideline catches, imagining ourselves the NFL heroes our fathers watched as they reclined on lime-green plaid couch sets in our family rooms, sipping Rheingold beer, snacking on cheese curls and adjusting the color on our new TV sets.

Every sport had its fantasy life on Benson Drive. The Herzogs, down the street and across, were the only ones with a driveway flat enough to make an outdoor basketball hoop worthwhile. With snow mounds framing our foreshortened court, Chris Coleman, Scott and Peter Herzog, Duane Gentile and I played pick-up games in our thin-soled Converse

Chuck Taylors. Our hands and feet were cold and numb, but in our minds we were hot. We were John Havlicek, Pete Marevich, Wilt Chamberlain.

Once, reality even came close to surpassing our dreams of glory.

*　　*　　*

"Hey batta, batta, batta! Hey batta batta!" The taunts flew from every direction. "You can't hit it! You can't hit it!"

"Keep up the chatter!" Coach Hauck called to the field, to the bleachers peopled with moms and dads, sisters and brothers.

It was the end of a long season of dusty elementary school ballfields and only the flag wilted in the summer heat. It was the last regular game, and the waning sunlight was taut with the tension of twelve-year-olds playing for their lives, of parents leaping from worn wooden bleachers to shout at umpires, strike-outs, bad calls. It was time to choose the All Stars.

It was the bottom of the ninth, score nine to eight, two outs. I was playing first base for the Cardinals, lunging left to right on legs lanky with new growth, playing off the bag, barely containing my delight. I knew we could win. I knew we *would* win.

"Come on, Dave! Strike him out! You can do it, Dave!"

Dave was in another world, a world where he heard neither my shouts of encouragement, nor the screams from the sidelines, nor his Dad the coach yelling at him to remember the plan.

Dave placed himself on the pinnacle of the pitcher's mound and stood as still as the sky at dusk. He fixed his stare on the catcher, and for that instant, time stopped. Just for that instant. Then he wound, recoiled, and shot a perfect fast ball directly across the plate.

"Stee-rike three!" the umpire called, punching the air to his right with his pudgy fist.

We had won the league championship.

The All Star Little League championship tournament spanned the month of August, when we played every other town in our district. At the end of August, we won the district championship. Then we played the other districts, and we won that championship, too.

We never found out for sure if we were the best in the state, although we believed it as if we really had played and won that final game against Wilton. Scheduling conflicts and rain delays made us co-state champions with Wilton that year.

Both teams traveled to New London for the regional playoffs. Wilton dropped out after the first game; we battled on through the third, which we lost in a heartbreaker—and on a bad call—to New Jersey.

The score was tied one all, and a New Jersey player called safe at first later went on to score the winning run. A picture printed in *The Journal Inquirer*, my hometown paper, showed the play at the decisive moment and settled all debate—that runner was out, no doubt about it.

By then it was too late. There is no instant replay in Little League, and we were out of the tournament. New Jersey may have won that game, but they went on to lose, and for that we were grateful.

South Windsor made us local heroes anyway, with a homecoming banquet at the country club. Not only did we bask in the sun of our proud parents' attentions, but Dave Smith, *The Journal Inquirer* sportswriter and photographer, attended the event. His enthusiastic coverage lives lodged between the yellowed pages of albums in at least 12 attics.

After a meal of rare roast beef, watery string beans, mashed potatoes with gravy and all the Coke we could drink, the celebrities spoke. This was before it occurred to famous athletes and their agents to charge a fee to perform such duties. Tony Conigliaro and Frankie Frisch earned only their meals and the respect of 12 young boys on a small town Little League All Star team.

After the speeches, Tony C and Frankie autographed baseballs and dinner programs. We had our pictures taken together, and made a big splash in the next day's edition.

Those pictures capture our looks of beaming pride and surprise. There we are with Tony Conigliaro and Frankie Frisch. There we are with the coaches. In the photos, I look directly at the camera, my eyes wide and expectant. "All-American heroes," the caption reads, "the Cardinals may not have won the regional Little League championship, but they've won the hearts of South Windsor."

That fall, we licked our wounds by joining a midget football team sponsored by the JayCees. Even our coach got in on the action. Maybe we just couldn't get enough of each other, or maybe it was just the pure physical pleasure of sport. Whatever it was, it drew us back together in mid-September.

I was chosen co-captain and quarterback. Lanky, 125 pounds at 12 years old, I was at the maximum weight limit to play, and I had to diet before each game, when both coaches and the referee showed up with an official doctor's office scale. Chris Coleman played guard and he too had to diet.

For us, a diet meant eating two Big Macs instead of three, and only a small order of french fries. No vanilla shakes or apple pies. Starvation wasn't an issue, nor was a lack of fuel in the form of carbohydrates. We burnt it all off so fast, it was a wonder we were able to keep growing at the same time.

We won every game we played that year. Our bright red jerseys, white football pants and blue helmets glowed in the autumn air, a stark contrast to the multicolored leaves that rimmed the fields. My sister, Lisa, and my girlfriend, Linda Regulbuto, were cheerleaders, rooting from the sidelines, their red, white and blue pom poms shaking, their ponytails flying, cheeks glowing in the cold autumn air.

We finally lost in the regional championships, by one touchdown to Tolland, a team of big, brutish boys in blue and gold, one of whom scored the winning touchdown in the fourth quarter; he ran the ball right up the middle, where I was linebacker. I missed the tackle, lost us the game.

Coach Hauck was great about it, but I was inconsolable. We were so close. I was almost the hero. It took me a long time to get over that play. And I never forgot how it felt to lose, to be so close, again, and again to lose.

I vowed I would win the next time opportunity placed such an occasion before me.

Chris Coleman finds me out on my back porch, my favorite place to settle at day's end. The sun is receding, the air is cooling, and off in Old Man Wells' pumpkin field, the birds are finishing their evening meal.

Chris settles back into an old blue-and-white mesh lawn chair, cracks open a soda. His he drinks straight from the can. I take mine from a straw when Chris holds it for me to drink. Occasionally, I have to remind him. "Hey, let me have a sip of that, will ya?"

Life is hard, and the years have weathered both of us. We sit, neither of us over 40, facing not each other but the darkening woods, enveloped by dusk, and talk about times gone by, the way I've seen old men do, sitting out on a porch somewhere, looking off into the fading evening, telling stories that move, vivid as cinema, before their eyes. We talk about the apple wars, about basketball courts ringed by snow, about how the town has changed.

Of all the kids of our childhood band, I'm the only one who left town and stayed left. Now I too am back, living just half a mile from the street where I grew up. The orchard where we played is smaller now, but its trees still bear fruit and the Orchard Hill store still sells apples and cider each fall. The old Orchard Man must be long dead. For all we know, a new generation of wild boys roams those hills, fighting whoompy stick wars and running from a bogeyman of their own imagining.

All those long ago summer twilights seem to accumulate here in my South Windsor backyard. They populate my dreams these days, as I sit, immobilized, and contemplate the dusk. Now, as then, the evening is riddled with mosquitoes and the oak and maple, birch and ash trees loom over me like distant, benevolent parents, whispering secrets in the dark.

The same trees, or their relatives, sheltered us back then, under their full swaying branches, while multitudes of fireflies swirled around us flaring in intermittent epiphanies. The trees speak to me now. When I was ten, I never noticed if the trees talked. I was too busy. Now I have plenty of time to listen, and they whisper secrets, words I can't quite make out. The fireflies still swirl, though their number is diminished—no one knows why—but their revelations burn just as brightly as they did all those years ago.

Wild Blue Yonder

September 1981

On 17 September, I was inducted into the Air Force in New Haven. I went with my hair still long, although I'd decided against wearing the ruby earring. I was one of two officer trainee candidates sworn in, along with 15 enlisted men.

The other officer trainee was Kevin Denton, a nervous little guy who had gotten his brown hair cut Marine style for the occasion. Kevin came up to my armpits at best, and he was clearly a man who had worked hard to compensate for his small stature. To complete the odd picture he presented, his head was much too small for his body. Kevin was also the type to wear his every feeling on his face. I could tell I would always know what peak or valley he was traveling at any moment, and that his excursions up and down his emotional geography would be frequent and extreme.

After the induction, the most unceremonious ceremony the military has to offer, they handed out the airline tickets and transport information. The induction center officer looked first at me, then at Kevin, and then back at me. Finally he handed the thick manila folder to Kevin, perhaps figuring Kevin was the more reliable of the two of us. Appearances can be deceiving, however, even when the man in question sports a Marine buzzcut.

Kevin's anxiety locked into high gear as soon as we loaded onto the bus headed to Kennedy Airport for the flight to San Antonio.

"What do you think I should do with the tickets?" he asked me. "What do you think I should say to the enlisted guys?" All the while he was nervously fumbling with the thick manila packet in his lap, his eyes unable to settle on a focus. "Have you ever flown before?" he continued. "I've never flown before."

What the hell was this guy doing in the Air Force? I wondered, not too quietly. He reminded me of an anxious little lap dog, just looking for reassurance and a pat on the head. Clearly the responsibility of the tickets was more than he could handle.

"Why don't you let me handle those?" I offered. The look of relief he shot me made me feel like a hero and a heel at the same time.

The flight was uneventful, but by the time we deplaned, loaded onto a bus and were driven to OTS—Officer Training School—at Medina Annex at Lackland, it was 0200 hours.

We were rushed upstairs into the barracks and pushed into rooms. Since Kevin and I had arrived together, we were roomed together. Fortunately, I was too exhausted to worry about what to do about Kevin. We fell asleep immediately, only to be awakened at 0500 hours. All of us OTS candidates, we assembled on the sidewalk in front of the barracks, where we lined up into columns in a sincere imitation of attention. With my long hair, I stood out among the crowd of clean-cut, sleepy young recruits.

As we marched to the chow hall for our first military breakfast, the Liberty Bell March—the opening song to Monty Python's Flying Circus —blasted from the loudspeakers. Hardly the music I expected to hear at OTS, my first day in the Air Force. I wondered if they knew what this music was, what it might mean to a boy of the seventies. I struggled to keep a straight face, march in time and pay attention, all to the tune of Monty Python. Every other step I wanted to break out into a John Cleese goosestep, first to the left, then to the right, then a rollicking pirouette. That probably would have ended my career right there.

I kept pace as best I could, but here we were in this military setting, I thought, and the soundtrack was farcical, not what I expected: John Philip Sousa, maybe, or the Wild Blue Yonder, but not the Monty Python march.

After breakfast, first stop was the base barber shop, where there was no choice of style or length. Only the three barbers who knew only one cut: the OTS buzz. When I realized I would win the center barber, the one with the eyes that looked in two different directions, I experienced a moment's regret. Before I could digest this feeling, however, he took the buzzer up in his hand and over it went. I watched my hair fall into the multicolored heap on the floor. The warm Texas air met my shaven scalp like a damp towel, and I heard the barber say, "Next."

OTS wasn't easy for me, because I couldn't make my socks smile in the classic Air Force sock fold, or pleat my underwear in perfect squares, or clean the theoretical dust out from under my metal frame bed. It seemed I always had enough demerits to keep me bed posted most weekends, a punishment that imprisoned me in my room, reading, writing letters, trying to figure out a way to sneak past the duty officer out front. But the marching and saluting and classroom work weren't that difficult, and I did well in those departments. I just never got enough sleep because of the pace.

Kevin remained my roommate, and while I had come to expect this, I felt a little bit like a kid at camp who has been assigned the dweeb as his buddy.

Kevin was struggling in OTS, too, but for different reasons. He lay awake nights before he was scheduled to be flight captain, the next day's march leader, and practiced his commands up at the ceiling.

"Good morning, Mr. Mess Checker, *sir*," Kevin intoned to the darkness. "Flight 910 reporting for chow."

The darkness never answered, but I lay in bed rolling my eyes. Kevin corrected himself. "No, *no*, that's not it. Good morning, Mr. Mess Checker, *sir*. Flight 910 reporting for 0830 chow. No, no, that's not it." On and on he droned into the night, until finally I could take it no more.

"Kevin, just go to sleep!" I screamed.

To his credit, I suppose, Kevin was undeterred.

"Forward, harch. Half right, harch. Flight halt!" he ordered the darkness.

Next morning, he was always so exhausted from lack of sleep and nerves, he messed up all day long. He made mistakes and then had to write demerits or redo his entire flight march. All in all, Kevin was totally miserable and probably would have preferred to be an enlisted man, to mesh in with the crowd rather than be put on the spot in OTS.

In the end, Kevin showed up at Vance Air Force Base for pilot training with me, but washed out not even halfway into the program.

I finished OTS on 29 January 1982. Surviving meant I could proceed to the next level of training, FSPOT ("FISHPOT"), flight school pilot officer training. I had gotten through the rigors of OTS, proved I could endure the rules, put up with the crap. Now the Air Force would test me to see if I had the soul of a pilot.

Sue and Dad came down for the ceremony, where the graduating group passed in parade review in our Class As, the Air Force full-dress uniform: Air Force sky-blue jackets, round, blue bus-driver hats finished with a black patent leather beak, highly polished black leather shoes, sky-blue trousers belted with a shiny chrome buckle, dark-blue necktie knotting up the collar of a light-blue shirt.

The day was hot, even for January in San Antonio, and a slight breeze ruffled the flags as four T-38s flew in salute overhead. The Air Force Band played marches. Most of the newly minted second lieutenants didn't seem to mind the heat. We were getting the hell out of OTS, and getting the hell out of Lackland, so a hot day in the sun in full dress uniform seemed like a fair enough bargain.

After the march in review, Dad and Sue each pinned shiny gold bars on my shoulders. I was a butter bar, a brand-new second lieutenant.

We spent the next few days sightseeing around San Antonio, and I enjoyed the thrill of not being locked in my room because I couldn't make my socks smile. Sue and Dad didn't care if my socks talked. They were just glad to see me.

*   *   *

February 1982

A crew of freshly minted second lieutenants, we were the Air Force equivalent of college freshmen, naïve, innocent, exploding with vitality and ignorance. Our flight instructors liked to tell us that we were "All velocity and no vector." Actually, they liked to bellow this at us. We translated it as "All balls, dick and no forehead." Either way, they were right. We had a lot of energy and no idea how to channel it.

We arrived at UPT—undergraduate pilot training—in our fresh Air Force haircuts, shiny Air Force-issue flight boots, brand-new flight suits. We were very proud of ourselves. At the same time, we wanted to look our best for our new flight instructors. We were freshmen, out to make our mark, and we knew that first impressions have a lasting impact. We all wanted to make a good first impression because we all intended to last.

UPT is where I met Mike Bready. He is the sort of guy people are naturally attracted to, the outgoing, sincere type, blessed with charm and a genuine and unique sense of humor, a trait that served him well during those early days of training.

At six feet, Breeds could be an imposing guy, but with a head topped by brown scraggly curls that contribute to his unruly appearance, he is more disarming than intimidating. He has dark, compassionate eyes that search to see if you understand what he understands, what the real script is all about.

Dark-skinned and hairy, Breeds always had trouble with the grooming aspect of pilot training. You could see the line on his neck where he stopped shaving, the hairs on his back sticking out around his collar like so much fur on a teddy bear in shirt and tie. He seemed naturally to fall into potentially troublesome situations but always survived and flourished, despite the rigors of UPT.

A green mountain boy from the Vermont Air National Guard, Breeds arrived at Vance Air Force Base in beautiful Enid, Oklahoma in preparation for a final assignment to fly F-4s back in Burlington, provided he could survive flight school. As much as we could, we helped each other through the rigors of that year: learning to fly, taking flight tests, passing check rides. But we had separate rooms at the BOQ—bachelors' officer quarters—so Breeds was on his own when it came to housekeeping.

Located directly next to the flight line were two one-story brick buildings side by side, like a grammar school and middle school on a single lot. One was the T-37 building, the other the T-38 building. Next to them stretched the flight line, 15 acres of tarmac, a huge parking ramp on which 70 T-37s and 50 T-38s posed neatly, all glistening white in the cold, clear Oklahoma winter.

Inside the T-37 building, a long, wide corridor stretched from end to end. Off it sprouted the doors to the individual training rooms, each labeled with a letter of the alphabet indicating separate groups of instructors and students in a different phase of training. The floors were brown and white checked linoleum tile onto which tracks of fluorescent lighting cast a greenish-yellow pall.

One morning, Breeds and I walked into the F flight briefing room for the first time. Just like everybody else, we had heard the rumors that F flight was the toughest flight of instructors on the line. We entered the brightly lit room as a group: there's safety in numbers, after all.

A group of very stern-looking instructors greeted us. From their faces, it was clear that their primary purpose in life and in this flight was to intimidate. Turns out it was not too difficult a job with the flock of wide-eyed would-be pilots that we were.

In the F flight room, the cinder block walls were earthen brown down below and cream white up top. Against this indelicately painted wainscoting background were etched the patches of previous classes and aircraft in various phases of flight. Some were landing or taking off on imaginary runways, others streaking across the sky in formation, and some twisting in acrobatic maneuvers.

Arranged neatly around the room stood nine, circa 1960 military-issue steel desks, what we called battleships. In front of each, three or four blue plastic and steel chairs were aligned. And at the front of the room a wooden podium painted with a giant white "F" for F flight commanded our attention. Behind this ranged an enormous green chalkboard on which the instructors sketched notes for study or test dates.

Our flight commander, one Major Chet Guerin, was a short, slight man with a narrow face and close-set eyes. He walked around with a pissed-off look on his face all the time, and I could never tell if that was for our benefit or if he was truly pissed off. It didn't matter much, since the result was the same. He kept his brown curly hair shorn close to his head and sometimes wore Air Force–issue silver metal frame eyeglasses. The retro fashion statement only added to his unpleasant appearance.

That first day, he told us that his job was to "wash you all out." Needless to say, this put the fear of God into us. Into me anyway, and Breeds, too. And Guerin nearly achieved his goal. By the end of the program, almost fifty percent of the class was gone, out with the rinse water. Most of them courtesy of the major's efforts.

In UPT, we first trained in the T-37, a twin engine, side-by-side two-seater jet built by Cessna back in the '50s and '60s. It's called the Tweet because of the loud, high-pitched whine it makes while idling on the ground.

They call the very first flight a student takes in a T-37 a dollar ride, because the new students give their instructors a dollar as a sort of payment for a fun time. In keeping with Air Force tradition, we decorated our dollars: drew F-16s on them, or cut out photos of faces and pasted them over Washington's face, or traced the outline of the pyramid with red magic marker. Anything that stood out and showed you made an effort, because the instructors displayed the best dollar tickets on their desks.

Just like in FSPOT school, a certain percentage of each class washes out of UPT due to air sickness, and if it was going to happen to you, it would likely happen on your dollar ride. We knew the instructors were placing bets on who of us would make it and who would not.

Since they were doing most of the flying, they asked us what maneuvers we wanted to see. "Do you just want to go up and fly around a little bit," they asked us, "or do you want to go do acro and spin?" Some of the students you could read like a book. The nervousness and anxiety playing on their faces instantly revealed their preference: get up and down as quickly as possible.

I was in the other group, the ones who looked like kids at a carnival, excited and anxious to get up in the air, wanting to see it all for the first time. Cuban-eight, barrel roll, clover leaf, loop, and spins: I had no idea what any of these were, but I was determined not to be intimidated.

That first ride was fun, although I couldn't tell up from down as we twisted and turned through the acro maneuvers. I experienced G forces dragging on my body for the first time and just being upside down in an airplane was thrill enough for me. As we entered the first spin, the instructor began quoting spin recovery procedures at me, but I didn't hear a word. I was staring out the front of the cockpit watching the world slowly peel by, losing all track of the parameters I was supposed to watch, like altitude, air speed and yaw direction.

Once we returned to the runway, I actually started to notice a little queasiness. That feeling of nausea when you're hot, but the cold sweat is rushing out of your body, your stomach turns inside out, and you just want to put the world on hold and lie down for a minute. It only lasted a short while, though. That was the only time I ever felt sick during or after a flight.

T-37 training was a very tough six months. One week you could be doing fine and the next week find yourself on special monitoring status within a ride of busting out of the program. It seemed as though the pressure never let up. Classroom academics, simulators and flights filled our days. We learned contact flying—take-offs, landings, acrobatics, spins, stalls—flying on instruments and in formation. Like getting a drink from a fire hose, you maybe got a little water in your mouth during UPT, but what you mostly got was wet.

There were different ways to go down the drain, and they had an acronym for every one of them: MOA (manifestation of apprehension), SIE (self-initiated elimination), and FTP (failure to perform).

For a while it seemed as though a student a week all of a sudden just wasn't there anymore. If someone's chair was empty one day, you knew why. Flush.

We spent a lot of time speculating about who would wash out and why, or who had and why. Usually you knew who was in trouble. Maybe he was on SMS—special monitoring status—not a good place to be. Or sometimes we were surprised when somebody who seemed to be doing well suddenly decided this was not the right career path and would SIE. It was a bumpy ride for everyone, even if you made it through.

Breeds and I did not go unscathed, either. We each had our share of busted check rides, trouble with Cuban-eights or instruments. But we survived. Somehow.

Mostly it was luck of the draw. A lot depended upon which instructor pilot you were assigned. I was lucky because I got a new guy named Matt Neuenswander, call sign "N+11." Still a second lieutenant himself, he was a little more sympathetic to the plight of us newbees. Although he worked us extremely hard, he did not ridicule or belittle us the way some of the other instructors did.

One poor student who suffered from this incessant ridicule was Eugene Ziwak. As we sat in the briefing room one day, Eugene's instructor pilot, a senior major, stood spinning a model of a T-37 slowly toward the floor like an out-of-control airplane. At the same time, he screamed at Eugene at the top of his lungs.

"What are you going to do, Zi-wak? You're out of control!" the major shouted. "You're going to crash, Zi-wak! What's the boldface procedure?"

The entire room became as quiet as a library on a Sunday morning. Students and instructors alike stared in any direction but Eugene's as his face bloomed a stunning crimson, and he struggled to maintain his composure and remember his procedures. "Sir, uh, sir, I uh," he stammered, his wet eyes bulging from his red face. He couldn't remember, what with the instructor spitting at him.

The instructor slammed the plane model into the floor, where it broke into several pieces that skidded across the room, hitting chair legs, other students' feet, that unmistakable sound of plastic skipping on tile, a sound that seemed to echo in the stillness.

"You're dead, Zi-wak!" The major still wasn't done with poor Eugene. "Your flight is cancelled today, Zi-wak. You don't know your procedures. And besides, you can't fly. You're dead!"

The rest of us suddenly found ourselves trying to look busy in the hope that we would not be the next victims of this tirade. We sat there, immobilized by fear, frantically trying to remember spin recovery procedures, hoping against hope that this instructor had satiated his need to belittle one of us. We relaxed again only when he left the room, a few minutes after the shaken Eugene, not to be seen for the rest of that day.

It wasn't all torture, though. We had our moments of levity, many of them provided by Breeds himself. Not that he set out to entertain us. It's just that he had a way of causing bizarre things to happen around him.

One fine Oklahoma day a state senator happened to be visiting Vance Air Force Base. The wing commander, eager to show this senator the best side of his operation, decided a trip through the students' BOQ would reflect positively on the base. Unbeknownst to Breeds, and unfortunately for the wing commander, he selected Breeds' room as the BOQ showpiece.

The wing commander couldn't have taken more than one step into that room before he quickly and wisely decided that a different room, any room, might be a better choice.

What that wing commander saw when he opened the door is left to the imagination. Not long after, however, a call came down to the flight line that Michael Bready was to report to the wing commander's office in full dress blues within the hour.

Breeds wasn't sure he was even in possession of full dress blues, so a few of us ran back to the Qs to help him throw together a uniform. I donated my tie and trousers. Others contributed jacket, shirt and hat. Breeds used his own shoes. The shine was less than blinding, but they would have to suffice. He wasn't about to take the shoes off of someone's feet. The shirt off someone's back, yes. But not the shoes. Even Breeds had his limits.

He reported to the wing commander and returned a short time later to announce that he would endure a room inspection the following day at precisely 1200 hours, presided over by the wing commander himself. Orders were that he should be standing at attention in "his" full dress blues when the appointed hour arrived if he wanted to continue his military career.

The ensuing 24 hours saw Breeds move at a pace unusual for one so low key. Epithets could be heard echoing up and down the corridors as all manner of garbage flew out his front door and into the paved yard below. Two weeks' worth of empty beer cans, newspapers, magazines, unwashed laundry, TV dinner trays and stray lampshades formed an uneven pile in the yard. Odd shoes, expended fire extinguishers, spent shell casings, plastic bags with moldy sandwiches, fast food containers, even his bloody wisdom teeth plugged into a stoppered test tube came flying out the door. Every once in a while bystanders would hear him exclaim, half in wonder, "Oh. *That's* where I put that." But it all went into the trash, such was Breeds' dedication to his commander and his career.

The next day, precisely at 1200 hours, the wing commander approached Second Lieutenant Michael Bready as he stood proudly at attention in front of his room. Wafting from the open door the strains of "Moon River" could be heard. A potted African violet, tilted at just the right angle to show off its perfect array of pastel blooms, decorated the coffee table. The contents of two entire cans of floral air freshener perfumed the room. In his drawers, his socks were smiling, his underwear lay flat and folded in perfect Air Force squares. Inside his closet, each hanger was spaced exactly one inch apart, all the clothes neatly pressed and folded over the hangers.

The wing commander was impressed enough to let Breeds continue his pilot training, but not before we placed him on "double secret" probation, our way of joking about the commander's uncanny ability to come up with new and bizarre punishments. It was then that we, his fellow would-be pilots, awarded him the wing commander's special Good Housekeeping seal of approval.

UPT was tough, and not just because of the surprise room inspections. We were far from home and enduring the test of our lives. Plus, for a couple of New England boys, Enid, Oklahoma can seem like the armpit of the earth. It is perfect for flying, though. A flat, low landscape, red clay soil punctuated every couple of miles with a collection of small buildings that hug the earth and allegedly constitute a town, population 300. Not even a fast food place. Just a gas station, maybe, a co-op silo for the local wheat or soy farmers, a few houses.

Out there, the land is divided into squares: north, south, east, west. Neat, orderly farm fields, plains. Almost like those early pioneers had it in mind to lay it all out so that the student pilots at Vance Air Force Base would be able to follow those section lines in their flight paths and find their way home.

During UPT, I had an alternating schedule by weeks: one early week, pre-dawn roll call for academics, flight line training, morning flights; one late week, noontime roll call, late afternoon flying. The thing I hated most about pilot training was getting up at 0400 hours for those pre-dawn rolls. But the thing I loved the most about flying was walking out on the flight line early in the morning, before the sun came up, when the air was still and a little cool, and the flight line wasn't yet loud with the noise of jet engines.

It was best to be the first one to start my engine and taxi out to take off before the sun rose, the smell of burning JP-4 jet fuel stinging my nostrils as I brought the airplane back to life. The jet engine was cold, unanimated steel and aluminum, waiting for me to stoke it into warm flying fire. Once I got up, took a few turns, it became part of me, alive.

As I soared up over the rooftops, left the red earth behind, I always thought of all the people back on the ground who were still asleep in their warm beds, missing this glorious sensation of entering the sunrise. I pitied them. They missed it. I didn't. As much as I hated getting up in the morning, I loved that solitary early morning flight into the rising sun.

Morning punctuality had never been my forte, though, and I had a long-standing reputation for oversleeping. I was late every day of my life for high school and college. But even at Fairfield University, a Jesuit school, very few of my professors managed to get really angry at me. Some kind of dumb luck got me off the hook every time, or maybe it was that awkward charm my mother always told me I have.

Major Guerin was not impressed with my awkward charm, however. I found him oddly immune to my crooked grin and sheepish explanations, and I continued to have problems until a single incident cured me forever.

One morning at Vance when I was living in an apartment complex off base, I got up late for a pre-dawn roll call. Once I managed to focus on the red digits glaring at me from my alarm clock, I leapt into action, sure that if I hurried, I'd make it to the base on time. I zipped up my flight suit, grabbed my flight boots, combed my hair, ran a razor over my face and raced out the door to my brand new Mazda RX-7 (black with red pinstripes, the perfect pilot's car—and perfect for speeding to the base at moments like this).

In my haste, I decided a short cut along the back roads of Enid would best serve my needs. At 70 mph and in total darkness, the narrow, two-lane pavement whizzed by, empty farm fields on either side of me.

I was making good progress until I spotted some flashing white lights up ahead. They looked sort of like the headlights of an oncoming car, but they were flashing in an unsteady, broken pattern. In the confusion of the early morning darkness, still bleary from sleep, I couldn't figure out what those lights were attached to or what they meant.

So on I sped.

As I started to near the lights, I became even more confused. They didn't seem to be moving closer to me, but they were still flashing. I flipped on my high beams, and in that instant, I felt a cold rush of shit to my heart. Suddenly, I realized what those lights meant.

My high beams illuminated the dull brown shape of freight cars rumbling over a railroad crossing. At the same moment, I remembered this was the point where the railroad tracks crossed the road. Those flashing lights were the headlights of the car parked on the other side of the crossing. The intermittent, irregular flashing transformed into the headlights of that car shining through the undercarriage of the passing train.

My early pilot training came in handy. I slammed on the nicely responsive Mazda RX-7 disc brakes, hit the clutch, started a skid and prayed the car would stop in time. I started to fish tail to the right, played into the skid, a trick I learned during those icy New England winters when I was late for East Catholic High, flying down the road in my mother's Oldsmobile Vista Cruiser station wagon.

I slid to a stop not two feet from the tracks, my car parallel to the train now and pointed in the same direction, so close I could feel the heat of the giant metal wheels on the rails, the sparks crackling in the dark.

I sat there in my Mazda RX-7, dwarfed and ignored by the speeding freight train, and I banged my steering wheel.

"Shit, shit, shit!" I hammered the words against the wheel. This was really going to make me late. No thought of my near brush with death in a fiery train crash crossed my mind. Instead, I cursed myself for choosing this short cut, straightened out the car, and after the train passed, a good three minutes later, I took off toward the base, my speed undiminished.

The fear of being late for morning roll call and incurring Major Guerin's wrath was ten times worse than the thought of being blown to bits under the wheels of a speeding freight train in deepest Oklahoma.

I arrived on time, but just. As they were closing the door to the briefing room, I strolled in, no sign of my recent encounter with tardiness—or death—on my face.

It wasn't until later, after I got to work and had a few extra minutes to breathe, that reality set in. I noticed I was shivering under my flight suit, that it was soaked with sweat, not just under my arms, but my whole body, like I had just taken a cold shower. In a way, I guess I had. I had almost died under that freight train.

All that day, I relived the moment just before the train came into focus in the dark. Like a bad dream that won't go away, I kept seeing myself from a distance, speeding down the road, peering into the night, and each time, terror rammed into me like I had hit that moving wall of steel.

The train incident cured me of tardiness. I started to set the alarm a half hour earlier. I disabled the snooze button. Lifelong pattern reversed. Problem solved.

That Major Guerin was one powerful guy. More powerful than a speeding locomotive, or at least meaner than one.

We worked harder during those weeks than I ever worked before. We also played harder. We needed to blow off steam, release some of the pressure that built up. There was that famous Hawaiian Luau, when we roasted a pig and Breeds kissed it on the lips. There were Fridays at the O Club, when we drank shots to the tune of oldies like "Witchy Woman" and "Rolling on the River."

It wasn't until near the end, when we entered formation flying, that we were pretty much assured we would graduate and progress to the T-38 phase. Even then, there was still the threat that you would later wash out of the program in T-38s.

But graduate we did, and when we moved to the T-38 building, we were just like the instructors said, all velocity. We were picking up in the vector department, though. We were becoming upperclassmen. Now we would fly the T-38, a faster jet, more like a fighter, where the instructor sits behind you instead of next to you. At last we would be supersonic—faster than the speed of sound—and fly a lot more solo rides, more formations. This was the part of the program those of us who wanted to fly fighters enjoyed the most.

For me, it all came together when I flew the T-38. I didn't exactly sail through, but things slowly got easier. The students who remained at this point were those who were probably going to make it. The instructors were more interested in teaching flying than intimidating us. The airplane was faster and more fun. And as we became more proficient, the instructors gave us more responsibility and leeway to start making decisions on our own. After all, we were on final approach to getting our wings. We were going to be Air Force pilots.

At the end of UPT, the instructors rate each trainee for a specific track: FAR (fighter, attack, reconnaissance); TTB (tanker, transport, bomber); and IP (undergraduate pilot training instructor pilot). Your track depended on how you did in pilot training. For the most part, the best guys go to FAR, the rest to TTB or IP.

Ritual called for us to wear our flight suits to assignment night down at the Officers' Club. In one of those ceremonies that seem to define the military, we were to learn our assignments in public, with all the other trainees and their spouses and girlfriends present. Not one of us knew for certain what his fate would be, but we all had our hopes, every one of us. Until they called your plane, though, you couldn't be certain. Such exposure called for significant lubrication, an activity in which we already had plenty of practice.

Once we were sufficiently prepared, the flight commander called each trainee's name. The pilot in question navigated to the front of the room, usually with some difficulty, and stood before the crowd to await his destiny. Once the commander had said a few words about the trainee in question, he flashed a slide of an airplane up on the wall, and this was how the student learned what plane he would be flying and what direction the rest of his life would take.

Finally, it was my turn.

"Lieutenant Donnelly," the commander boomed. I stood, made my way up front, my heart pounding so hard I felt dizzy, but my face a mask of nonchalance. Or so I hoped.

"Lieutenant Donnelly here managed to get through UPT with relatively few setbacks. Just the usual check-ride busts, Donnelly."

Here he looked me up and down, while the audience had a chance to issue the requisite guffaws. He was making me wait, I could tell, but I wasn't going to let on how much I wanted to know. I kept my eyes front and center, smiled a little, but not too much, like this wasn't such a big deal. I half wished I wasn't so drunk. In my heart I was praying. Praying for a fighter. Would I get it? Would they send me to FAR? Everything I had done, from signing on, to FSPOT, to UPT, had all been for this moment.

The flight commander made me wait one more second. The room got relatively quiet, although Breeds found the opportunity to call out to me. "Hey D!" he yelled. "What's it gonna be?" I smirked in his direction, but my armpits were drenched. He'd get his.

A picture flashed on the cement block wall. It was an A-10, the Warthog, a tank attack plane. My number one choice. I was going to FAR. I would be a fighter pilot.

A cheer went up from the crowd. "Hey, Big D! Way to go!" I hugged the flight commander, who bear hugged me back, slapped my back as I ran to hug Sue, Breeds, anyone else I could grab.

Breeds got his F-4 assignment, just as he had hoped, despite his grooming problems. I paid him back in kind when it was his turn to learn how he'd spend the rest of his life, but a happier night we never shared.

We had only a few more weeks together, training at Holloman Air Force Base in New Mexico. After a Saturday skiing the slopes of Sierra Blanca, Breeds and I found the bottom of a bottle of Johnny Walker. We talked then of our lives and how lucky we were. And then our paths parted.

I didn't see Breeds again until he was best man at my wedding. After that, he left the Air Force to fly L1011s for a major commercial airline. He lives in Vermont now with his wife and young daughter. Flies to Europe twice every other week. Spends the rest of his time at home, on his farm.

Amyotrophic lateral sclerosis. Gary Cooper as Lou Gehrig retiring from the Yankees with a brave speech before a sell-out crowd. "Today I consider myself the luckiest man on the face of the earth." A perfect Hollywood moment. Great speech, great man, heroic wife. Funny how you never see Gary/Lou suffering from the ravages of later-stage ALS. You only see him being brave.

ALS is a degenerative neurological disease, and there's nothing Hollywood or romantic about it. The disease is almost always fatal. But then again, so is life. It's just that with ALS, you have a better idea of when and how the end will come.

In my case, it first showed itself with that weakness in my right leg. In neurologist's lingo, I experienced massive loss of anterior horn cells of the spinal cord and motor cranial nerve nuclei in my lower brainstem. This is what caused the weakness and muscle atrophy (amyotrophy). Deterioration of the nerve sheath caused by degeneration in my motor cortex resulted in upper motor neuron symptoms (lateral sclerosis).

They seem to have all the names figured out. They know how ALS progresses. They just know next to nothing about what causes it or what to do about it.

Men are almost two times more likely than women to fall victim. Mean age of onset is 57 years, with two-thirds of patients falling between the ages of 50 and 70 at initial onset. I guess that makes me and all the other Gulf War vets with ALS lucky, since we hit this jackpot so young.

There is no treatment for ALS, and there is no cure. Current therapy consists of a daily dose of an experimental drug—"The first agent that extends tracheotomy-free survival in ALS patients!"—and the experimental drug myotrophin, with which my wife injects me twice a day, alternating left abdomen, right abdomen, left thigh, right thigh to reduce scarring, as well as regular visits from my occupational and physical therapists, Susan and Terry.

Neither drug is really thought to do much, but they are all there is right now. The physical therapy controls the rate of atrophy and minimizes edema in the extremities. Aside from this protocol of care, I am on my own.

And on my own, I ingest huge amounts of vitamins. Three thousand milligrams a day of vitamin C, 800 milligrams of vitamin E, both of which are thought to be especially important in protecting the outer nerve cell sheath. Sublingual B12 (what my mother calls "bilingual"), antioxidants, CoQ10 and other dietary supplements thought to slow the disease's progression. No one can say for sure if any of this will help, but I do it just in case. I do it to do something. I do it for my mother, who will not rest if I am not taking my vitamins.

I've read all their books and I know what they say will happen to me. I know in a way those medical textbook authors can never know, because I have felt myself progress through their neat disease "phases."

ALS is a disease for which there is no definitive test. It's diagnosis by exception, where over a period of months they rule out all the other possibilities, leaving you always hoping it will be something less grave, less horrific.

I have my information from the source, one of the most renowned ALS researchers in the country, Dr. Robert Brown at Massachusetts General Hospital. And while the astronomical incidence of ALS among Gulf War veterans indicates a rare cluster, which clearly intrigues him, he just doesn't know what to make of it or what to tell me.

When I first saw him in April 1996, Dr. Brown assured me that if there were a treatment, he would know about it. If there were a cure, he would be sure I got it. And even he wasn't sure I had ALS at the time. He tried to answer the questions I didn't want to ask. All he could say was that time would tell. But I kept getting worse, and all the neurologists kept pointing me in the direction I did not want to go. Down the path that Lou Gehrig walked before me.

Dr. Brown was right. Time told.

All the doctors, all the answers, the reading, the talking with the social worker at the UCONN ALS clinic, with Father Jerome, my priest, none of it really helps, as much as I love Father Jerome. When I was using a cane, I knew the walker was next. Even so, I honestly never expected to need it. I was glad for the walker when I finally started using it, though.

After that, I knew the wheelchair would come, that I would lose my hands and arms after I lost my legs, but I never really believed I would need a wheelchair. Now I'm in a wheelchair, and I sometimes wake up in the middle of the night and forget what I am. I try to move my hand to scratch my face, or shift onto my back, and it all comes rushing back to me in the lonely dark. The hand doesn't answer. The body doesn't move.

I try not think much about what happens next.

Velocity and Vector

August 1983

Tucson was the training base where anyone in the Air Force slated to fly the A-10 Warthog goes for an initial four-month course. There are no two-seat A-10s, so the very first time a pilot gets in one and takes off, it is solo all the way. Trial by fire. That first flight, when I lifted off the ground, raised the gear handle and the flaps, and looked down at the desert below, I thought, man, this is it. I have made it.

Pilots talk about situational awareness, and this is probably the hardest thing to teach someone, because a pilot must be born with it. Either you have it or you don't. SA is an intuitive awareness of where you are and what's happening around you.

A pilot receives many inputs when flying—visual inputs, seat-of-the pants inputs you pick up from the aircraft movement, audio inputs from radio transmissions—and they all come together to create for the pilot an awareness of the environment. Pilots with good situational awareness tend to excel in flying, especially flying fighter jets. I learned in Tucson that I was blessed with superb situational awareness, even for a fledgling fighter pilot.

It all felt natural to me. I was top gun in my class and a distinguished graduate from the program. An ace fighter pilot in the making. I had never been happier in my life because I was where I was supposed to be, doing what I was meant to do. I couldn't believe they were paying me money to fly these jets, to test myself against the forces of air and altitude.

From Tucson, we were sent to Alexandria, Louisiana, a foreign country for Susan and me. It was the land that time may have forgotten but the Air Force still remembered often enough to station young pilots there. We went to England Air Force Base, where I joined the 23rd Tactical Fighter Wing, 75th Tactical Fighter Squadron, a unit with roots in the American Volunteer Group that flew the P-40 in China during World War II. I was familiar with the P-40 because I used to assemble models of it when I was a kid, paint tiger teeth on its nose.

In Alexandria, I had two days to find a place for us to live before I had to go to TDY—temporary duty at Fairchild Air Force Base near Tacoma, Washington for land survival training—and leave Sue on her own for three weeks.

At Fairchild, the first two weeks of land training involved classroom instruction on survival techniques and prisoner of war resistance, followed by a week in the woods. I was in my element. We sampled the local flora and fauna, learned that ants taste like citrus, but without that nasty rind, that grasshoppers are a little tougher and you have to make sure you tear the hind legs off or they get stuck in your throat.

But most of the time we ate like kings. We found an orchard bursting with ripe Macintoshes, with which we filled our rucksacks for our time in the woods. I managed to sneak some hooks and fishing line in with me and we dined on roasted apples and brook trout, cooked over an open fire in the forest. I also taught my fellow students how to make whoompy sticks, and we fought our very own whoompy stick wars in that Washington orchard, 30 grown men flinging ripe apples at each other, laughing at the top of our lungs.

This was grown-up army, though, and it became even more real when we were locked up in the simulated POW camp. Here we learned resistance to torture, interrogation and other techniques of abuse, all as close to the real thing as possible. There was no Chinese water torture and we all came home with our fingernails, but it was real enough to be no fun at all. It was something to be endured and to learn from. Not something anyone would want to volunteer to repeat and only some of which I am free to recount.

At one point, they took us from cells where they had locked us up in a kind of solitary confinement, put canvas bags over our heads and lined us up single file, right hands on the shoulder of the next prisoner, left hands behind our backs. We were marched outside and into another building, and even though I knew this wasn't for real, it was hard not to be a little afraid. I had no control at all, no sense of what would come next. I could feel my senses sharpen, like an animal waiting for a blow, ready to flinch.

When we got to our destination, wherever that was, we were made to stand with our backs against a wall while people around us screamed insults, pushed us around.

"You asshole!" A disembodied voice met my ear. "Up against the wall!" The voice had an arm, and I felt a shove toward the left, where the wall hit my shoulder, hard.

The arm forced me down, into a sitting position, shoved me forward into "the box," a space so small that my knees came up to frame my cheeks as I felt my head being pushed down, a door meeting the curve of my taut spine. But before the guard could close the door, so tight was the space, he had to shove me deeper into the box, pushing the door up hard against my back. Instantly, my legs fell asleep, my knees began to ache from all of my sports injuries. It was hard to breathe with the canvas bag over my head, and I had to talk myself, silently, into calmness.

And then the music started, loud, martial music, filled with the sound of marching boots and shouted commands. Not exactly mood music. But then again, I guess it was. I fought the panic that rose like bile in my throat, the tears that welled up behind my eyes, my lids pressed shut under the itching canvas.

I counted to ten, slowly, tried to get my breath to keep pace with my counting, to slow my heart rate. Tried to find something else to occupy my mind, to keep from shouting "Let me out!" I thought of Sue, the smooth slope of skin where her ear meets her neck, of home, of family vacations on Martha's Vineyard, that first time we rented a Boston Whaler and Dad let me pilot it around Edgartown Harbor, the warm July sun, the cool ocean breeze.

I have no idea how long they kept us there. It could have been two or three hours, it could have been ten minutes. I lost all track of time. But when they opened the door behind me, I thought I would spring out like a Jack-in-the-box. All I wanted to do was lie on the sweet earth and straighten the legs I could no longer feel.

"Stand against the wall!" The voice again. A nice thought, but impossible, since my legs were not about to obey any commands at the moment, and since I couldn't see to find the wall at any rate. I felt four hands grab me under the shoulders, force me to my feet, slam me against the wall, where I managed to stay upright to endure the minutes of verbal abuse that followed, my legs stinging as the blood returned to every capillary. The hands then dragged me off to a room, where I learned firsthand what the enemy could do to make a person talk.

The party wasn't over yet. Not by a long shot. But that's the part I can't ever repeat, the part of the story I am sworn not to tell.

Then it was back to Alexandria and life in a new jet, a new squadron.

A pilot's first day in any squadron is fraught with nervous anticipation, excitement, anxiety, all these things, all at once. The pilot is brand new to the airplane, to the squadron. He doesn't know anyone, has never been in a fighter squadron before. He doesn't know how he'll be, how the other pilots will be, whether he'll measure up, even if he was top gun out in Tucson and his reputation preceded him.

The squadron commander in Alexandria was Bob Coleman, a model teacher, patient, strict but fair, and a true leader. He let it be known from the start what was expected of new second lieutenants in his squadron. There would be no slackers. Everyone would work hard and pull his weight. Mistakes were acceptable and expected, but crimes would be punished to the maximum. It was all right to screw up, learn from it and go on. But if a pilot broke a rule on purpose—if he flew too low, for example—he could say goodbye to his Warthog.

The squadron was filled with guys with names like Bluto and Pinto, Muck, Butter and Crawdaddy, Bullet and Sweez. For a time, I became "FNA" for my favorite expression: fuckin' A. Fitting in was not a problem.

The flying was challenging, and the weather was always exciting in central Louisiana. But there was plenty of open air space, miles of thickly wooded bayous and farm fields sliced by winding, muddy rivers and streams. The Red River runs right through Alexandria—the very same Red River that would later guide my final flights in Texas—and it served as our major navigational tool.

The work was hard, and it wasn't all just flying around the lush Louisiana landscape. Young lieutenants spend hours locked away in the squadron safe, studying deployment, employment and threat information. Our mission was to deploy to Europe in case the Soviets ever invaded from the east. The Warthog was supposed to destroy the legions of Soviet tanks expected to rise over the Fulda Gap, so we had to study plans to fight that war, as well as visual recognition of tanks and battlefield equipment and threats—surface-to-air missiles (SAMs) and anti-aircraft artillery.

We had to commit all this to memory, because once the balloon goes up, it's too late to start studying. And skimming over the earth at 100 feet or less into the jaws of enemy fire is no time to be struggling to recall the range of a certain SAM that has suddenly appeared on your radar warning receiver. Besides, hell hath no fury like a squadron commander when a pilot messes up in front of the mission-ready certification board.

That was the life. It was tough, but we loved it. When you go to work and never know if you'll make it home at night, when accidents happen every day that kill your friends and shatter your soul, esprit de corps and morale are genuine, not empty slogans bandied about by generals and politicians in a false attempt to pump people up or win public support.

In Louisiana, I was far from home and yet I felt all was right with the world. I knew I was born to fly, to rouse my buddies at midnight and cruise the deepest Louisiana backwoods till dawn, to live and work surrounded by people equally dedicated to finding the place where life intersects death and together to walk the razor's edge.

*   *   *

May 1984

For the wedding, we returned home to South Windsor. By 1984, Sue and I had been together for three years, and she had followed me through our early days of new love into the hard times, from UPT in Oklahoma to Alexandria, Louisiana. I figured if she could handle living in the places we had lived and still find her way, then she was meant to be an Air Force pilot's wife. My wife.

On a clear, hot Saturday, we gathered at St. Francis Church, an early 20th century sandstone structure with peaked stained glass windows and a high, vaulted ceiling.

Sue wore an ankle-length, old-fashioned wedding dress, with sheer, lacy sleeves and a high neck of transparent lace, a white silk ribbon at her slim waist, her long, brown hair piled atop her head in a crown of baby's breath and white roses.

I wore my Air Force mess dress: white waistcoat, silver epaulets, aviator's wings pinned to my breast, black pants with a satin side stripe, a black bow tie, white shirt, black cummerbund.

The wedding went off without a hitch, but for the altar boy who passed out in the middle of the Mass, an event captured for perpetuity on the wedding video. His slow but final decline to the marble floor, the rush of three of us at once to gather him up—my Dad, Tim, and me—and carry him out into the air. Mike Bready, ever the gentleman even if he wasn't very neat, stepped up to the altar to stand next to Sue during the commotion, so she wouldn't be left alone at the altar.

The reception took place at the Ellington Ridge Country Club, where 13 years before we had celebrated that Little League state championship. As the day came to a close, the sun set in a red glow off the balcony, where Susan and I danced our wedding waltz. I was a proud man and happy, surrounded by my family and friends, in love with my beautiful wife, and ready to take off, after a short wedding trip to Martha's Vineyard, for Alexandria and another two years of flying the A-10.

January 1987

We left Alexandria in 1986, headed for Tucson to fly the OA-37. Only a year after I got there, though, the Air Force decided to retire the aging fleet of FAC aircraft we had been flying and replace them with the OA-10. It was basically the same aircraft as the A-10, but instead of actually attacking, the OA-10 orbited over the battlefield and coordinated with the ground Army FACs to direct other incoming aircraft laden with bombs, rockets, missiles and anything else they could think to load.

When I became an instructor, I used to tell my students that a successful Air Force career required a pilot to recognize three key facts: timing is everything; it's nice to be lucky; and there is no justice. While I would later come to understand the truth of my own words, in Tucson, luck and timing conspired to my benefit. I was chosen to be among the first to fly the OA-10. As part of this new unit, a few of us were called upon to participate in the TD and E—tactics, development and evaluation—for the OA-10. We were like test pilots, assigned with defining how the OA-10 would best be put to use in combat.

New jets were not all I was testing back in 1987. I may have been an Air Force fighter pilot, but at home I was a new father, a task I saw as at least as challenging, even if it wasn't life threatening.

Erin Caitlyn Donnelly came into the world on April 10, 1987. From the day she was born, we could tell she was a special child. All parents think that about their children, but Erin truly was. She demanded a lot of attention, walked by nine months, and spoke in full sentences at one year. Erin never ceased to amaze and captivate us and anyone else who met her.

Witnessing the birth of your child is an unparalleled event, even for a fighter pilot used to thrills and spills. I had not been looking forward to attending the birth, since I've never been good around hospitals or blood—my own or anyone else's. But I wasn't going to miss this. Not if I could remain conscious, anyway. I reserved a spot in the corner of the delivery room and told the attending physician not to be surprised if he suddenly saw me in the prone position taking an impromptu nap when things started to happen. This all from a man who never once got airsick. Fortunately, that corner of the delivery room went unused, and I was conscious for Erin's entry into the world.

I don't think I breathed once during her birth, so it's a miracle I didn't pass out. I watched, transfixed, my eyes glazed with love and wonder as her tiny, perfect body met the air. This was all the joy I'd ever need, I decided in that moment. Her first wail of bafflement stung my heart. I was born to protect her, to guide her.

After that, life changed for Susan and me, the way it always does for new parents. There were endless days and nights when it seemed that all we did was alternate between feeding Erin and changing her diapers.

While I may have become a family man by night, by day I still lived the wild life that pilots are reputed to live. There was a memorable Arizona seafood feast, for one. My buddy Jimbo McCauley and I were tasked to take a commercial flight to Massachusetts to pick up two additional OA-10s slated to join the squadron. Rather than waste a rare trip to New England, we decided to supply the squadron with some much-needed Atlantic-style nutrition. We posted signs advertising "Operation Crustacean, order your pound and a quarter fresh Maine lobster, $7.75 each."

When we took off, we had orders and cash for 75 lobsters, and an arrangement to pick up our cargo the next day. We billeted overnight at my parents' house, and my Dad drove us up to Massachusetts the next morning. The lobsters came conveniently packed in ice, newspaper and cartons just big enough to fit into the cargo pods. And off we took, a flying clambake.

Turns out Jimbo's fuel tank wasn't feeding properly, so we had to make an unscheduled stop in Ohio, but the technicians were unable to repair the jet. With 75 lobsters kicking around our cargo pods, we didn't want to waste too much time. We pressed on after refueling. Jimbo had to stop again in New Mexico to refuel again, but I continued on with my precious load. I radioed ahead so that the ground crew could get the water boiling, the butter melted, the corn shucked. No need to ice the beer: the beer was always iced in Arizona.

When I landed, we pulled 40 terrified but living lobsters from my cargo pod, where they had all escaped from their wrappings and were scuttling around the darkened hold, looking for an outlet, which we were happy to provide. By the time Jimbo landed, an hour or so later, a full-scale Arizona "clambake" was underway.

He found us up to our elbows in melted butter. We cracked the red shells of those New England lobsters, sucked out the sweet, nutty flesh like we hadn't eaten in weeks. Jimbo pulled his usual beer stunt, spraying foam across the picnic tables, but no one seemed to mind. We were having too much fun.

Operation Crustacean was a singular affair, but there were many other spectacles and adventures: Mexican meals the likes of which no easterner could imagine, with fresh white corn tortillas overflowing with seared beef, pulled chicken, refried beans, and the greatest salsa on the face of the earth. There were desert dirt bike rallies, squadron quail hunts and pig roasts. There was the squadron softball team, which almost won the base championship. There were the late nights playing the game of Crud.

We were together—Sandy Sandkamp, Nutter Nutterfield, Hoss Barker, Zuke Zaccaro, Willy Culbertson, Miller Lite, Jimbo McCauley and Bud Jackson—a team of men, a family of pilots, skating across the mountain tops, seeing life from the pilot's God's eye view of the world. We lived the high life, and we tested the limits of speed, both in the air and on the ground. We were lucky, and we knew it.

*   *   *

April 1989

The airlines were hiring, and a lot of pilots were choosing to separate from the Air Force in favor of a civilian aviation career. The decision weighed on me, too, because either way, I figured I'd get to keep flying.

It was more a question of what I'd be flying, where I'd be living, and how much control I would have over my own life. But when the Air Force initiated the pilot bonus program and offered me an additional $12,000 a year, the choice became even tougher. When they said I could fly an F-16 anywhere I wanted, the decision made itself. F-16 or L-1011. Put that question to a fighter pilot and there's no contest. The Air Force it would be.

In April we sold our house in Tucson and packed what belongings we needed into our Mazda 626 and a beat-up old Mazda pick-up truck—we had traded in the RX-7 and sold the Pinto long ago. We loaded Erin, now two and very talkative, into the 626 and started the long drive to Tampa, where I would undergo F-16 training at McDill Air Force Base before we went off to Hahn Air Base in Germany, where our belongings would meet us.

The drive took us three days, what with stopping for Erin, coordinating our route in our separate vehicles, and resting up for the next stint. It took us east through Arizona's Saguaro desert and the arid southern New Mexico wasteland to Alamogordo. From there we went on to San Antonio, then across to Mobile, and on to Tampa the next day. We arrived at McDill on a Saturday afternoon, all three of us ready to arrive, but no one more than Sue and I, who had taken turns driving with Erin.

The F-16 class was made up of trained F-16 pilots who had been out of the cockpit for a while, one of whom was "Woody" Wood—later to become my operations officer in the Gulf War—Air Force and Navy aggressor pilots, and one other ex-Warthog driver. I got the distinct impression most of the others didn't think I would do very well in the F-16 course, because the A-10 is a much slower aircraft and the missions vary so much between the A-10 and the F-16.

I set out to prove them wrong.

Almost all of the other pilots had flown with radar before. But the A-10 didn't have radar, so this was totally new to me. When I started to dig through the manual to try to figure out how radar works, I found myself more than a little overwhelmed by all the technical jargon.

When we covered radar in academics, the instructor started to blow through the material like we all knew exactly what he was talking about—range-while-search, track-while-scan, air-combat mode. Trouble was, it was all new to me. When I dared to raise my hand to ask a question, a round of moans rose from my classmates. It was quickly decided that I and the other A-10 pilot would stay after class for individualized radar training, freeing the other students from the torture of having to sit through remedial instruction.

I struggled through those three months. The classroom work was difficult enough, with all the new aircraft systems, emergency procedures, and operations manuals to memorize. But the first time I got in that aircraft—after I had been in Tampa for about three weeks—I knew I was going to fly the F-16 and love it.

After just 30 hours of training we set off for Germany. Sue and I decided it would be best for me to go over first and find a place to live before she followed with Erin. The Air Force could not guarantee us a house, and base housing had a six-month waiting list. Such was our introduction to moving overseas with the United States Air Force. Here are your tickets. Have a nice life.

I arrived in August 1989, and immediately checked into my new unit, the 10th Tactical Fighter Squadron. As for housing, it took me a while, but I finally found a place in the small village of Peterswald, about a half hour from the base. We lived there for six months, until another pilot moved back to the U.S. and vacated a beautiful A-frame house in the rural village of Reich. We rented a U-Haul and moved in.

Hahn was notorious for the worst weather of any U.S. base in the world. For a pilot with only 30 hours in the F-16, this presented some unique challenges, unlike any other flying difficulties I had ever encountered.

The F-16's missions included air-to-air combat, air-to-ground combat and nuclear strike. We had to fly check-out missions in each of these areas, followed by check rides, where a standardization and evaluation pilot accompanied us to be sure we were flying according to procedure.

There was also a certification briefing in which the pilot sat before the wing leadership and briefed his own plan of attack, followed by an intense question and answer period. They were probing for weak points in the pilot's knowledge about aircraft systems, threat systems, attack planning, anything that could make the pilot a liability rather than an asset in a war. I got the check-out phase behind me in short order and found myself mission-ready in an F-16 by November 1989.

In December, the 10th Tactical Fighter Squadron deployed to Incirlik Air Base in Turkey, for one month of WTD—weapons, training, deployment. This was a semiannual stint to give pilots some air time, since we were socked in at Hahn most of each winter.

While we regretted leaving our families behind, we looked forward to the wide open flying environment offered only in places like Turkey, with its broad turquoise skies, still air, numerous mountain ranges undisturbed by turbulent weather, and radar-free airspace. All this allowed us to improve our combat training and get in the most training time per flight, while cutting down on non-mission essential flying time.

It was a pilot's dream. Just the squadron and the airplanes in an exotic foreign country with nothing to do but eat, sleep and drink flying.

Together, the squadrons flew what we called surges—around 60-70 sorties a day. If we were scheduled for air-to-air combat training, we were assigned a clean jet with no external wing tanks or bomb racks. A clean jet meant we could fly three sorties in a row and never have to get out of the jet or shut down.

Everyone wanted that schedule every day. You would take off, head about 20 miles away from the base and start your air-to-air engagement. It was full out, balls-to-the-wall after-burner and high Gs. You could fight all the way down to minimum fuel, glide in to land, go through the hot pit to tank up, take off and do it all over again. Each sortie was about 30 to 40 minutes.

Or else you would be scheduled to practice weapons delivery training, in which case the jet was equipped with external fuel tanks and bomb racks loaded with BDUs—bomb dummy units. When these detonated, they sent up a plume of smoke that let you score your hits.

Bombing flights usually entailed a long, low-level flight that snaked through the mountains and valleys. You could see entire towns where electricity was still a fantasy, and in many places, houses without glass in the windows. I remember peering down out of the cockpit once and seeing a caravan of people walking, picking their way along a mountain trail, their mules loaded with their possessions.

There I was, skimming a few hundred feet over the earth at 480 knots—about 800 feet per second. I must have looked to them like an apparition from the future as I whizzed over their heads. To me they certainly looked like they had just landed from their own time machine, their dark, hungry faces staring up at me in wonder.

When we weren't flying, we had no problem finding ways to amuse ourselves, shopping on Market Alley for carpets, gold, brass, Turkish towels and other trinkets for home. We bargained en masse with the merchants, who always loved to see a passel of American fighter pilots plying the alley.

Sometimes, we'd go to places like John Belushi's or the Falcon, or the BP gas station, which doubled as a restaurant where we ate kebobs and sampled Effies, the local beer, a brew too heavy on formaldehyde and too light on hops for more delicate palates. Fortunately, we didn't suffer from delicate palates.

To celebrate Christmas, we threw a party in the quad, a square open space set in the middle of a low-hung row of buildings that housed pilots from all over Europe. A truly shabby set of quarters, especially by Air Force standards. Gaping holes in the walls were not uncommon. Some showers consisted only of a pipe sticking out of the wall and pointed slightly floor-ward. And more than one very well-used window air conditioner fried itself or short circuited at least once each sultry night.

That Christmas celebration started out innocently enough. Budweiser in abundance, piles of pistachio nuts—a local favorite—and a barbecue with hamburgers and hot dogs procured from the base commissary. At some point, we sent the wood fairies—the lowly lieutenants—out to scrounge wood for a bonfire.

Before long, the barbecue pit in the center of the quad was overflowing with the wood fairies' successful fuel search. Older members of the squadron, myself included, were busy affixing the four ends of rubber surgical tube high up on the shelter supports. Several more members, whose mission it was to fill balloons full of water, returned with ammunition.

Target practice began forthwith. The water balloons were inserted into a pocket attached where the two surgical tubes came together. One person stretched the tubes to their fullest, while another inserted the balloon.

Cars parked in an adjacent parking lot served as targets. After a few spotting rounds, the order was given, "Fire for effect!"

By this time, our small Christmas bonfire had become a raging inferno, the flames reaching so high they licked precariously at the overhanging electrical wires that had previously gone unnoticed but now were brought to our attention by the dripping of the plastic wire coating into the bonfire, which itself created small blistering explosions that bubbled and crackled nicely on the wood.

It wasn't until the security police car screeched to a halt in front of this Christmas party that the crowd spontaneously burst into a rousing rendition of "White Christmas," perfectly in tune and in unison, at least to our ears. The squadron commander, always the first to react, met the security police officer before he could reach the bonfire or see the water balloon slingshot.

Lt. Colonel Ed "Julio" Houle convinced the policeman that this fine group of pilots merely missed their families during this holiday season and were not up to anything dangerous. The policeman seemed suspicious at first, but as the volume of singing increased, he relented, but made us promise to let the fire burn down.

Ah, Christmas in foreign lands?

Back in Germany, the flying was exciting and intense. With so many different missions and so many different flying units from all over the world, there was never a dull flight. Air-to-air simulated combat against American F-15s one day, low-altitude intercepts against German F-4s the next. When we least expected it, Canadian F-18s showed up to take part in the fray. And British Tornados flying so low you couldn't distinguish between the aircraft and its shadow. This type of flying is no longer allowed in Germany; it was in November of 1990 that the Berlin Wall fell and the high state of readiness, the reason for low-level flight training, no longer existed, much to the relief of the local residents and to the disappointment of pilots.

Just in time, for it was in August 1990 that Saddam Hussein invaded Kuwait, and the specter of Americans at war loomed for the first time since Vietnam. We were briefed by the intel personnel: Iraq had invaded Kuwait—the news was sometimes a little slow making it to distant outposts like Hahn. In the darkened briefing room, we looked at each other in confusion and the same question repeated itself: What is a Kuwait and why did Iraq want to invade it?

We were soon to learn for ourselves the answers to both those questions.

Within a month, as tensions mounted and Hussein strutted arrogantly across the world stage, the wing was notified that a squadron would be selected to deploy in support of what they were calling Operation Desert Shield.

Part III

Victory Takes Wings

    Whereat Michael bid sound
Th' Arch-angel trumpet; through the vast of Heav'n
It sounded, and the faithful Armies rung
Hosanna to the Highest: nor stood at gaze
The adverse Legions, nor less hideous joyn'd
The horrid shock: now storming furie rose,
And clamour such as heard in Heav'n till now
Was never, Arms on Armour clashing bray'd
Horrible discord, and the madding Wheeles
Of brazen Chariots rag'd; dire was the noise
Of conflict; over head the dismal hiss
Of fiery Darts in flaming volies flew,
And flying vaulted either Host with fire.

John Milton, *Paradise Lost,* Book VI

Lines in the Sand

Two days after Christmas 1990, we said goodbye at the Frankfurt airport. Sue, not yet showing with Sean, had fed Erin a little dramamine mixed in with her vanilla ice cream. Already the kid's eyes were at half mast. She'd lasted the three-hour drive down into the city from Hahn, and all she knew was that she was tired and cranky and that her grandmas and grandpas were waiting to meet her. She was only three. How could she know this might be goodbye forever?

The farewell. Sounds like it ought to be romantic, dramatic. Bogey and Bergman on the tarmac at the end of *Casablanca*. Why not me and Sue, my jet idling in the background, violins rising in weeping strains, an impatient wind teasing my white silk pilot's scarf? Sue bravely fighting the tears, my jaw taut, set, my eyes on the distant horizon, only a slight twitch in my cheek revealing my feelings, whatever they might be.

Actually, it was nothing like that. We stood outside the security gate while Erin played sleepily at our feet. I think it was with her Cabbage Patch doll. Sue and I were both so quiet. What do you say? Anything could be the wrong thing. We held each other tentatively, almost a little embarrassed.

"I love you, Q," I whispered. I stroked her smooth brown hair. "I love you. Take good care of Erin and baby. Take good care of yourself." Sue kissed me lightly on the cheek, on the mouth. "I love you too, Mike. Be careful. Do good."

I scooped Erin up off the floor and clutched her to my chest, trying to memorize the impression her small body made there. "Never forget how much Daddy loves you, Erin." At first she squirmed in my arms, but then she must have sensed the tension of the moment. "Don't worry, Daddy," she said very confidently as she patted my back. "Everything is okay."

It was the last time everything would ever be okay for all of us.

I kissed them both again. Then they slipped through the revolving door and were gone. The image of their faces, turned back in goodbye, became a photograph I would carry with me into war.

Suddenly the airport seemed very loud and very foreign. I didn't want to cry, not there. I hurried out into the cold and pointed the car back toward Hahn. We deployed the next day to Moron, an old bomber base in Spain that had been closed years before and that the Air Force had recently reopened to serve as a main staging base for aircraft headed into and out of the Persian Gulf area.

28 December 1990

Friday

My squadron, the 10th Tactical Fighter Squadron, has been called on to deploy to the Middle East to push the Iraqi army and Saddam Hussein out of Kuwait, which they invaded on 2 August of this year. The invasion is seen as an unprovoked aggression against a defenseless country. Though the UN has passed a resolution condemning this act and has called for Iraq to withdraw its forces, Hussein has refused to do so and continues to call Kuwait the 19th province of Iraq.

Before August 2, it looked for all the world like peace was breaking out all over.

My own feelings are mixed. There is excitement in the air. The drums of war are sounding and we are marching in time. I firmly believe that we are going to war with Iraq. I also believe that this is totally necessary. Hussein is a man without conscience and must be stopped. Anyone who cannot see that does not understand history or the nature of man. This is more than a battle over oil, although that is a part—a large part—of what I believe this is all about. I also believe that we have the means and the will to destroy him quickly. This is my goal and everyone else's goal.

I am ready to go. The waiting is the hardest part. I miss Erin and Sue already... I can't help but wonder what all our lives will be like in six or eight months from now.

General Chambers, 17th Air Force Commander, and General Galvin (four stars), United States Forces in Europe Commander, came to talk with us today before flying out to get here. Both talks were encouraging, straightforward and honest. Both see a war in the future!

They told us the models predict 25% attrition. That means that of the 32 pilots who flew to Moron, they expect eight to be shot down. We all looked around the room when Chambers said this to see who the eight might be. You could tell that not one of us thought he might be among the lost.

It was only two months earlier that we had flown at Zaragossa in preparation for deployment to the Gulf. Back then, Hussein and Bush were already trading insults as Iraqi troops settled into Kuwait.

We spent those autumn days flying, our nights playing, always looking for new ways to torment each other. The new-arrival initiation was one of my favorites. A decades-old Air Force custom, it involved a trip to the "Tubes," an ancient section of Zaragossa with narrow, winding streets wide enough only for pedestrians and lined with storefront saloons that promised tapas and tinto.

Newbees were forced to consume all sorts of exotic edibles—or inedibles, depending on your perspective—miniature fried octopus, stewed sheep's brain served directly from the split roasted head, fresh warm anchovies and olives, grilled calamari, sautéed skewered sweetmeats and other delectables that will remain forever unidentified and undigested.

We also swallowed great quantities of tinto, the local dark red new wine, so strong it tasted like bull's blood. Its effect was as powerful as bull's blood, too, and most newbees succumbed to the combination of strange new flavors before the evening was out.

My roommate that October was J.D. Hay, later a hooch-mate during the war. A husky guy with the smooth dark hair of a game show host, his face always ready with a smile, J.D. was an energetic, light-hearted type. Despite his easygoing ways, J.D. was a serious pilot. He knew when to knock off the shenanigans and get down to work.

On the other hand, he was never at a loss to find ways to thwart boredom. One Thursday evening after flying, we were crossing the base on our way to the Officers' Club to quench our thirst before catching the downtown bus. After a few quick beers, we somehow found ourselves standing in front of the club, staring at the marquee, one of those prefab lettered signs with moveable black plastic letters. It announced the usual base events.

Officers' Wives' Club Mah Jongg meeting Tuesday
Car wash Saturday
Sign up for our bake sale to benefit base beautification project

J.D. and I turned to one another. A mischievous grin played on his face. I loved that look.

"Are you thinking what I'm thinking?" he asked. Of course I was. Fighter pilots who fly in tight formation can read each other's minds. Or so it often seemed.

"That sign is just begging us to find better a use for all those letters," I answered.

We sprang into action. The rearrangement took us less than a minute, although we made it up as we went along, like playing a cross between *Wheel of Fortune* and *Jeopardy*. When we were done, we were more than pleased with our results. Letters we didn't need we dropped there in the dust for the Mah Jongg club to find.

**The next base ob/gyn clinic will be held at the Officers' Club
in the casual bar at 2000 hours on Friday night**

Exit, stage right, nonchalance our guide. Like teenagers after a prank, we couldn't keep the smirks from our faces or our pace normal. We sped past in the base bus, the loud guffaws from our fellow passengers our reward.

It wasn't all fun and games, though. We were preparing for war, after all.

Word had it that we would attack using medium altitude tactics, a move that troubled a lot of us. It was a change in strategy from previous briefings, and we knew the Iraqis possessed a huge arsenal of Soviet anti-aircraft artillery. The higher you are when you drop those bombs, the more likely you are to return to base. We worried to each other that this medium altitude strategy would place us in the middle of surface-to-air missile envelopes. Not a fun spot for a fighter pilot with four tons of bombs strapped to his belly.

By the time we arrived at Moron in December, the base was already crowded with many of the pilots who would fly in Desert Storm. This was no rehearsal. This time we knew we were going to combat. If we returned, we would return with the badge of honor all men covet. We would be combat veterans, men who lived to tell the tale. And if we did not return . . . Well, we would not return. If there was one thing they beat into our heads in pilot training, it was to acknowledge death as a daily possibility, but not to nurture that possibility with the thin gruel of worry.

Even so, that indescribable intensity of feeling common to every soldier on the cusp of war washed over us. Every moment became so beautiful it was often painful just to breathe. Our days were infused with the distilled intensity of time. We marveled at the sharp edge between shadow and light on a city sidewalk. The bite of garlic filled our mouths. The tinto poured again, pleasantly acrid, down our throats.

We were alive. Who knew if we would live to see another December?

I tried to imagine what it would feel like to be shot at. I had flown more than 1,500 hours of practice combat, but no one had ever shot at me in earnest. How would I react?

Then the orders came through. No time to worry about how I would react. I would soon find out. We prepared to deploy to the United Arab Emirates the night before New Year's Eve.

30 December 1990

Sunday

Everybody up at 0500 hours to go to the command post to brief for our flight to the Middle East. There is a very thick fog and we are glad we don't have to fly today! We brief the flight, go out and run the jets in the pre-dawn fog and then go to breakfast.

Talk is all centered around the Gulf and what is going to happen. Almost everyone seems to feel the same as I do about it. A lot of emotions hit all at once. We have to go to bed at 1400 to get up at 0000 hours for a 0130 takeoff. It is not easy to go to sleep in the middle of the afternoon. Especially when you are so wired about what is going on.

We wake up at midnight, shower, shave, shampoo and off we go to eat breakfast and step to fly. But the fog is still there, so we do all this for nothing and the launch is canceled. Now it is 0300 hours and we are all awake. We decide to stay up and watch TV/movies, play cards, and have a few beers. Some of us play basketball at the gym to relieve tension.

We finally took off from Moron late on New Year's Eve, after midnight. Foggy still, but not as foggy as it was the night before, not foggy enough to cancel the mission. And it was dark, no moon at all.

Shortly after taking off and joining our formation, we got above all the clouds and the fog. I looked out at the very, very dark night. So many stars. As we flew east to rendezvous with the tanker that would take us to the United Arab Emirates, I wondered what lay ahead. Four sets of F-16 six-ships flying in tight formation headed toward war, we filled the night sky like a dream, like a nightmare.

From the ground, we were invisible. But here in the night sky, we sensed that we were each of us the agent of some Iraqi's doom. This knowledge made us powerful. It also terrified us, on some unspoken level, for if it was true, then perhaps an Iraqi pilot, himself the agent of our own doom, was at this moment flying his anonymous flight westward into the night, to meet us and execute his task.

Still, we had only one choice, and that was to fly. I, for one, was comforted by the fact that I was flying an F-16, the envy of the aeronautical world. The sleekest jet in the air.

At 29,000 feet an F-16 is almost totally silent. Sitting there, bubbled against the night, the only sound some occasional radio banter, my gloved hands worked the control stick, the throttle. The cockpit instruments glowed whitish green, reflecting off the canopy, cocooning me in the darkness. It was cold outside, but the aircraft heating system kept me warm and comfortable.

The F-16 is a beautiful aircraft. Neat in the sky, responsive, uncomplaining, it's highly maneuverable. Its ancestors are ancient by air battle standards: one pilot, one engine, the model of self-reliance. But its technology is the most modern in air design. The pilot sits in a reclined seat, with a control stick mounted to the right instead of between the legs, and the throttle to the left. The stick and throttle hold upward of 20 buttons and switches that give the pilot almost complete control over the avionics: radar, radio, flight data navigation, weapons employment. Everything a pilot needs right at his fingertips.

A Maserati in the sky, we called it the "Sex Jet," the "Electric Jet," and although its official nickname is the "Falcon," we called it the "Viper." No matter what you call it, it's what every pilot longs to fly.

The F-16 even has its own song, but to understand it, you've got to know pilot talk. Once you know that Fishbeds, Foxbats and Floggers are Russian MIGs, and that Aim-Nine J and P are missiles, the song's message is clear. It's usually sung with ample lubrication and it goes like this:

RB Double-A Bravo (Red-Blooded All-American Boy)

I'm an RB double-A Bravo
And I fly the F-16
Better than sex and Mom's apple pie
It's the meanest little jet you've ever seen
It'll kick the shit out of Fishbeds, Foxbats,
Floggers and the F-15
I'm an RB double-A Bravo
And I fly the F-16

I once checked at six an F-five-echo
At seventeen thousand feet,
Loaded down with twenty-millimeter aim-nine J and P
I laid a bat turn down his throat
And shot him in his two front teeth
And I heard him scream from the fireball
"Damn, I just can't stand the heat!"

I've got a friend at Bitburg and he flies the F-15
Called me up, said come on down
You ain't seen nothin' yet!
So I kicked the tires, lit the fire
And over the Mosel we met
In twenty-two seconds he called me up
Said he wanted to change the bet

I'm an RB double-A Bravo
And I fly the F-16
Better than sex and Mom's apple pie
It's the meanest little jet you've ever seen
It'll kick the shit out of Fishbeds, Foxbats,
Floggers and the F-15
I'm an RB double-A Bravo
And I fly the F-16

Singing was not exactly on my mind as we crossed the Mediterranean, although I was grateful to be flying an F-16. For this flight, our airplanes were less sports cars than station wagons, loaded up with tons of live air-to-air missiles, bomb racks, fuel tanks, and electronic jamming pods—fully operational wartime loads. Most of us had carried and dropped live munitions before, but this was different. This was no war game over the Nevada desert.

I tracked our progress by the lights I could see down below, even from this altitude. The boot of Italy off to my left, Sicily just off to the south.

Less than four feet away off each wing another pilot sat glassed in his own cockpit, flying into his own private darkness. Were they each thinking of their lives? Were they afraid, as I was, that they wouldn't measure up? Were they afraid of dying? Which of us would return? I wondered. Would J.D.? Would Goo Goo? Would I?

We flew on, alone but together, joined by an invisible web of thought that traveled eastward with us across the vast black sky.

From listening to the radio banter, you'd never know we were headed into battle. When we talked at all, mostly it was to reassure ourselves that we were all still there, or to point out the sights on this rather unusual sightseeing tour. The monotony of our seven and one half hour flight was broken up only by these occasional laconic radio exchanges and the multiple air refuelings from our tanker.

Whenever one of us started to wander out of formation a little, the rest would worry. The main concern on a long flight like this was that a pilot might fall asleep. A message on the VHF band, the interflight radio, usually cleared the air.

"Hey, Sabre three. What's up?" was generally enough to bring a pilot back to full consciousness, if consciousness was indeed the problem. A quick reply like "Stand by, I'm busy," meant he was probably just trying to pee. But at least we knew he was still there, still flying.

"Check right, three o'clock low," my wingman called at one point, and we saw the lights of Libya far beneath us. The radio crackled to life. "As long as we're armed, maybe we should pay Mohamar another visit."

Others in the flight acknowledged the light-hearted conversation with "zippers," a double-click of the mike button that indicated they had heard the exchange and were in agreement. No words needed. I pictured my comrades smiling at the image of an impromptu visit to Khadafy.

I wondered about the guys who had performed that raid back in '86. What went through their minds as they peered down through the darkness and saw those lights? Had they thought, as I did now, of the whole of their lives? Had they wondered if they had done right? What they should have done differently?

Not all my thoughts were philosophical. At one point, I had to take a leak and in the worst way.

In a single-seat airplane, the only way to manage this is with the aptly-named piddle pack issued to each pilot. It resembles a large baggie with a neck, around which are attached plastic-wrapped aluminum wires. Unlike regular baggies, however, the piddle pack comes filled with two compressed sponges. To pee in midair, the pilot must unstrap his waist, unbuckle his seatbelt, finger through layers of flight suit, place the proper part of his anatomy into the piddle pack and proceed to urinate while flying an F-16 four feet off of somebody's wing at night, and a very dark night, at that. But when you gotta go, you gotta go, so you do what you have to do. Now that's what I call flying.

As we hit the eastern end of the Mediterranean, the sun began to rise and illuminate the clear day, animating the line between green water and brown earth. Since we were flying due east, the light shone directly into our eyes, and although we had tried to adjust our bodies' circadian rhythms to the Middle East dawn by taking off after midnight, I felt tired. Tired, but happy that day had come. The glare was so bright, right in my face, the dark visor on my helmet helped only a little. I had to concentrate by looking to the side, and not into the sun as it emerged huge and exotic over the edge of the earth.

Down below lay the eastern Mediterranean and Egypt. We could make out the Nile River to the right, and the Suez Canal cut a huge swath through the land directly beneath us. I felt as if I were flying over history. In reality, we were flying into history.

Just as we began to allow the relief of arrival to seep into our tired muscles, real life interceded.

First, without warning, our tanker announced that it was out of fuel and was leaving us. Thank you very much. Have a nice war. We were on our own. A little disconcerting to a pack of F-16s still several hundred miles from our destination. Then, the radio blasted to life.

"This is the United States Navy Midway," someone shouted so loudly the whole cockpit filled with the sound of panic.

"Aircraft proceeding on a heading of 080 at 30,000 feet, identify yourselves."

The voice repeated this message three times before it finally announced, in tones that obviously meant business, "Aircraft heading 080 over Dharan, this is the United States Navy Midway. If you come any closer without identifying yourselves, we will initiate action!"

At this point several of us in the formation finally figured out that the voice was describing us, and that we looked like a threat to them. We all screamed, half in jest, maybe more than half serious, into our inter-airplane communications radio, "Don't shoot! Don't shoot! It's us!"

We had arrived.

On land, our reception committee was small, an oversight resulting from the effects of excessive celebration on the premises the previous evening. The other two units were from Shaw Air Force Base and had been here since August. When we arrived, they were still recovering from their New Year's Eve party, where they had apparently enjoyed the cases of German wine we'd shipped down earlier in the week. Of course, we had planned to partake of that wine ourselves, but for the fog-in at Moron.

We parked the jets in the new aircraft hangars and were taken back to the base camp. Built years ago for German contract workers, it had always been intended as temporary digs for whoever lived there. Even so, it was a fairly well-equipped place, with hardened aircraft shelters at both ends and high-speed taxi-ways leading out to a huge runway.

January 1, 1990

Tuesday

We get a couple of briefings and then go to tent city. Home for who knows how long! All the pilots are in six-man hooches, though, not tents. Little trailer type housing. Better than a tent, but not home. We like it! It's like going back to college and fixing up your dorm room. My roommate is J.D., one of the best guys in the squadron. Talk about your basic, well-intentioned, honest guy! We get along good and have basically the same outlook about life, the same sense of humor.

We slept on folding Army cots and had little other furniture to speak of. We immediately set about trying to make our home as comfortable as possible, scavenged some plywood, got some planks to lay over the top of our cots. To soften up our slumbers, we placed our thin mattresses over the planks and then piled blankets or sleeping bags atop these.

Each room had a small desk area with some shelving. I fashioned a closet from my wooden foot locker, which I hung vertically on the wall, inserted some shelves, and then placed pictures of Erin, Sue and my family inside the door. It served as a pretty good place to keep my stuff and lock it up, not that that was required.

The other guys in our hooch are "Heebs" Mark Hebien and "Ragin'" Terry Bull. Since they have been rooming together for a long time, they are used to each other and match personalities well. "Hobo" Jim Long, who is also my flight commander, and "Bo" Mike Boera are the other two. Both good pilots.

The first night we go to the makeshift Officers' Club and have a couple of beers and then go to the mess tent for chow and then to bed. Needless to say, we fall asleep immediately and are comatose for ten hours.

What a way to spend New Year's Eve and Day.

Next day, the Shaw guys showed us around the camp: mess tents, post office tent, commissary tent, a PX-type of building, a chapel. Much to our surprise, they also showed us a pool, tennis courts, and an outside basketball court.

Luckily for us, we were in a part of the Middle East where we could actually get beer. To keep us honest and in honor of the laws of Islam, the local government issued two beer tickets per day, per person. Of course, nobody really paid attention to the rules, and you could pretty much get as much beer as you wanted—or needed—at the Officers' Club.

A large brown prefab building with a plywood floor and a homemade plywood bar, the inside of the O Club building was sheeted with white marker boards. These boards became a place where people recorded significant events, or made comments about one another, or just vented, scrawled what we used to call a hog log, except now it appeared on the walls. Sort of a collective journal of our lives.

Off in one corner stood a pool table, usually the center of a raucous crowd of pilots. There were no pool cues and only two balls, the cue ball and the eight ball, the only equipment needed to play the game of Crud, the pilot's version of the game of Life.

Behind the bar chugged an old chrome refrigerator, its glass windows frosty with the effort of chilling our beer. All we could get was Foster's and Heineken, imported to the UAE through the British expatriate club in downtown Abu Dhabi. It served the purpose, but it felt strange that we should be drinking Australian and Dutch beer in this most American of wars.

3 January 1991

Thursday

I miss my family already. Sent letters to Sue and Erin and Mom and Dad today. No mail yet.

Word from the world today tells us that our illustrious elected officials back in the U.S. want to pass legislation to prevent the president from going to war. However, they don't want to call a special session. They are all a bunch of pansy asses. They are sending a signal of weakness to Iraq and he knows it. That is what is going to cost more American lives. They only understand the public opinion game. It really pisses me off. They have got the guts of a sand worm. That is not a point of contention. It is pretty much mutually agreed upon.

I think a war is inevitable, although I would gladly give up the opportunity to go to war if Saddam surrendered without a fight. I don't see that happening.

The Shaw squadrons have had enough of desert life after five months and just want this to end. I don't blame them.

January 15 is only 12 days away now. I hope we will be ready when it happens. War will not be pretty. I'm sure it never will be or never was. It seems like such a waste, but I believe it is necessary because of the nature of man.

Sometimes I am scared, sometimes I am angry and hurt. Other times I am afraid to admit that I am excited about the chance to use my knowledge and ability to defeat someone like Saddam Hussein. Again, he does not know what he is up against.

I can't help but think that he has got something up his sleeve, though. We know that he has terrorist teams out and that he is crafty. I hope the higher ups have figured all the angles on this.

Peaceday, Warday

4 January 1991

Friday
(Peaceday)

Finally got in the air! First flight in country was pretty impressive. Went out over the Gulf to air refuel and then on a low level route to some simulated targets. Nothing but sand, camels and a few nomads out in the desert. Sand dunes and scrub brush are all you can see for miles. Once you get off the coast, there are no terrain features.

We do some high altitude attacks and then come back to base to land. We are going to do business (fly) the way the other two squadrons are doing it because they have been here for five months and we are the new guys on the block.

The 10th pilots have made a few mistakes in the first couple of days. I'm afraid we may be making a bad name for ourselves. McCaffrey punched off flares on a takeoff roll, and Taschner almost had a mid-air with another flight on the tanker. There are a lot of airplanes in a small area, so the chances of a mishap are high. The flying is going to be very exciting and very intense.

The weather has been great. Every day is sunny and warm. It's a great contrast after winter in Germany. It reminds me of Tucson.

One day early on they herded us all into the O Club, where they had set up rows of chairs. I found a seat with three of my hoochmates. Together with all the assembled pilots from Hahn, we sat facing the chugging refrigerator and the empty pool table. The windowless room hummed with air conditioning, the bare light bulbs suspended from steel rafters shedding hollow columns of light in our cool, dim grotto.

First the wing commander got up to say a few words. Then he introduced us to the wing weapons officer, Lieutenant Colonel Nordo North, who stood to brief us on a plan he called Desert Storm.

A tall, dark-haired man, Nordo's normally animated face was completely solemn that day. There was nothing humorous about briefing a room full of pilots for war.

"Gentlemen," he announced, clearing his throat in the waiting silence, "what I'm about to tell you is classified top secret. Anyone who has a problem with keeping his mouth shut is invited to leave the room at this time."

The room was still, all eyes front. No one moved.

"American lives depend on your ability to keep secret what you are about to see and hear," Nordo continued, scanning our faces, fixing as many of us as he could with his intense eyes.

Finally, we would find out what the higher-ups had in mind, how it would really go for us. For weeks now, we had wondered anxiously about that single, most thrilling and terrifying eventuality: what would happen when the fighting really started? Would this be another Vietnam? Would the war be influenced by politics? Or were they really going to let the military fight this one? We were all hoping it would be no-holds-barred, full throttle.

The briefing set our minds at ease. We were awestruck by what we learned. If the fighting did start, our attack would be massive on all scales short of nuclear. The coalition had planned total war against the country of Iraq as well as the Republican Guard in Kuwait. We were informed of the nature of the targets we would be hitting, many of which were the chemical and biological weapons production and storage facilities the Iraqis were known to possess.

In that 90-minute briefing, we learned that the U.S. and its partners would employ all of the assets available, including cruise missiles and every type of aircraft and munitions that existed. Except for a nuclear strike, of course. And it looked as though every minute or so in the first three days of the war some kind of explosion or detonation would be pounding Iraq and Kuwait. The number of aircraft involved was mind-boggling.

No target would remain untouched.

As he wound down the briefing, Lieutenant Colonel North paced before us, his frame relaxed yet confident. "I need not remind you, gentlemen," he stopped, dead center, "that this briefing is top secret. I ask you now to stand and swear yourselves to secrecy, for the duration of the war and forever after."

Forty pilots rose from their cold metal seats. After a few minutes of shuffling and chair shifting, the room fell silent once again.

"Please raise your right hands and repeat after me."

Forty elbows bent as 40 pilots raised their right hands. The solemnity of that pledge, the fervor and focus in that room, live with me to this day. I cannot reveal the nature of our promise, for that too was secret, but I can say that each of us swore never to reveal what took place there or what we were told. For that reason, I record here neither the contents of our pledge nor the details of our attack plan.

I say again only that no target would remain untouched.

As we left the dark, cool O Club to head out into the desert sunlight, a wave of pure elation hit me like a wall of light. I could see that every other pilot felt the same way.

J.D., Heebs, Ragin' and I walked four abreast across the dusty parking lot to the sidewalk that led back to our hooch. Eyes squinted behind aviator sunglasses, we must have looked like a cartoon, four identical fighter pilots walking in step, tall and powerful in our dark-green flight suits, our shiny black boots.

"Wow," I breathed, the first to speak. "What did you guys think?"

Ragin' answered for everyone. "Shit hot!"

We chuckled. It was a very good feeling to know that if we had to do this, it was going to be all or nothing. There would be no political handcuffs like back in Vietnam. They were taking care of us.

Sure we were scared. But the plan was a good one. Out of that mixture of elation and relief erupted the sense that if it did come to combat, at least we would be getting it right this time.

5 January 1991

Saturday

People around here are starting to talk about the days as either *wardays* or *peacedays*, depending on whether the news says the talks are on or off. We think there is going to be a war.

No flying for me today. Spent the day scheduling. Dueling responsibilities between myself and Major Jenkins. An ugly guy with no hair and a huge head. He has a cro-magnon man skull and brow and is a sight to behold. His nickname in the squadron is "Cro." I have a feeling I know why he was added to our squadron at the last minute, before we deployed down here. Colonel Houle won't admit it but I believe our illustrious leader from Hahn, Colonel Nordie Norwood, forced him on us.

Anyway, I have to deal with him every day, since I am the chief of scheduling. I'm sorry, but he is one of those people I just don't get along with. I was with him in the 23rd TASS also and I did not like him then either. He was airborne when Roland Perry died.

Those days before the war started, there was plenty of time to wait, plenty of time to think back across a life and let your mind catch on those slubs of time when everything changed. And when I encountered Cro, I couldn't help but think about Roland.

I first met Roland Perry during AGOS—air-to-ground operation school—at Hurlburt Air Force Base in Florida, early 1986. Our paths were parallel, as were our lives. For a time.

A slim, wiry guy, Roland was an ex-state-champion wrestler from Indiana with a great sense of humor. The thin brown hair that topped his narrow, affable face was a little long for Air Force regulations, but perfect for the Guard.

People—especially our wives—said we were similar in temperament. Not too somber, but as somber as we had to be to survive as jet fighter pilots. We were gung ho, but not to the point of obsession. We laughed at the same things, usually at each other, or at the other jocks who took their jet-pilot-selves just a little too seriously.

17 July 1986 was a clear, blistering desert day. Sky as far as you could see, no wind. A day made to skim a jet over the arid purple mountains. I was the duty desk officer, assigning people their airplane tail numbers as they stepped out the door to fly.

Roland was hanging around the duty desk, shoveling some leftover quiche into his mouth.

"Hey Roland," I ribbed, "real men don't eat quiche."

"Not only am I enjoying this quiche, Big D," he answered, his chewing exaggerated for my benefit, "but I made it myself last night." Then he hurled an unrepeatable epithet at me and swallowed the last of his meal. Minutes later, he stepped out the door to fly as part of a two-ship—with Bob "Cro" Jenkins.

I remember calling, "Hey, quiche boy, have a good flight!" as he strode out onto the flight line, parachute strapped to his back, helmet swaying loosely by the chinstrap as he swung it from his fingertips. Roland lifted his right arm in a backwards wave, but he never turned around.

About an hour later, word came back that an aircraft was down. A few minutes after that, we learned the call sign of the downed craft. It was Roland's. No one knew whether he had ejected or survived the crash.

Turns out he had done neither.

Because Roland and I were best friends, I was among those sent to tell his wife that Roland was dead. The four of us, Charles "Bud" Jackson, the squadron commander, plus a flight surgeon, a chaplain and I, put on our Air Force blues and drove to their beautiful house in suburban Tucson. We stopped at home to pick up Sue.

When we parked and got out of the car, Denise was just coming out to check the mail. At first she smiled when she saw me and Sue. But then she noticed the rest of us, the uniforms, and her comprehension was instant, complete.

The visit every pilot's wife dreads had arrived at her doorstep on a perfect July afternoon.

Sue and I spent the night with her and their two small girls, until her mother and other relatives could arrive. Denise and I sat up most of the night, unable to sleep, drinking coffee and talking about Roland.

The accident investigation team suspected that Roland had been diving to drop a simulated bomb on a target. When he pulled off the dive, he must have G'd himself out—blacked out due to the G-forces that result when you pull back on the stick to recover. Since Cro was airborne with Roland at the time, he was the only firsthand witness. It was Cro's testimony that led the investigatory board to its conclusion that Roland had G'd out.

It was all over so quickly. At the memorial service in the base chapel, the whole squadron arrived in dark-blue Air Force dress uniforms. The chaplain and the squadron commander said a few words, and then we filed outside with the color guard. Taps was played as a four-ship of OA-37 Dragonflies performed a flyby in the missing man formation: four jets in a tight, skewed vee in the sky, until the number three aircraft pulls straight up and out, in honor of the fallen comrade.

And that was it. Roland was gone.

It didn't seem fair that Roland should be dead, that Cro should live. Who made that bargain? After that, I always saw Cro as the reason Roland had died, although I knew of course that wasn't the case. Cro was just one of my least favorite people in the world. He had survived when Roland had not, although there's nothing in the world he could have done to save my best friend.

I didn't begrudge him his life. I just always wondered what really happened that day in the Arizona desert. And now Cro had to show up in this desert on the other side of the world.

But we were at war, and I had to focus, to make my aversion to Cro the least of my worries. Because he was in my face every day, though, I found myself thinking about Roland a lot. About how it would have been to have him here with us. About how accidents happen even to the best of pilots in the best of circumstances.

6 January 1991

Sunday
(Warday)

Iraq says it will attend talks in Geneva with Secretary Baker, but that it will never leave Kuwait. They shall be singing a different tune in about two weeks.

I flew up to the border of Saudi Arabia and Kuwait today with K.C. Schow. We did a mission called Eagle's Nest. Just to show them that we are there and to keep them uneasy. No action to speak of.

Logged a 3.5-hour mission with AAR [air-to-air refueling]. Tomorrow we are part of a 16-ship mass package strike into Saudi Arabia. Should be fun. I noticed again today what a beautiful aircraft the F-16 is. It has such sleek lines and looks so smooth in the air. It is really a dream to fly because it handles so well with just the touch of a finger. I'm proud to be a part of all this. I miss my family, though.

Mail call came every day at the ops building, where we each had a mailbox. So many packages arrived from home loaded with whatever our families seemed to think we might need—peanuts, homemade cookies, Slim Jims, toothpaste, film, gum, deodorant, candy, sunscreen, pictures from home—everyone shared whatever arrived. In our hooch, we set up a box near the door where we stowed all the goodies for everyone to grab.

Those days before the war began, the tension was high, but the waiting consumed most of our time. Whenever we were free, which was often, we played cards or read or hung out at the facilities. I've never had much use for tennis balls except when I could shoot them at friends in the tennis can bazookas we built as kids, so we spent hours grilling ourselves beside the swimming pool, or playing a pick-up game of basketball. January is about the only month you want to be in the Arabian desert, when the daytime temperature is bearable, maybe 80 to 90 degrees, and the nights are bright and cool. Very pleasant, really. Here I was at war, and I was going to go home with the best tan of my life.

Just across the fence an Italian air force unit was stationed, a cause of some distress for many of us. Although the Italians had to live in tents, the aromas that emanated from their chow tent testified to their true priorities and contrasted sharply with the reactions our food usually induced. It was unbearable at times, especially for a boy whose Italian grandmother arrived each Sunday bearing a pot of homemade sauce, meatballs and sausages. And although we shot frequent yearning looks in their direction, those Italians never invited us over. They had no trouble asking the American female service members to eat, though.

Their luck wasn't all good. The Italians flew Tornados, and one from our base was shot down the first night of the war. The pilot was killed, but the weapons officer became one of the first prisoners of the war.

7 January 1991

Monday
(Peaceday)

Flew in a 16-ship of F-16s today. The flight went pretty well, all things considered. Makes me think that the combat plan of mass package attacks is viable, but I still wonder about the "medium altitude" versus the low altitude attacks. Logged a 2.3. Weather is fine.

Talked with Sue and Erin on the phone. They both sounded well and in good spirits. It was nice to hear their voices, and Sue said there was stuff in the mail for me, am looking forward to that. I miss them both and if I ever get to hold them again I will do so with a love of life and sense of appreciation I cannot describe.

The missions are in for the go-to-war plan. They look very tough, i.e., heavily defended targets. Yes, I am scared. So is everyone. My biggest fear is that I will not measure up.

Tomorrow I am in a 24-ship package which features the Air Force Chief of Staff himself. General (four stars) McPeak. What a dog and pony show that will be! I am excited, though.

The McPeak briefing orders came down strict and direct: You will have highly polished boots, clean flight suits, and fresh haircuts, and be in your seats one half-hour before the general's arrival time.

On the appointed day, at the appointed time, we waited dutifully in our seats. All of us had arrived early, our hair cropped close, boots polished, flight suits neat. I even got a whiff of Aqua Velva.

We were ready but we were also bored. It was show time, and it all seemed like such a huge waste of time, given what we would soon be up against.

I sat with my flight formation, Goo Goo, my wingman, to my right, Buck Richards on my left, nervously picking his cuticles, and K.C. Schow, our flight lead, next to him.

A major from one of the Shaw squadrons was to brief and lead the 24-ship of F-16s. Four F-15s would accompany us as air-to-air escort, one of which was a two-seater in which the general would have a captain or a major instructor pilot as seeing-eye dog to fly with him and keep him out of trouble.

Naturally, we were all anticipating some kind of speech out of the general. Here we were, about to go to war, planted in some desert thousands of miles from home and country. And for the first time, we were about to meet the Air Force chief of staff. A little leadership was definitely in order. We figured he would pump us up, tell us what heroes we were. How the folks back home were so proud of us. Et cetera.

The crowd hushed as a colonel entered and quietly informed us that the general was about to make his entrance. Then, the doors at the side of the room swung open.

"Room tench-hut!"

We bolted up from our seats as one and planted ourselves at attention: hands at our sides, stomachs in, chests out, chins up, eyes front.

Like everyone else, I fixed my eyes to the white projector screen up front. Fighter pilots have excellent peripheral vision, though, and I could see McPeak as he entered. A tall, very thin, very plain man dressed in a general's uniform carefully made his way to the front. Wan and frail, he looked more like an actuary than a general, an actuary who had been on a starvation diet of bean soup and water.

I was glad I was not going to be his seeing-eye dog. I didn't exactly get the sense he was a powerful person or even someone who could find his way around the sky in a jet. This was the Air Force chief of staff?

"Be at ease," the general ordered, almost in a whisper.

His eyes cast down to the pale orange shag carpeting, McPeak never once looked up or acknowledged our presence. Instead, he walked to the chair at the front of the room marked with a naugahyde blue patch emblazoned with four white naugahyde stars on the back.

He sat.

"Proceed with your briefing, major," he breathed tonelessly to the tense man standing at attention up front.

The major pulled himself together, and we dutifully listened to the briefing we had already heard twice before during the practice runs we had endured in anticipation of the general's visit.

"Are there any questions?" the major asked the hushed audience when he finished.

The room was quiet for several seconds, until a captain up front raised his hand to ask a prearranged question about back-up targets.

"I'm glad you asked that, captain," the major said, as if he were really contemplating how to answer. He spelled out his memorized response for the general's benefit.

"If there are no further questions," he announced, "that concludes the briefing. Step time in 30 minutes."

We sat quietly in anticipation of any words the general might finally have to offer on upcoming events. Hello? We were about to go to war. Words such as "The nation is with you, gentlemen," or something might be appropriate. Anything. Sir.

Instead, the general slowly and laboriously raised himself up and proceeded directly to the door at the side of the room from which he had entered, his eyes still on the orange shag carpeting. With a whoosh, the doors fell shut behind him.

The room deflated. Several seconds of silence followed McPeak's departure. None of us knew exactly how to react. Pumped up we were not.

A low buzz of worried murmuring slowly creased the silence. I turned to K.C.

"Wa-al, hit me on the head 'n call me Shorty," I drawled, "that wasn't exactly inspee-rational now, was it?"

"Yeah," K.C. answered, "General Patton he ain't."

As we made our way into the life support room where our flying gear was stowed, everyone offered his own interpretation of the briefing. Some of the pilots had heard of McPeak and told us this was standard. But those of us who had no experience with him were left wondering exactly who this man was and how he had got to be the highest ranking man in the Air Force.

We struggled into our gear, which was stowed on rows of pegs and hooks lining the walls. Each pilot was assigned a place to hang his G-suit, helmet, gloves, harness, survival vest and ground chemical warfare mask. We suited up and stepped out to fly.

The flight, too, was something of a letdown. We had all been excited about the prospect of flying with the Air Force chief of staff. But once up in the air, we neither saw him nor heard from him. There was some scuttlebutt that maybe he never really flew in the mission. That he came to the briefing, showed his face, and went home. He was a nothing, a non-event.

We could only hope the war would not be the kind of anticlimax his visit had been. And that this guy was better at planning wars than he was at inspiring pilots.

8 January 1991

Tuesday
(Warday)

Today I flew as number 17 in a 24-ship of F-16s to attack a simulated target in Saudi Arabia. There was a cell of five tankers, four F4-Gs, 2 EF-111s, four F-16s and French Mirages as aggressors. It was impressive seeing all these fighters in the air at one time. The flight went well except for me missing a frequency change to the strike frequency. It worries me because that is crucial, especially when people are shooting at you. I have to be flawless if I am to survive the ordeal.

Tomorrow Baker and Aziz meet in Geneva. We're all waiting to see what is going to happen now. Iraq has said it will never back down and Bush has said it will not be long after 15 January that we will use force to move Iraq out of Kuwait. Thus, *warday* today. There is no doubt that the U.S. and its allies will be successful in defeating Iraq, possibly in a short time, too.

I can't help wondering what Hussein has up his sleeve. I also wonder what the cost will be in lives. There is no one in this unit that I would want anything to happen to, not even Cro.

9 January 1991

Wednesday
(Warday!)

The talks between Baker and Aziz in Geneva failed, so it looks like all the days between now and 15 January are going to be wardays. It's amazing to me that a man like Saddam Hussein can let so much of the world be against him and not be willing to change, give in or at least be willing to save some of his own people's lives.

He must have some trump card that he feels will change the way this war is going to come out. I hope he doesn't.

10 January 1991

Thursday
(Warday!)

Brigadier General Gloster came to talk with us and really pumped us all up. He had a few real pearls of wisdom to enlighten us. He swore up and down and cursed a lot and let us in on some really secret info. The quote of the day was "The quickest way home is through Baghdad." That got a real rise out of the crowd. There is now absolutely no doubt in any of our minds that we are going to be in fight soon.

There is something about the thought that someone is going to be shooting at me that really scares me, and yet I feel more anger than anything else. Courage is nothing more than being able to put your fears aside and do your job. I am not afraid for myself, but more for Sue and Erin and my unborn child.

We've been told this on numerous occasions, there is no target in Iraq worth dying for. I fully intend to be holding Erin and Sue in my arms when all this is over.

We are now under the impression that Iraq will probably start this war and will most likely try to draw Israel into it. Now we are so close to the deadline and Saddam is clearly not willing to give in. By this time next week we will be dropping bombs on their heads. I venture to say that it will be a short war. I would say that the way they have the air campaign planned, it may not even take that long!

I miss my wife and child and I've only been away for two weeks. I feel better knowing that they are in good hands and okay. No mail yet. I'm wondering how my mom is holding up to all of this. This is a lot of pressure with both Tim and me in the military right now. I pray this all ends in a good way and that we can get the family back together again.

11 January 1991

Wednesday
(Warday)

Flew a 2.2 today. It was a 14-ship package of just 10th jets led by the squadron commander, Lt. Col. Houle. The flight did not go all that well, but I had a good ride.

Saddam is not going to back down and, thankfully, neither are we. We are expecting a pre-emptive strike this weekend sometime. History in the making and I am part of it. I feel absolutely no remorse or guilt that that guy is soon going to be blown to bits and that his regime is going to fall. It is a shame that so many people are going to die, just because of one man's desire for power. The world community cannot let this happen and they cannot let him go unpunished.

Within a week we will be dropping bombs and getting shot at. It is going to be a very dynamic and tense situation that will border on the edge of insanity. Hopefully, it can be contained and ended quickly. Let us hope!

The base is being shut off tonight and security has been increased. Makes me feel better. We spent tonight digging a bunker in the front of our hooch. Sand bags stacked in a square. Something to hide in, in case we are attacked.

Cro was taken out of the scheduling office by Woody. Much to my relief.

14 January 1991

Monday

No flying today for me. Studied in the safe for a while. Ready to go. We loaded almost all of our bombs and missiles and the whole wing is ready to launch. Some are on standby, but I am not one of them. It is 2230 hours and in about 24 hours the deadline will have been reached and all-out war is going to be taking place on this planet for who knows the number of times. A lot of people will die and it will be quick and violent. I believe the plan we have and the leadership that we have are doing this right. It looks like it is going to happen.

Goo Goo was told today that he will not be flying on my wing when we go to war. He will be part of the mission planning cell. He was pretty hurt and has been moping around all day.

We've been here for 14 days. Tomorrow the battle begins. I will go to my crew chief to tell him my jet will be called SuzyQII. Hopefully, he will put some nose art on there with this saying.

While his English was perfect and he sounded as American as the rest of us, Goo Goo jumped into Spanish whenever he got wound up. I don't know how he got the call sign Goo Goo. Maybe it was his olive-complected, slightly chubby babyface and puppy-like personality, his round dark-black eyes, the tousled mop of curly black hair through which he was constantly running his fingers.

Goo Goo was a good guy, even if he wasn't yet the pilot the war would eventually make him. When they told him he wasn't going to fly at the start, he came to me.

"What happened, D? Why won't they let me go up?" he asked. He was very upset. His slightly bulging eyes were wet, his hands were restless. We were sitting outside the hooch in two old lawn chairs. The sharp night sky prickled with millions of desert stars. Besides our voices, the only sound we heard was the base generator humming, keeping our beer cold and our engines warm.

Goo Goo wanted to know what the boss told me about why he was being taken off the schedule.

"Goo Goo," I said. "I gotta tell you, they're worried about your performance. They've been noticing that you seem to be making some mistakes, lately."

He cursed, spit into the sand. Looked away from me.

"The boss man said they're the kind of mistakes that are unusual for you. Unacceptable risks for the squadron. He didn't say what exactly, Goo Goo, just something about nervous mistakes. I figure maybe you're out of formation position lately? Or screwing up your ground ops?"

A pilot performs ground ops with the crew chief, who's waiting at the jet when the pilot arrives to prepare to fly. The pilot walks around the plane to inspect it, checks the maintenance record, straps in with the crew chief's help, starts the engine and goes through a series of aircraft systems checks. Only then is the pilot ready to taxi for take-off.

Goo Goo was my wingman. I told him that the boss hadn't asked me if he should ground him. He had merely informed me that he was going to sit Goo Goo down.

Goo Goo became visibly upset.

"What am I gonna do, D?" he wailed.

I was worried about him. And I could imagine how he must feel. He goes to war and when he gets there is told he won't be flying, at least not in the first couple of days. What do you write home? How do you live with yourself?

"The thing to do," I told him, "is to prove them wrong." I tried to calm him with my voice. "It's a challenge, Goo Goo, like flying a fighter jet, like being here, so far from home. You have two choices of what you can do with this."

He tilted his head back and looked up at the stars.

"You can either fold and prove them right," I continued, "or you can go out and work hard and win their respect by doing the best you can do."

The night was very beautiful, the black bright sky immense. "You're right, Big D. That's what I gotta do."

He looked at me and smiled.

We sat for a while in the desert night, leaning back against the mesh webbing of our lawn chairs, our chins tilted up to the field of stars overhead. Tomorrow the clock of the world would strike the deadline and we would be at war.

Crossing the Fence

15 January 1991. The deadline. We awoke to a state of heightened alertness. Airplanes were loaded up with munitions, fueled and ready to go. Pilots were busy making last-minute plans to put together packages of planes from the other squadrons.

Some of the packages had 50 or more fighters in them, and none of us were used to operating with so many aircraft at once. Needless to say, a huge amount of coordination was required on the part of the pilots, especially because some of the planes were located throughout the Saudi Arabian peninsula, including Navy jets flying off carriers in the Red Sea and Persian Gulf. We called these giant packages "gorillas."

15 January came and went. The eerie silence before the storm descended on the base. Still no war. Still no change. Just the long wait.

16 January 1991

Wednesday
(Warday)

Well, it is the 16th and nothing has happened in the world yet. We gather around the TV in our makeshift O Club to watch the news and find out what the word is back in the States. No flying for me and they cancelled tomorrow's sorties. Something is afoot, but I don't know what to think.

I got a letter today! Grandma Flo, and she mailed it on 29 December, so I guess the mail takes almost three weeks from the States. Other letters should show up soon.

When the war finally started, I was fast asleep in my bunk.

Early on the morning of 17 January 1991, probably 0400 or 0430 hours, the first wave of 40 aircraft took off from our base for a dawn raid on an oil production facility in Iraq. Since our camp was near the departure end of the runways, those of us still asleep in our hooches were jolted from sleep by the roar of a sequence of 40 F-16s in full afterburner.

Because of the number of aircraft and the live munitions on board, a 20-second spacing separated each aircraft as it left the ground. I lay in my bunk in the dark, counting the jets and timing the distance between launches. It didn't take me long to figure out that 40 aircraft taking off in full afterburner 20 seconds apart added up to 13 minutes of uninterrupted, unadulterated noise. The sound of freedom. By the end of the string of take offs, nobody was still asleep in our camp.

"Hey Big D," J.D. whispered through the dark after the last jet had burned into the distance. "You awake?"

"No, J.D.," I answered. "I can sleep through anything. You know that." What did he think? Of course I was awake.

"Cut the crap, big guy. You know what this means, don't you? It means they started. You and I are at war, buddy."

I could hear him roll over in his bunk. He let out a sigh. I couldn't tell whether it was a nervous sigh, or just a sigh of relief. It had finally begun. J.D. was scheduled to fly in that afternoon's go. I lay on my back, arms up behind my head, wondering what today would bring for me, for J.D., for all of us.

"Yeah, J.D. I know. By tonight you'll be a combat veteran. Maybe even have a few Iraqi MIG notches on your belt." I was trying to sound cool, I guess. "You think this thing will last long enough for me to get a mission in?" I was a little worried I'd miss out on the chance to see some combat. I wasn't scheduled for a flight until the next afternoon.

"Don't worry, D. There'll be plenty of war to go around." J.D. was already up. No point lying in bed speculating. We figured we might as well head out, grab some chow and go over to the ops building to find out what was going on.

The first wave was due to return to base around 1000 hours, and most of us were there to greet them. We wanted to make sure 40 aircraft returned, that no one was shot down.

In the middle of the flight line tarmac we stood, the desert sun beating down on us. Necks curled, we checked the first formation as it dotted the horizon, then the second. Out of the distant sky they appeared, first four specks, as inconsequential as insects, then another four, and another. We counted aloud to 40 as the jets passed overhead in tight formation. All had expended their bombs but still had their external fuel tanks and wing-tip missiles. All but one.

The number two in the sixth four-ship was clean: no external fuel tanks, no bombs, no wing-tip missiles. The F-16 carries air-to-air missiles on the tips of its wings, and the fact that this jet no longer had its missiles meant there had probably been an air-to-air engagement with Iraqi fighters. In an air-to-air engagement, a pilot punches off his external fuel tanks to improve maneuverability and speed.

The clean jet generated much excited chatter on the ground. Maybe he had engaged an Iraqi aircraft. Maybe he had shot one down.

The newly minted combat pilots made their way back to the ops building, where we waited to greet them and hear their stories amid much hand shaking and back slapping and high fives all around. They had survived the first attack.

Finally, the pilot with the clean aircraft walked in, but instead of a look of pride, he wore his helmet bag over his head. More than a little embarrassed, he confessed that he had inadvertently pushed some of the wrong buttons in midflight, dropped his fuel tanks and fired his missiles. He was a wingman, just a young kid. Maybe he had gotten a little too excited, but who could blame him? Everyone laughed, but mostly we were glad to see that they had all made it back.

We sat through a quick debriefing about what the first pilots had seen, and the second mission launched out, J.D. among them. Most of us spent more time in the safe reviewing our attack plans, the threats, and the tactics we were to use the next day. A small stuffy room in the bowels of the ops building, the safe housed all the classified documents. A cipher lock kept the bad guys out, not that there were any bad guys in the ops building.

17 January 1991

Thursday
(WARDAY!)

We have access to CNN news and I am able to watch it by the hour to keep up on the world situation. Talk about your "prime time" war. Instant TV news accounts of what is going on, while it's happening. It amazes me to know there are so many brave men out right now, fighting in a very intense, life-threatening situation while I sit comfortably watching the news. In no danger whatsoever. The only danger to us here is a terrorist threat and security around here is very tight. I feel semi-safe and try to stay alert to any unusual situations.

According to CNN, the attacks by the F-117s were very effective. They were able to penetrate Iraqi airspace with impunity. They dropped 2,000-pound bombs on key command and control facilities in the middle of the night. They were also able to hit various SCUD missile sites and were so effective that the immediate threat to Israel by SCUDs was wiped out.

Tomorrow is my turn. I fly a late takeoff to go and bomb a fighter base halfway between the Iraq-Saudi border and Baghdad. The target is defended by light and heavy AAA, a Roland II surface-to-air missile system. It is not the most heavily defended target but it is also not something to let your guard down on. It will be intense.

Not so much scared now as I am excited about it and angry enough to feel aggressive about it. There's no question in anyone's mind that at least the first 12 hours of operation of Desert Storm has been an outstanding success. Better than probably expected by the generals involved.

Despite our massive attacks, Hussein is still defiant about his stand on Kuwait. He referred to our attack as but a cool breeze that blows by the Iraqi army. He says that they are unscathed by all the attention and attacks and insisted that Iraq will make the U.S. pay a large dividend in blood for invading Iraq. I can't help but think that maybe he has something very powerful and malicious up his sleeve.

As I write this, the second wave of night attacks has begun. So far we have lost no aircraft or people to enemy fire. I feel confident that our raid in the afternoon will go well and will be a warm up to what will follow next. Downtown Baghdad.

We are all carrying 2,000-pound MK-84s, two of them. We are ingressing the target at about 25,000 feet and rolling for 45-60-degree releases of about 16,000 feet. At that altitude and those ranges, we cannot easily be seen by people on the ground. In fact, we are almost invisible. We get escorted into the target by F-15s and F-4G Wild Weasels.

The news today announced that we had launched 1,000 sorties in the first 12 hours of the operation. So far there are reported to be only three jets lost. An F-18 from the Marines, a British GK-1 Tornado, and a Kuwaiti A-4. Altogether this plan seems to have been put together well and at least initially executed well. I hesitate to be too comfortable or confident about the outcome, though. It is not going to be easy and it won't be over until the ground forces move into Kuwait and take it back from the Iraqis.

One last thing. I got a package from home today that was filled with all kinds of goodies. It had a picture Erin drew and a lot of sweets in it. Nice to finally be getting some mail. Must get to bed. Got a job to do tomorrow. Love you, Sue.

It must have been around 2300 hours that night when J.D. and one of the other pilots in our hooch returned, but Heebs, Ragin' and Hobo were asleep. We really could sleep through pretty much anything, even impending combat flights. Though J.D. and company tried to keep the noise down because they knew we were all flying the next day, I woke up when J.D. came into our room.

"Good to see you, Daryl," I croaked, but I really meant it. It *was* good to see him. "How'd it go?" I sat up in my narrow cot.

"Oh, good, you're awake." J.D. dumped his gear on the bare floor next to his bed, fell backwards onto his mattress. It sagged under his weight, despite the plywood base.

"It was awesome, D. No other word for it. We blasted them. Blasted them!" He started to get undressed, and the excitement in his voice told me he was still pretty worked up.

"The weather kind of sucked, but we got our attack in and I think we bombed the hell out of them. It was really cool." In shorts and a t-shirt now, J.D. leaned back against the wall. His words rushed out in a stream.

"The F-15s were out in front of the package and there were some Iraqi MIGs airborne. We could hear the F-15 talking to AWACS [Airborne Warning and Control System] and sorting targets, and then we hear 'Fox from one' and then 'Fox from number three.' A little while later, we hear 'Splash one bandit' and then 'Splash two bandit.' They got two kills, D. We were sitting in the back of the package trying to find the action on our radars, but we were too far back."

I wanted more detail. Did anyone get shot down? Was there any triple A? What about SAMs (surface-to-air missiles)? I figured I could have my own personal debriefing here with J.D. Maybe it would help me tomorrow.

"We all came back together, the whole package," he continued. "But when we got into the target area there were SAMs flying every which way and triple A way below us."

He was breathless with accomplishment, like a kid who had gotten away with something. "The weather was clear over the target, so we dropped on sight." By now he had crawled into bed and was leaning up on his elbow, facing me.

"Dude," he started up again, "we rolled in from 24,000 feet. I was about 55 degrees of dive and I put the pipper on my target, pushed the pickle button and let those puppies fly. Man, I looked up in the HUD and I was supersonic. Those bombs were really moving when they came off the airplane. Ain't nothing like it."

We never talked about whether he was scared, or whether I was worried about my flight the next day. We were fighter pilots, not therapists in training. And we didn't want to jinx each other. After a good half hour of chit chat, J.D. started to come down and I decided the best thing for me was to get some sleep.

"You'll be great, Big D. Now go to sleep," J.D. ordered as he reached up to pull the chain to the bare light bulb suspended from the rafters.

I fell asleep trying to picture the scene J.D. had just described for me and wondering if my own mission the next day would be anything like his.

We were scheduled to go after a place called Tallil Air Field in Iraq, to bomb the runway and taxiway complex so the Iraqis couldn't use it. We brought four F-15s along for air cover as well as four F-4 Wild Weasels, whose job it was to shoot missiles at the enemy's SAM sites if they tried to shoot at us. Also, two EF-111s accompanied us to jam the enemy radars and prevent them from locking onto us. All together, we were a package of 40 airplanes, a real gorilla.

We briefed for our mission in the same room where the General McPeak show had occurred. This time, there was just a little more electricity in the air. No need for feigned attentiveness. This brief was the real thing and the General McPeaks of the world seemed as far away as the moon.

The mission commander took his place up front, briefed the flight details. All 40 of us found the rim of our chairs the only comfortable place to position our butts as we furiously scratched notes on our line-up cards, reviewed our maps to be sure they were in order. The intelligence officer briefed the current situation and threats. The weather man covered the weather, which by now had started to worsen from northern Saudi Arabia and southern Iraq. We spent a lot of time on weather back-up delivery plans in case weather prevented us from seeing the runway complex. Then we suited up.

Since our unit was from Europe, we were supposedly the most prepared of all the units, but we were the only ones who had to fly with antiquated .38 caliber revolvers. Everyone else had the new 9 mm Baretta automatic pistols, a weapon I would have preferred to have with me if I went down behind enemy lines. They issued us about 20 rounds of ammunition, and we each loaded five rounds into our revolvers. You leave the barrel underneath the hammer empty so that if it accidentally discharges, you don't end up with a hole in your stomach. Our loaded revolvers we stowed in the holster sewn to our survival vests.

The usually jovial five-minute bus ride from the ops building to our aircraft was quiet, each pilot absorbed in his own thoughts or studying the information on his line-up card, all the while balancing the pile of gear at his feet. We each carried a helmet bag, map bag, chemical warfare mask, and escape and evasion kit, all of which fit into the cockpit in any available spot we could find. Crammed into our survival vests and flying harnesses, we filed off the bus looking like a parade of Michelin men, our G-suit pockets stuffed with maps, notes and those twin necessities, water bottles and piddle packs.

Pre-flight, my first mission. I circled my jet slowly, performing all my checks, opening access panels, looking for leaks, making sure the jet was ready to fly me to Iraq.

Holy shit, I thought, this is really gonna happen.

I kept reminding myself to concentrate. I didn't want to miss something critical. The crew chief approached me during pre-flight. "Looks ready to go, sir," he said. Then he asked me a question. "Sir, is this your first mission?"

"Yes," I answered, wondering if it showed.

"Well, you don't seem very nervous." He looked at me with what must have been either respect or disbelief.

"What's there to be nervous about?" I asked, wondering as I said it where this assinine comment had come from, given how I felt.

The crew chief gawked, his eyes wide, clipboard clutched to his chest, as if to say, I'm glad it's you and not me, buddy. I think we were both a little shocked at my response. I know I was. But I had to continue the Joe Cool charade, when really I was just trying to concentrate so I didn't screw something up.

I climbed the ladder and folded my long frame into the cockpit. The crew chief followed me up and helped me strap in. Then he tapped me on the shoulder. "Good luck, sir," he said. "Good hunting."

Getting 40 F-16s started-up ready for taxi and take-off is a huge orchestrational problem. Weapons crews swarmed over the jets, pulling all the bomb and missile safety pins. We pilots organized ourselves to be ready for take-off at the appointed time and in the right order. None of us had ever pulled off such a massive flight.

They put the 10th pilots in the back of the package, among the last to take off, because the other two squadrons had been there since August and knew their way around the AO—area of operation. We were the tail-end Charlies, and I was somewhere near the end of the tail end. Not the best place to be in any package and certainly not what I would have preferred on my first combat mission. But there I was.

There we all were. Me, K.C. Schow, Mongo Cerbins, Ragin' Bull, Ivan Thomas, Shiv Kapoor—my wingman in Goo Goo's place—Snuffy Smith, Hobo Long, Biff Motlong, Lunar Lawson. Together, we were bringing up the rear of our first Desert Storm combat mission when only two months earlier we had been dancing in the streets of Zaragossa, lubricated with large quantities of tinto, our bellies warm and full of Spanish delicacies.

We took off at 20-second spacing and formed into our four-ships, each four-ship maybe a mile or two behind the last. From our base outside of Abu Dhabi, we followed each other all the way across the Persian Gulf up to northern Saudi Arabia, where five KC-135 air-to-air refuelers were waiting for us. Our plan was to put eight F-16s on each refueler, four on each side, and fill everybody up with gas before going in to drop our bombs.

We were a monstrous swarm of machinery winging north in a glowering sky, each KC-135 a mother duck with her eight little ducklings trailing dutifully along. The tankers flew in a giant oval, forming an enormous racetrack pattern in the air. From the back end of the package, where we flew on the last tanker, I could look forward and see four other tankers, each surrounded by eight F-16s, all strung out before us. Several miles off the right wing as we flew north into war, two more tankers flew alongside us with F-15s and F-4s on their wings. Up ahead, the mountainous black cumulonimbus clouds we were about to enter loomed, a solid wall of weather.

18 January 1991

Friday

My first flight in combat. I flew in a package of 40 aircraft to an airfield in Iraq. It was a 4.7-hour flight. The attack took place right at sunset and there was a lot of weather in the area. We almost aborted, but finally made it to the target area.

As soon as we hit Saudi Arabia, the weather really started to get bad. From my vantage point, it looked like your basic "delta sierra" weather—dog shit in the sky. Luckily, the F-16 has radar, so at least we could keep track of where everybody was. The clouds were so dark and dense, though, I thought for sure we were going to lose some airplanes, go lost wingman and crash into each other. The conditions were perfect for a disaster.

I had gone into this kind of weather with this many airplanes only once before, and it was an experience I had not planned on repeating, certainly not while en route to a war.

The last time I went through something like this, we gave it a name: we called it the Baton Rouge Bomb Burst, for the way each jet flew blind, like bomb shrapnel propelled randomly through the air.

It was back in 1983. I was still a young lieutenant, still new to fighter jets, still new to the sky. It was one of our practice deployment exercises out of England Air Base, and we were scheduled to fly our entire squadron—24 A-10s made up of six four-ships each loaded with extra fuel tanks and any other equipment that might be needed in the expected theater of operations. The weather was standard central Louisiana cold front from the north meets warm front from the Gulf of Mexico. In other words, thunderstorms, rainshowers, reduced visibility and generally dog leavings throughout the entire region.

We were all hoping the deployment and flight would get canceled. But the powers that be ordered the squadron into the air, north into Arkansas, east into Missouri, then south into Alabama, back west through Mississippi and into southern Louisiana, and finally back to Alexandria. Total flight time: 4.0 hours.

Most of the flight entailed moving in and out of that dangerous weather and trying to avoid the thunderstorms. I was number four in the lead four-ship, with Crawdaddy Barton, and another second lieutenant, Don Butter, on the squadron commander's wing. Our commander, Colonel Bullet Bob Coleman, flew the lead. We were a bunch of young pups being tested by the boss.

Three and a half hours into this grueling flight, we were coming into southern Louisiana from Mississippi, about to make the turn north over Baton Rouge and home to Alexandria. We had begun our descent and managed to avoid most of the bad weather. Patches of green earth and brown water flashed by several thousand feet below us as we popped in and out of intermittent cloud decks. All of us tucked in as close as we dared to go. Up ahead, an ominous black cloud formation loomed like a column of smoke from the fires of Hades.

"Tuck it in tight, boys," the boss's voice crackled in my ears. The lightning bolts that shocked the sky up ahead were interfering with radio transmission.

"It looks pretty dark up here," he continued. Crawdad, Butter and I did our best to make sure we didn't lose sight of each other as we passed into the darkest, meanest cumulonimbus I had ever seen.

The violent weather tossed our little airplanes like so many matchsticks in a hurricane. We were buffeted around the sky so rapidly it made our heads spin, which isn't something any pilot needs when he's trying to keep track of which way is up and who's next door.

Just before we entered the cloud, I checked my position: I could see all three of the other aircraft around me. In the cloud, all but one had disappeared. I could see only Butter on my immediate left. Then Butter's fuselage vanished into the dark, and all I saw was his wing, a dark green plume extending out of the murk, my only reference point. Soon, that too was gone, and I was left hanging in the sky on a flashing green light attached to Butter's wingtip.

My hands were soaked with sweat inside my flight gloves as I worked the stick, rudder and throttle, trying for all I was worth not to lose sight of that green light, my lifeline. All was in vain, though, because soon the light vanished. I jammed the stick to the right, mashed the radio switch on the throttle and shouted into my microphone, "Four's lost wingman!"

"Three's lost wingman," Butter called, his voice splitting with the panic I felt.

"Two's lost wingman," Crawdad echoed. Number one was flying on instruments, out in the lead.

We had all gone lost wingman. We had all lost sight of one another in the muck.

My heart drummed adrenaline through my veins as I struggled to remember the correct procedures. Get on the instruments, a voice screamed in my head. Frantically I worked the controls, trying to recover my aircraft to level flight.

There we were, 5,000 feet above the earth, traveling at 300 mph, four of us within three feet of each other, and not one of us could see the other. It was like we had entered a tunnel of liquid night.

I had learned about spatial disorientation in class. But nothing teaches like experience. Suddenly I became an expert in spatial disorientation.

Colonel Coleman came over the radio as he called into Baton Rouge radar control.

"Baton Rouge, this is shark one flight. I need three additional IFR clearances to England Air Force Base." IFR clearances are instrument flight rules clearances, and no air traffic controller likes to give too many of these away, especially not all at once. Each IFR is a lot of work for the controller and requires a great deal of air space, which in turn requires the controller to coordinate the flights with other controlling agencies in the area.

Meanwhile, we tried to keep the rest of the group behind us from entering that cloud, but the next four-ship went lost wingman as well. Now they required four separate additional clearances. That was eight individual clearances Baton Rouge had to come up with in a hurry. "Wait a minute," the controller radioed back to Colonel Coleman. "You can't do that." He obviously had not quite grasped the severity of the situation. The squadron commander's answer made our circumstances clear.

"You don't understand," Coleman said in a commanding tone that even got my attention. "It's already done. We are lost wingman and we need your undivided attention, and NOW!"

I listened in disbelief as the radar controller again tried to resist.

"I don't have time to debate this with you," the commander announced, his voice hardening. "I have four aircraft up here in this soup and none of us can see one another. If you don't help us now, there's a good chance we're going to run some aircraft together. You and I don't want that, now, do we?"

Discussion over. We continued to battle to control our jets, get our new clearances from radar control, change our squawk—our radar identification—and turn to our assigned headings and altitudes.

At last the controller issued us our new clearances, but when he tried to get Crawdad to turn to a certain heading, maintain a specific altitude and change his squawk, Crawdad, in his slight Louisiana twang and a few octaves higher than his normal speaking voice, answered directly. "I'm flyin' *this* altitude, *this* heading and *this* airspeed. I'm squawkin' what I'm squawkin'. And I ain't changin' a thang." Never in the history of the 75th Fighter Squadron had so much information been transmitted in so few words.

It took him long enough, but the radar controller must have finally gotten the message. "Okay," he answered, and offered no argument.

The remainder of the return flight was uneventful, and we landed back at the base a half hour later, all of us about ten years older. As we walked back into the squadron, Colonel Coleman was the only one with a smirk on his face. The rest of us were ashen white from our recent adventures in space.

"How do you boys like flying fighters now?" he had asked with a grin.

That was all of eight years earlier, and I hadn't seen weather like that since, and I certainly never thought I would encounter it while en route to my first combat mission. I soon realized though that we were going straight for that evil cloud. This is not going to be good, I thought. Not good at all.

It was like driving down a crowded Autobahn at 150 mph in a thick fog. All I could see was the jet right next to me, and I couldn't take my eyes off of him because if I did, I was dead for sure. I couldn't really look at my aircraft instruments to tell what my altitude was, whether I was upside down or sideways, or climbing, or diving.

My body was coated with a slick sweat inside my flight suit. In a way, I was grateful that I had lived through the Baton Rouge Bomb Burst. At least I had had some practice. I wondered whether the pilots around me had ever gone lost wingman before. A prayer seemed like it might be in order, or a song, something to send up to heaven by way of a message.

It was well past Christmas, but it was a Christmas tune that popped into my head. Maybe it was the tension, maybe it was a way to relieve the tension. Anyway, I just kept singing it to myself, all the way into those clouds. The tune I sang went something like this:

Jingle Bells: The Marine Corps Version

Fuck, fuck, fuck!
Fuck, fuck, fuck!
Fuck, fuck, fuck fuck fuck!
Fuck, fuck, fuck,
Fuck, fuck fuck fuck
Fuck fuck fuck fuck fuck fuck Fuck-uck!

It summed up nicely how I felt at the moment.

We finally got the tanker to climb to a different altitude and turn to a different heading to slice our way out of the weather. I was grateful when we left that dark mass of cloud behind us. I felt my heart return to its normal rhythm.

Miraculously, everyone managed to get gassed up. I think the mission commander up front was close to canceling the mission altogether, because it looked like the weather up ahead might be bad enough to prevent us from making our target. We pressed on anyway. There was a certain amount of pride at stake. The F-15s, EF-111s and F-4 Weasels met us en route to the Iraqi border, as planned.

After we drew away from the tankers, the mission commander came up on the radio.

"Collie flight," he commanded. "Go tactical formation."

The four-ships answered in order, "Collie 5," "Collie 10," "Collie 15," and so on. We spread our aircraft out so that numbers one and three in each four-ship were lined abreast of one another about a mile apart. Numbers two and four were then 1,500 to 2,000 feet off their respective leads, about 30 degrees back. We called this formation "fluid four." Each four-ship was then one to one and a half miles behind the previous, so that the entire package of F-16s was a good 10 to 15 miles long. From the ground we must have sounded like what we were—death in the sky.

As we crossed the border of Saudi Arabia heading north, the cloud deck carpeting the earth obscured our view. We were maybe at 24,000 feet and if I looked out to the sides, I could see towering thunderstorms all around us. In fact, we had to turn the whole package to the northwest for awhile to get around one huge column of storms.

Finally, after hours of flying, refueling, dodging the weather and each other, we crossed the fence, flew over the Iraqi border. My stomach was tight. This was the moment I had trained for. Would I live up to that training?

I was too busy flying to be scared or worry too much about what would happen next. The actual mechanics of flying an airplane were second nature to me, and I spent most of my time staying in formation, monitoring the radar and radar warning receiver, cross checking my map and monitoring the radio to keep my situational awareness up.

My hands were busy on the stick and throttle, my head swiveling on my neck like a wobbly-necked dachsund on the back shelf of a Dodge Dart. I constantly scanned the instruments and the sky ahead. I was sweating again inside my flight suit, probably from a combination of nerves and excitement. I double-checked and triple-checked all my switches to make sure I was ready for whatever happened. Inside my flight gloves, my hands were slippery with sweat as my fingers flicked the rows of switches that surrounded me in my cockpit.

"Collie flight, fence in," the mission commander ordered, and 40 F-16s performed their fence checks over enemy territory. We switched our master arms on to prepare the bombs and missiles to employ. Chaff and flare dispensers flicked on, self-protection against enemy missiles, as well as jamming pods, to block incoming radar. We also changed our squawks, changed the IFF (identification friend or foe) to the preset frequency. We were ready. We were ingressing the target area.

I was at war.

"Collie flight, go strike frequency," the mission commander ordered again, his voice crackling with static. A strike freq order means no reply is required—or allowed. A flight goes to strike freq as it crosses into enemy territory, ready to drop its load. We were approaching our targets and the closer we got, the faster my heart pounded in my chest. I became aware of the sound of my own heavy breathing. My nerves and the shot of energy that tensed my muscles jolted my brain, kept me alert.

About twenty minutes after we crossed the fence, the mission commander called, "Collie flight, weather back-up. Repeat, weather back-up."

We were almost on target. I went into radar mode inside the aircraft and located the runway complex. Then I found my end of the runway. I was even able to get a good enough picture that I located my DMPI—designated mean point of impact—my target, the intersection of a main runway and a taxi way. This was it. The moment of truth.

"Collie two eight, go close formation," I called, when the time came to prepare to drop our loads.

"Roger," Shiv responded. I glanced to my right to see his aircraft closing on me. I was glad Shiv was my wingman today.

"Stand by to drop," I called.

I could hear people talking on the radio, "Heads up, Collie, triple A below." No surface-to-air missile warnings. I looked out in front of the aircraft, to the sides and down, saw little gray puffs in the air. It occurred to me that those must be triple A fire, but they were low, just above the clouds, probably 5,000 or 6,000 feet below us, maybe more.

Suddenly, a huge explosion and a great black cloud filled the air. Holy shit, I thought, what was that? I wondered if it was a missile or some huge anti-aircraft gun. It wasn't until we got down onto the ground later that I learned that someone in front of the package had dropped bombs that fused and detonated in the air. That was one mean explosion.

I checked out the aircraft in front of us, the F-16s up ahead, and saw the bombs fall in pairs straight down through the clouds, a scene straight out of a World War II or Vietnam movie. I could almost hear the whistle. In reality, the cockpit of an F-16 is totally silent but for the crackle of the radio and the whine of the radar warning receiver when a missile locks onto you.

Just a quick glance and then I had to bring my attention back into the cockpit, get my radar lined up in the center of the target.

I even turned on my onboard video camera and switched it from the radar picture up into the HUD, the heads-up display. I wanted to tape how I centered up all that data and released my load.

"Ready, ready, pickle!" I called to Shiv on the interflight radio, and my airplane shuddered as the two 2,000-pound bombs fell away toward earth.

Someone called out a SAM, but I never saw it. As soon as we dropped our bombs, we hit the burners and got our butts the hell out of there. I had two thoughts come to me at this time. The first was that I was born to do this stuff, and the second was that I wished we had seen more activity. That sounds silly, but it's what I thought. This is not a game, it's real, but it was the most exhilarating thing I've ever done. I wondered if I had killed anyone and I wondered if it would bother me. It doesn't. I'm too far removed at 24,000 feet.

When you're going into the target area and you have bombs on board, you're busy watching for threats and getting ready to blow something up. You feel big, macho and strong. But as soon as you drop your bomb and your mission is complete, you're ready for that hard curve to the south and an immediate "Let's get the hell outta here."

The flight en route to our target was adventure enough for my first day of combat. Turns out our return trip was even more fun. We reformed our formations as we headed back south toward the border. Aircraft everywhere.

No one was real interested in finding that nasty weather again, especially since night was coming on. First we had to try to locate the tanker to gas up for the trip home. It got pretty hairy. Not only were we uneasy about flying back into that weather at night, but the tanker pilots were a little bit excited about being that close up to Iraq without an escort.

Since it was still early in the war, we didn't know whether Iraqi fighters would be following us south. After we refueled, the tankers requested that we fly on their wing all the way back to our home base in the UAE. We agreed to escort them, but instead of flying direct, they flew due south into Saudi Arabia and then turned to the west and toward the UAE, lengthening our flight by probably 45 minutes to an hour.

By the time we got back to the base, it was late. While it was located outside of Abu Dhabi, it was far enough away that the city lights really didn't help our night navigation or light up the airfield area at all. It was a very, very dark flying environment at night, an environment that would prove fatal to one tired pilot later in the war.

We were exhausted after we landed. All in all, it had been a grueling 4.7-hour flight, our first day of combat, and we had encountered some of the worst flying weather I had ever seen. Still, we were way too pumped up to go to sleep. We took our films and all our flight material into the ops building to debrief and prepare for the next day's mission.

For me that first flight went just like a training mission. Even though we had to go to our back-up delivery, everything seemed to work just fine.

And because we couldn't see the ground, there was no way for us really to tell whether we hit our target or not. But you know when you have 40 F-16s each dropping two 2,000-pound bombs, that's a lot of iron and explosives to be falling on one runway complex. Even if we didn't exactly hit our DMPI, I have to think that their people had a little bit of their fight taken out of them, at least enough to slow down their operation severely, if not completely take it out.

I had done it. I had not only survived my first combat mission, I had performed well. All those years of training had kicked in when I needed them. A belated surge of fear swept over me as I lay in bed that night, waiting for sleep. But I battled it back into its dark corner and fell away into unconsciousness with a half grin on my face.

19 January 1991

Saturday

Nothing much today! Iraq has launched its second SCUD attack on Israel and so far, no retaliation from them. The missiles are very ineffective so far and Hussein's attempt to bring all the Arab world in to this war is failing. He must have more up his sleeve, but we don't know what yet. We sent out some F-16s today to try to find these mobile SCUD launchers and take them out. We'll have to wait to see how effective they are. I am on the board tomorrow for a dawn launch to go to Baghdad to pay a little visit. See how it goes!

20 January 1991

Sunday

Today I flew a 6.6-hour sortie to western Iraq to try to find some of the SCUD missiles to take them out with CBU-87 (CEM). It was a pretty exciting flight due to all the changes that took place. We had some bad weather in the target area and then some trouble finding the tankers.

It seems I was celebrating my success as a combat pilot a bit prematurely. Not that I was cocky. I was just proud that I hadn't succumbed to fear. But my second mission made my first seem like a walk in the park.

We had already briefed for another bombing run to Baghdad when they called in a last minute mission change to western Iraq, near the border of Syria, to chase SCUD missiles. Although we were glad not to have to go into downtown Baghdad, the fact that the change came last minute made it more difficult to get our huge package of airplanes to a target we knew little about. We had to air refuel three times: once in eastern Saudi Arabia, once in western Saudi Arabia, and once after the attack on the way home. And since it was another late afternoon raid, we had to air refuel and fly home in the dark. The whole experience turned out to be a very rude awakening.

En route to the second air refueling track, we questioned whether the target information was correct and what the weather might be in the target area. Then, to make matters worse, we found out that one of the air refueling aircraft dropped out and part of our escort of F-4s, F-15s and EF-111s would not be arriving. The mission commander, a guy from a Shaw squadron, decided to air refuel the first half of the package and take it into the target area with what escort we had. That left us in the back, stuck trying to talk more gas out of the tanker pilots so we would have enough to attack.

As we started our run north into Iraq and switched our radios to strike freq, another surprise greeted us.

"Boxer one two," my radio squawked, "SAM launch, right, one o'clock low."

"Heavy triple A, left, two o'clock, medium altitude." The voices were excited, breathless, a little shaky.

As we approached the target area, the escort aircraft were bingoing out. They were out of gas and egressing, leaving us in the lurch. By now, the front half of the package was leaving, but not before they had really stirred up the hornets' nest. We saw white streaks shooting skyward, and gray, white and black popcorn balls exploding up ahead.

On the ground, the vast expanse of desert was punctuated with earthen berms and revetments. Tan-colored sand blanketed the earth to the horizon in every direction, the entire landscape sliced by a highway running north/south. Out in the distance, to the left, plumes of black smoke rose from the ground where bombs had recently detonated. Intermittent muzzle flashes blinked on and off, what must have been the triple A guns.

Farther to the north, I watched two F-16s diving at the ground, and I saw their munitions separate from their aircraft. A huge billowing white plume of smoke, a misfired or damaged SCUD, shot up from the ground and then rolled and flew parallel to land, forming first a giant corkscrew and then rocketing back down to earth, where it exploded in a monstrous black cloud of smoke and blasted sand.

Then, wouldn't you know it, the aircraft I was flying decided it needed a vacation. The radar shut down a couple of times, so I had to restart it, wait for it to go through its warm-up cycle before I could reset it and know if it was going to work. The F-16 is a visual bomber and uses its radar to supply accurate air-to-ground information to put its bombs on target. I really wanted that radar working, so I wasn't about to give up on trying to get it back online. After a few minutes of panic, I had finally got it running again when the fault light in my jamming pod flashed repeatedly. Apparently it, too, wanted the day off.

I was busier than a one-legged man in an ass-kicking contest, trying to complete all my fence checks and recheck my systems, half listening to the excited voices on the radio, while I took in the action we were about to enter. At the same time, I had to keep track of my other flight members, look at the map stretched out on my lap and search for my target.

We were entering the target area when my radar warning receiver suddenly emitted a high-pitched wail. I looked down at the display screen. It was telling me an SA2 radar was looking at my aircraft.

"Spiked! SA2!" I called, as calmly as I could.

"Roger same," Shiv came back.

I looked around to try to locate the SAM. A few seconds passed, eons, and then the warning tone changed. Now a loud warble, the radar warning screamed "Missile launched!" into my headset. I furiously searched the area where the missile should be coming from.

"I got launch here, Shiv," I told my wingman.

"Four same," he answered.

"No joy," I came back. "No joy." I couldn't find the missile.

"Four same," he repeated.

We had a saying during the war: when the pig squeals, it's time to dance. The high-pitched warble coming from my radar warning receiver sounded a lot like a pig squealing, an invitation to dance if ever I heard one. It was time to start moving that airplane in the sky to keep the missile from hitting me.

"Tally ho, missile eleven o'clock low!" someone else called. Since I didn't see the missile, and had missile launch screaming in the radar warning receiver, I figured we were locked up pretty good. I had to assume that missile was headed straight at me.

"Hang on, Shiv," I called. "Chaff now!" and I rolled the airplane over onto its back, pushed the power up to mil, full, and took her down, my body locking against the Gs as they worked to pull me down into unconsciousness. Shiv followed me through the maneuver.

Several seconds later we pulled back out of the dive, dragged our noses around in a hard turn in an effort to lose the missile, if it was indeed tracking us. Soon after, the radar warning receiver calmed down. So did we. I let my thigh muscles relax, felt the blood flow back into my heart. I took a breath. A deep one.

We pointed our noses back into the target, but we were unable to find or see any SCUDs. With the rest of the package egressing, gas running low, Shiv and I rolled on the SA2 site, the smoke trail it made when it left the ground a perfect white finger in the sky pointing out its target—us.

I fingered the pickle button on the stick and maneuvered the bomb fall line so that it ran through the center of the SAM site. The pipper started its steady march up, so that it ended up directly over my target. My right thumb mashed down hard on the pickle button, ready to blow them away. Death unleashed from above.

The sky was pocked with holes of blue in a cast of gray clouds as we pickled off our bombs, the solid thump, thump shaking the aircraft, letting me know that the load had fallen away toward its target. The silent puffs of grey and white smoke now became our concern as we recovered from our dive and started a twisting climb up toward the relative safety of altitude. I grunted with the sudden Gs, tensing my muscles up against the inflated bladders that encased my stomach and legs, forcing the blood into my brain so that I wouldn't pass out.

Then we pointed our noses south. It was time to go home.

We headed out of the target area, climbing back up and reforming our flight, but there were so many F-16s in front of us, I couldn't tell which one was K.C., my flight lead, so I couldn't pull into my formation. "Rock your wings, Boxer two five," I radioed and scanned the sky for any F-16 in front of me rocking its wings. I spotted him. Ten o'clock, about three miles and slightly high. "Close it up," I radioed to Shiv, and we began to make our way over to K.C.

But the party still wasn't over. Suddenly, the radar warning receiver came back to life—the damn pig was starting to squeal again. The mission commander called for a climb to get us above the cloud deck over our heads, because at that moment we were a giant moving silhouette against the sky, sitting ducks in a shooting gallery. This time, we would outrun the thing.

"Burners now," K.C. ordered. K.C. is a great pilot, and he turned out to have a cool head in combat. Maybe he had a tendency to stick around the target area a little too long, but I couldn't worry about that now.

I rocked my wings for Shiv to move in to close formation on my wing and threw the throttle forward over the hump into full AB, the radar warning receiver all the while screaming "Missile launch!" at our six o'clock as we punched into the cloud deck. Going up!

What happened next threw my heart from its usual position, up and forward to lodge against my adam's apple. With the radar warning receiver still screaming, I heard a loud KABOOM! The jet rocked and shuddered violently. I got thrown forward in the seat, my feet tossed off the rudder pedals.

Aw shit, flashed through my mind, I'm hit.

Then I heard Shiv speak.

"Hey lead, looks like you've had a compressor stall."

A compressor stall is not that unusual in the damn Pratt and Whitney engines we called "coal burners." They were great when they first came out, in the 1970s, but by 1991, these engines were old news. The stall occurs when the turbine coughs, and the aftershock can send a pilot rocking around the cockpit like the world has ended.

After several seconds during which I worked at repositioning my heart in my chest, I came back with my best John Wayne.

"Yeah, but she's working okay now," I drawled, as if I hadn't just seconds before thought I'd glimpsed death on my instrument panel.

Somewhere around 30,000 feet we shot into the clear air above the cloud deck and came upon a breathtaking scene—airplanes everywhere, each writing its own history in the sky. Our contrails told the tale of our departure and our success in multicolored streaks that striated the orange-purple heavens. Vapor spoors that follow jets across the stratosphere, contrails emerge from the condensation that develops when heated jet fuel meets cold air. They looked almost fluorescent in this light, plumes of cold fire illumined by a setting sun.

Everybody made it out of the target area and came home. So far the wing has not lost anyone or any airplanes. However, we have not been too effective due to the bad weather covering up his airfields (our targets). It will not last forever and soon we will hammer him into submission. Right now the pressure is on us to find those SCUDs to keep Israel from getting involved in all of this. It is a risky business and not easy in an F-16. The bosses say do it, so we do it. Such is war.

Crud

One mission a day per four-ship was not enough. We needed to get more missions out of ourselves and our jets, and Abu Dhabi was too far away from Iraq to make that possible. From base, every mission entailed at least an hour and a half flight just to get to our targets, which added up to commuting wear and tear on jets and pilots alike. There just weren't enough hours of daylight.

That's when they sent us to KKMC, King Khalid Military City, a single, out-of-the-way runway in Saudi Arabia, about 50 miles south of the Iraqi border. An FOL, forward operating location, the A-10s had been using since the start of the war, KKMC became our new touchstone, the place we pre-positioned fuel and bombs so we could launch up to three missions a day into Iraq.

Now that we had a home away from home, we removed the external fuel tanks from our aircraft so we could each carry four bombs instead of two. We took off out of the UAE in four-ships and flew up to Saudi Arabia on the wing of a tanker stationed with us outside of Abu Dhabi. After tanking up just south of the Iraq-Kuwait border, we ran up and down the highways hunting targets. We dropped our bombs and then flew back into KKMC, always in a hurry to land, because by this point we would be close to running out of fuel.

25 January 1991

Friday

It's hard to believe that it's been five days since I last wrote in this book. The days run one into another and you lose track of the date and what day it is. Since Monday I've flown two more combat sorties. Tuesday we went up into western Iraq and demolished an early warning radar and electrical intelligence gathering center. It was a 6.1-hour flight but well worth it because the post-strike assessment is that we took it out. The eyes and ears of western Iraq are gone. SCUD hunting should be easier now.

The next day I flew a 4.1 strike to Tallil AF south of Baghdad. The weather was not great and so we were only partially effective. It's frustrating driving all this way and then finding the target partially obscured. Press on!

At KKMC, maintenance personnel reloaded the bombs and refueled the aircraft, and we were off again, back over the border, where we dropped our new load on yet another target, or maybe the same target as before. Then back to KKMC to reload, refuel and do it all over again. On the last mission of the day, instead of landing, we hit a tanker out over the Persian Gulf and flew all the way back to the UAE. All in all, they were long days, nine hours from take-off to landing back at Abu Dhabi. But we looked forward to them because we really felt like we were accomplishing something for the war effort.

Yesterday, a Saudi pilot killed two Iraqi "Mirages." Fox II kills on both of them. That, I think, is good for the overall war effort. Help keep this alliance together. Saudis protecting the homeland.

The Mirages were headed to the Gulf to shoot Exocet missiles at the Navy. There has been a lot of intel about the Iraqis and Iran being in cahoots. There is talk that we are now in peril of attack here from Iran and from across the Strait of Hormuz. That scares me.

From KKMC, a four-ship flew three missions a day, instead of just one, each jet dropping three loads of 8,000 pounds of bombs. That translated into one four-ship dropping almost 100,000 pounds of bombs on Iraq *every day*. The roar must have been immense from the ground, ceaseless, perpetual thunder.

We were hammering Hussein and could only wonder why he was offering so little resistance. One theory was that he was about to use his chemical weapons, but we agreed that even if he did, it would have little effect on the outcome of the ground war.

I was supposed to fly on Thursday, but our tanker supply dropped out so we were scrubbed. Needless to say, it was an emotional roller coaster. We were in our jets with the engines running when we were cancelled. However, any sane man would never pass up the opportunity to get out of having people shoot at him.

Last night I was on the night mission planning cell. We stayed up all night long and broke out the air tasking order (ATO) from headquarters and planned the missions for the guys flying the next day. It's now 1200 hours on Friday afternoon and I have the day off to sleep and relax. Tomorrow I fly in the late raid. No idea what the target will be. We have started to concentrate on the Republican Guards. Hopefully we can break them soon and put an end to all of this.

Today I got all kinds of mail. A real pick me up. Plus, a package from Susie. I'm gonna have a lot of letters to return. Sue and Erin sound as if they are doing well. All of the mail is from before the hostilities started. They all say they hope the deadline will come and go and peace will be realized. It's hard to believe this was eight days ago. I wish there was some way I could reach them to let them know I am okay! They must be really worried.

Alfred Mongo Cerbins. He got his call sign from his size. A giant of a man, Mongo was at least six feet four and of equally substantial girth. We often wondered how he squeezed his enormous frame into the cozy cockpit of an F-16. Roomy it ain't.

Mongo was chosen to go up to KKMC for a week to be the "ramp rat," to coordinate rearming and refueling all the aircraft on their turnaround trips. Mongo's was the face that greeted me one January morning when I climbed down the ladder from my jet.

By now, Goo Goo was flying my wing. While he had had to sit out the first few days of the war, the boss finally cleared him to go. And he was doing a good job. It must have been the prewar nerves that got him. Nobody held it against him, since we all felt it. It was just that Goo Goo let it show.

K.C., Buck, Goo Goo and I had just landed after the first of that day's missions. The weather was clear, perfect flying skies all the way into Iraq and back. In that part of the world, on a clear day you really can see forever, and in this case, forever extended all the way from KKMC to beyond the Iraq border. The flat desert skyline shimmered under a rising sun for a full 50 miles and on into the vast, empty horizon.

"Hey, Big D," Mongo grunted up at me from his spot down on the tarmac, "how'd it go out there? You get any?"

"Mongo, my man, how you holding up?" We pitied Mongo his ramp rat assignment. Living conditions at KKMC were considerably more austere than at Abu Dhabi: tents instead of hooches, no air conditioning, and general misery from a pilot's perspective since you couldn't fly. At least it was only an eight-day assignment. I wondered what he had done to deserve this. It was usually the older lieutenants or the younger captains who pulled ramp rat duty, and Mongo was neither. The rest of us were stuck back at the base as FIDOs, fighter information duty officers. Fortunately.

"Great," I answered with the easy, cruel sympathy of the powerful for the meek. "We hammered the hell out of a triple A site north of Kuwait

City, up towards Basra." I didn't want to gloat too much. If I were Mongo, I'd hate to hear the stories from pilots as they returned from their bombing trips.

"Yeah, great D," Mongo answered, turning away from me. He seemed to be taking it just fine. But in that big hulk of a back he could probably find room to hide a lot.

Buck, Goo Goo and K.C. converged on us from where they'd parked their jets. After greetings all around, Mongo told us a tale of life at KKMC. Turns out it was not all boredom and jealousy. Turns out it was also dangerous. Only later would I come to understand just how dangerous.

Mongo struck a pose against my jet, his arm up on the wing like he owned it. "Life can get just a little monotonous when you're counting jets instead of flying them," he began. I could see that Mongo was settling in for a long story, and I had to pee like a race horse. Apparently I wasn't alone.

"So what's the punch line, Mongo? Some of us have places to go, people to bomb." Buck could be just a little mean at times. A skinny little guy, maybe five feet tall, Buck was no one to be acting like he was Mr. Ace Pilot. He had not proved very good at controlling his fear in the sky and had been asking a lot of questions about obvious things. Besides, he talked too much on the radio for a wingman and had a hard time finding the right frequency. On the other hand, Mongo was asking for it. We didn't have much time between flights.

"They were having this cookout for us visiting crew," Mongo continued, his big face flushed. "I had just filled my plate and sat down at a picnic table when a brick on the table blares out 'Alarm red! Alarm red!' Around here alarm reds are common as flies on a dead Iraqi, so I just ignore it and start plowing into my food." A rather unwelcome image comes to mind, of Mongo launching into a huge plate of chili, macaroni salad and lime jello.

"I'm wolfing down my chili, trying to remember where I put my mask, you know?" he continues, knowing he has us now because we've had our own scares with NBC alarms, nuclear, biological, chemical weapons attack alerts. "All of a sudden, I hear this BOOM! at the same time that I feel it, and I know it's the sonic boom of a Patriot leaving its launch tube. So now I know this is serious."

There goes the plate, I think. Lime jello, chili, macaroni salad everywhere.

"I dash the 50 yards back to the truck to get my mask. Even with the sprint and dropping my plate, I have the mask on in under 10 seconds. We were okay, though. I watched while the two Patriots went up and searched the sky for the SCUDs. I'm hoping they live up to their freaking reputation, you know? Then I see the two contrails find the first SCUD and blow it up. They needed three missiles for the next SCUD, but they got it. Each one of them babies kept arching up and up, farther back, until BLAM! the third one found the SCUD."

Well, I think, what a nice way to start your second mission of the day, the mental picture of Mongo's abandoned meal mixing with images of chemical weapons raining down over KKMC. I made my way to the head and left the others talking with Mongo. A few days later he was back at Abu Dhabi, flying.

27 January 1991

Sunday

Flew a 5.5-hour mission today. Went 200 NM [nautical miles] up into Iraq, west of Baghdad and orbited over Al Assad AF. We were looking for SCUDs reported to be in the area. We couldn't find them, but we bombed our original target, a weapons storage bunker complex. We took some AAA from the airfield, but most of it was small caliber. I think you can say we have achieved air superiority when we can orbit at 20,000' over an air-field 200 NM inside of enemy territory and they don't even come up to meet us. I have to believe that the Iraqi military is really hurting.

Estimates of how long they will all last vary a lot. Conservative view is up to a year. I don't expect they can hold out that long, not with what we're doing to them every day. However, I do think up to three or four months would be realistic. The Army says mid-February before they are ready to attack. This is good, because it gives the air power longer to work on the Iraqi army in Kuwait. I personally would not want to be on the ground there even if I was in a shelter. Word from the front is that the A-10s are do-ing a good job of making life miserable for the enemy.

Going in and out of KKMC, I saw A-10s, some of them with the desig-nation of my old FAC squadron, the 23rd TASS (tactical air support squadron). Others had the teeth painted on the nose—the 23rd fighter wing, where I was assigned from 1983 to 1986.

I wondered if I knew any of the pilots. In fact, I was dead sure I did. I recognized their voices on the radio. It was like a reunion of sorts, only we weren't celebrating anything. Yet. But we were flying together over an-other desert in another part of the world, and their presence brought Tuc-son to mind, those days in the OA-37 and OA-10.

Not long after Roland Perry died, Dan "Sandy" Sandkamp showed up in Tucson from a stint in the A-10. I was by then an instructor in the OA-37 and showed Sandy the ropes. Although he couldn't replace Roland, Sandy and I got along and became great friends.

Sandy is one of the few lucky fighter pilots actually to survive a plane crash. It happened after he got caught in the wake turbulence of some A-10s, as he was attempting to land. The pressure altitude of the runway, the wind conditions, and the large number of aircraft landing in front of him at George Air Force Base in Victorville, California, all conspired against him. He found himself sinking rapidly into the desert. His A-10 slammed into the ground, shearing the gear and fuel pods, tossing dirt, rocks and vegetation. Luckily, the jet stayed upright and Sandy was able to open the canopy and egress on his own. He sustained only minor injuries. At least from the accident.

Pilots talk of the Air Force tradition of eating its own, that special way it has of diverting blame from itself and onto its personnel, a tradition I came to experience firsthand once I became ill. In Sandy's case, the higher-ups tried to blame him for the crash, which would have meant the end of his Air Force career. But he was exonerated in the end, since he was only doing what the tech orders described as correct procedure in such a situation.

I wondered if Sandy or Nutter, Hoss or Jimbo was sharing this Arabian sky with me now. I wondered if I had crossed flight paths with any of them. I wondered if we would all survive this war to live more good times like we did all those years ago in Arizona.

> I'm glad to hear that the "Hog" [the A-10] is doing so well. I always knew that was a good A/C [aircraft]. Given the right circumstances it can be devastating.

Our targets changed throughout the war. Some days we would be after something strategic like an airfield, or just tanks, or armored vehicles. Or else they would send us out for bridges on one of the two rivers—the Tigris and the Euphrates—or we would be given sections of river to patrol. If we saw any sort of river crossing or bridge building going on, we would try to hit it.

We also went after the Republican Guard. The only thing we were instructed not to strike were bridges close to towns, because we weren't carrying any of those laser-guided munitions the generals were so fond of demonstrating on CNN, and we didn't want one of our bombs to stray into a surrounding town.

28 January 1991

Monday

We, I, was not tasked to fly today, so I took the day to rest. I have a cold, but it won't stop me from flying. Bag some rays. Get ready to plan tomorrow's mission. Again after the Guard. We have six MK-82s each. They are 500 pounds each.

Nice day today! It's starting to get hot here. Word up from the front is that the oil spill has been slowed down. Good news.

Baghdad has again said that it will make the Allies pay. He (Saddam) claims the Allies will all die, in the "mother" of all battles. Who does he think he's kidding? So far he has used the SCUDs on civilian targets, then puts POWs on TV, then he releases millions of barrels of oil into the Gulf. By these actions, he is showing the world that he is an animal and that the allied nations are correct in fighting him now, instead of later.

Next, I think we will see the chemical and biological weapons come out. If he does this to anyone, but especially to Israel, I think Baghdad will be vaporized!

By the end of January, the hog log in the O Club was a smeared, multicolored history of the war, pilots scrawling their wisdom in green, red, black and blue. Some messages were adorned with accompanying artwork, which led us to conclude that there was a reason these men were flying jets and not painting murals. Still, I guess you could say it was art, of a sort. Art and history at once.

But it was history for the moment, not for the ages, history as we lived it every day. Much of it related to the weapons, good and bad, when it wasn't about the CNN correspondents and their inaccuracies.

"The F-15E Eagle's booster thruster is a SCUD buster and John Sweeney is a CNN buffoon," someone recorded on the wall. The F-15 afterburner has never been called a *booster thruster* and John Sweeney obviously had no clue.

Someone else recorded a few other CNN gems: "When I heard what I heard, believe me, I wished to hell I had not been at ground zero," Peter Arnett. "If this is a surgical strike, I don't like being this close to the operating table!" Bernard Shaw, 17th floor, Al Rashid Hotel, Baghdad.

When we weren't watching CNN or recording the day's events on the hog log, we were blowing off steam by enjoying a game of Crud, a game every pilot knows. Played on a snooker table with just the cue ball and the eight ball, no sticks are used in the game of Crud. It's just the pilot and his balls.

The eight ball is set at one end, in the center of the table, and a player from the opposing team uses the cue ball to try to hit the eight ball into a corner pocket. Play alternates between players on opposite teams, and continues until a member of one team is able to knock the eight ball into a corner pocket.

Players must shoot from the ends of the table and not the sides, and take care not to shoot out of turn, or let the eight ball stop moving before they hit it. Violators have a life taken away: all players start with three lives, and when you lose all three lives, you're out of the game. You're dead.

If a player shoots the cue ball from the side and not the end of the table, he is called by the referee for "balls," referring to the part of a male anatomy that must not cross the end of the table. The winner is the team that has members remaining alive when the other team has run out of lives.

Where the game of Crud comes from no one knows, but the tradition may have its roots in the resilience of pilots. To survive, a pilot must have more than one life. He must also know that it is not up to him to count the lives he has used or the lives he has left. He must always play as if this life is his last and only life, and hope that his fellow pilots do the same.

29 January 1991

Tuesday

Today I flew a 3.6-hour sortie into southern Iraq against the Republican Guard. We dropped four CBU-87s each. The most impressive thing was that there was a steady flow of A/C into the area. Bombs are falling there 24 hours a day.

There was very little in the way of air defense there. We dropped our bombs on a concentration of vehicles. There were a lot of things burning on the ground. The A-10s were in there killing tanks. The Iraqi Army cannot hide. They are being obliterated. Hussein must not know what is really happening there.

This is so easy, there must be something going on behind the scenes. We are all wondering what the trick will be that Hussein will pull out next. I'm betting it is chemicals. I hope not.

I wonder if I killed anyone today. I don't worry about it much, though. I think of it more as dropping bombs on things instead of people. I'm trying to destroy their ability to fight. I'm saving the life of our boys down on the ground every time I take out some of them. Besides, they sure as hell are trying to kill me, too! I don't intend on letting them. That is all cold hard fact.

Every day I fly, my heart rate jumps up, my nerves are on edge and I take everything and everyone seriously. When I cross the border into Iraq/Kuwait, it's the most alert, cautious and intense time of my life. Everything depends on it. I'm fighting for everything I believe in. I love you, Sue and Erin. My family must be going crazy at home. I wonder where Tim is now.

3 February 1991

Sunday

Today is my birthday. 32 years on this earth. Yahoo! Not really much to celebrate because of the war and all.

It's 1200 hours on Sunday afternoon and I'm sitting in our makeshift O Club, alone, watching CNN news. Hussein launched more SCUDs last night. I had to work all night in the mission planning cell so I am not flying today.

So far I have flown nine times. I guess that is really not all that much, but it is about average for our squadron. We have really started to hammer the Iraqi Army in Kuwait. We are on them 24 hours a day. Every time they come out into the open they get killed. They tried an assault on a small border team this week (Khafki) and were basically annihilated. A lot gave up or were taken prisoner. Hussein is trying to get the U.S. to start the ground war. Another last ditch effort by a desperate man.

Saddam, we're coming for you! It won't be long now!

From our wing, we lost three aircraft during the war. One pilot, a guy named Dale Cormier, crashed just 17 miles from the base one night after flying three combat missions out of KKMC. They determined it was probably spatial disorientation. Just got confused, lost his point of reference, thought up was down and down was up and flew straight into the ground, all the while thinking he was pointing his jet to the heavens.

One day when we were flying jets from the Shaw wing, we went up to Kuwait to hit a target. We were scheduled to come back to base to fly the missing man formation for Dale Cormier's memorial.

I was supposed to be the one to pull out of the formation as the number three. On this one day, though, it seems my bombs just didn't want to release from my aircraft. I tried everything, even an emergency jettison, any kind of jettison. Those damn bombs just would not separate. I had to fly from Kuwait all the way back to the UAE with four 2,000-pound bombs strapped to my gut and then land the thing. Trying to land a jet loaded with live bombs is like skimming a crate of eggs across a driveway at 300 miles an hour and hoping none of them break.

Even so, I was not nervous. Apprehensive, maybe, after everything I had done to try to make those bombs come off. I was afraid they would suddenly decide to come loose just as I touched down. Obviously, that never happened, but at the time I couldn't have known I'd live to tell the story.

I found out later that as I landed, people were lining the runway, taking pictures and videotapes of me landing that loaded aircraft, to see if something loud, memorable and fatal would happen that they would have witnessed and recorded.

I suppose it's just human nature, hoping to record the gory details of an F-16 and its pilot getting blown to bits as he tries to land with 8,000 pounds of munitions strapped to his wing. I disappointed them, though. It just wasn't my turn.

Michael in his T-38 at Vance Air Force Base in Enid, Oklahoma, 1982.

Michael and Susan on the evening of their wedding day, May 25, 1984.

Four F-16s flying in formation over the German countryside. Michael is flying wing in the first pair, in the second jet from the bottom, labeled 10th AMU (for Air Maintenance Unit), 1989.

Michael in full flight gear posing in front of his F-16 on the base in Abu Dhabi during Desert Storm, January 1991.

Michael, wearing a Red Sox hat, standing in front of his F-16 on the base in Abu Dhabi during Desert Storm, 1991.

Homecoming. Michael arriving at Bradley Field Airport in Windsor Locks, Connecticut in June 1991 and being greeted by his parents, Rae and Tom Donnelly.

Family portrait: Michael, Susan, Erin and Sean, taken in Wichita Falls, Texas in late 1994.

Michael in the backyard of their South Windsor home, November 1997. (Photo by Brad Clift, *The Hartford Courant.*)

How Do You Spell Victory?

We were running out of targets. The war was not over, though, because Hussein was not backing down. No one could figure out why, or what he thought he could achieve with his entire military pounded into oblivion by almost 30 days of non-stop bombing. He kept promising he would send the war home with us.

Up at KKMC and on the front lines, chemical weapons alarms were as common as gnats. Intel briefings assured us repeatedly that these were all false alarms, that no chemical weapons had been employed to date, a great relief to all, of course, because it meant they believed Hussein was not likely to use them.

Not once were we ever briefed on a chemical or biological weapons threat, and our worries about Hussein's use of these munitions were limited to what he might try when the ground war started. Mostly we were convinced that he was already defeated, that our complete and total victory was just a matter of time.

We also knew that George Bush had made a promise to Saddam Hussein: if he used chemical weapons, the coalition forces would drop a nuclear bomb on Baghdad. Maybe he was not such a madman after all, we thought. Maybe he understood the power of that threat.

By now, most of the military targets in Iraq had been destroyed. We were traveling deeper and deeper into the country just to find something to bomb, and when we arrived, we could locate only a few desolate revetements out in the desert, most of which were empty or decimated by some earlier mission.

A few times, we found pontoon bridges or river crossings. We would go in and take them out. Once, Buck Richards and I found a couple of pontoon bridges on the Tigris, and we hit both of them. I actually saw my bombs hit. Right in the middle. I looked down and back and saw huge chunks of metal fly through the air, turning and twisting, water spraying everywhere. There was no bridge left after that. I don't know if there were any troops on it or nearby.

It was these missions, when we hit targets on the ground and watched them blow up, that were truly satisfying. But there were others when we went in and tried to hit targets and the munitions either failed to work because they were so old—some of the stuff we dropped was made back in 1970 or '71 for the Vietnam War—or else we had the wrong kind of fins on our bombs and they wouldn't fly accurately.

You could have a vehicle lined up, or a building, or whatever, and the bombs would leave your jet and get into what the textbooks called a PIO, pilot-induced oscillation, although this problem was not pilot induced. The bomb separated from the aircraft, but the fins weren't big enough to guide it, and it would wobble in the air like a cartoon bomb heading for the Road Runner. Unlike the cartoon, however, the bomb would miss the target. Those days were frustrating. Except for the people on the ground. On those days, Allah was with them. Those bombs just weren't meant to find whoever we were targeting that day.

For all the missions we were flying, it wasn't surprising that we had our share of weapons malfunctions. And we became so intimate with those weapons that we named them. There was the Crowdpleaser, the MK-84, a 2,000-pound bomb, very accurate and with a large blast effect, named for the huge fireworks effect it launched on detonation, the kind of fireworks blast that makes a languid Fourth of July crowd say "Ooooh!"

The Ladyfinger, an MK-82, 500-pound bomb, had a very small blast effect. Loaded on triple ejector racks, a pilot would carry six of these at a time. They created a lot of drag and weren't very accurate. Most pilots preferred Crowdpleasers when they could get them.

Sparklers, on the other hand, a CBU (cluster bomb unit), were so called because of the way they looked when they detonated. They often had fuse and canister problems. Still, they were effective on trucks and troop positions.

We also liked the bomb we called the Gift That Keeps on Giving. Another CBU, it was time-delayed to detonate randomly, well after you left the target area.

And finally, there was Molten Jism, my favorite. A CBU-87, this weapon, when its submunitions detonate, is like lethal popcorn, especially when it hits anything that produces secondary explosions. It's like throwing a strip of firecrackers on the ground. Its depleted uranium core made it especially effective against tanks.

February 13, 1991

Saturday

   I have flown ten sorties in the last ten days. I don't know how much longer this is going to go on, but we are all ready to be done with it and go home.

   It's funny too because it has only been about three weeks. Not long at all as far as wars go. Air power has really been smacking Hussein good and we can keep it up for a while without much problem. So, I think we will, at least for a little while, before we start a general attack. Hopefully that will be an overwhelming success and not take long, so we can go home. Let's hope.

   Needless to say, but, I miss Sue and Erin and all my family and look forward to being home. I wonder sometimes if I'll make love to Sue again. I can't wait to hold her in my arms. Life seems so precious now. I can't wait to hug and kiss Erin.

By now Kuwait was burning. Not the whole country, not Kuwait City. Only the most flammable thing in Kuwait itself: the oil. Iraq had set fire to the legions of oil wells that punctuate the Kuwaiti desert, transforming the vast arid plains into the fields of Hades. Towering spumes of liquid fire shot into the sky, spilling acrid black dust over thousands of miles, rendering the air unbreathable for Kuwaitis, for allied troops and for the invading Iraqi army. And who knew what Hussein was incinerating with that oil? Was it just the oil going up in smoke, or was he also burning something more pernicious?

On our way into and out of the Kuwaiti theater of operations, we flew over these burning oilfields, through thick skies choked with ominous black clouds, clouds of spent oil staining the poisoned air, clouds so thick and high we were forced to fly on instruments because we lost sight of the ground and one another in the murk.

The burning of Kuwait was scorched earth policy at its finest. If Hussein really intended to attach Kuwait, then the booty was undoubtedly the country's oil wealth. By incinerating it, Hussein was showing us he knew he wasn't going to be able to keep the country he coveted. If he couldn't have it, no one else would have it, either.

Saddam Hussein had shown himself to be a world enemy, by threatening to use chemical and biological weapons, by actually using them against his own people, by intentionally spilling millions of gallons of oil into the Persian Gulf, a pristine body of water remarkable for its beauty, transparent, liquid turquoise teeming with life. Saddam Hussein was not just an enemy of the coalition, not just an enemy of Kuwait. He was an enemy of life itself. We came to think of him as death on two legs, the devil incarnate.

16 February 1991

Tuesday

I have to pull night duty officer (NDO) and there is no flying for me on these days. Sleep in the day and work at night.

The war goes well, relatively few losses compared to what we have done to Iraq. I don't think they understand what we are capable of and how we would fight a war. Hussein is an idiot. He could save a lot of his lives and he won't. Some time in February it hits the news that he was almost killed by F-16s attacking a convoy along the route from Basra to Baghdad. That would have been fine. But, no cigar! The fight goes on.

We never knew from day to day where we would be flying, what our targets might be. One day we might scour Al Taqqadam air field west of Baghdad under a hail of triple A and SAMs. The next might find us patrolling the roads in and out of Kuwait City, where some traffic still moved.

The ground war started three days ago. The initial reports are very good. Minimal casualties on the coalition side with up to 20,000 POWs. Army is making great strides. This is all good news. The end of the war is near! Today Baghdad announced, unofficially, that it was willing to leave Kuwait. U.S. and allies rejected it because they want Hussein to acknowledge the U.N. resolutions and publicly state that. Meanwhile the war goes on! A SCUD hit in Dharan today and killed 22 people. That bastard is going to pay!

To bring this up to date: So far, I have flown 29 sorties and have logged 100.4 hours. An average of 3.46. Since we left home on 29 December 1990 I have flown 37 sorties and 124.7 hours.

Once the ground war began, they sent us up to the battle areas to perform close air support, to coordinate attacks with the Army, to be sure the targets we bombed were enemies, not friends. But the ground troops were moving so quickly, it was hard to keep up with where they were. We were always afraid of hitting friendlies.

One day, we got handed off on the attack frequency to a British forward air controller who gave us coordinates and information about a pocket of Iraqi tanks the coalition forces had bypassed on their rush through the country.

On the way from the initial point to the target area, we saw a bunch of vehicles. They were in the wrong coordinates, but they looked like enemy tanks. It was actually K.C., who was leading the flight that day, who said, "Let's look up further and see if we can find anything at the briefed location." I don't know what made him say that, but I came to be very grateful that he did.

We pressed on, and we did find some scattered tanks at the area we were briefed on. That's where we dropped our bombs. I think we probably hit one or two of them, but it was hard to tell because of the weather and the sun angle. Right after us, as we were leaving the target area, a couple of A-10s checked in on the same frequency, so the forward air controller tried to describe the same target area to these A-10s.

We checked off freq and flew home.

Later that afternoon we were in the ops building when K.C. was called to the phone to answer some questions about our mission. Turns out that several British tanks had been shot up in that area by some A-10s, probably with maverick missiles. They had struck the wrong target. Nine British soldiers died in the assault.

War is by nature confusing. Train and plan as much as we do, and still these things happen. What a tragedy, both for the soldiers who were killed and the pilots who dropped the bombs. There but for the grace of God, I thought.

The mishaps became more common the more likely our victory seemed, as if a communal sense of complacency clouded our judgment. It worried me. Like we couldn't get out of our own way fast enough to win this damn war and get the hell out of this place.

One day we were coming into KKMC when word came over the radio that an OA-10 Nail FAC pilot was all shot up. When I flew OA-10s, Nail was our call sign—I was Nail 75. Chances are I knew this guy, flew with him back in Tucson. He was coming back to KKMC to try to land. The talk was of aircraft hydraulics system problems and engine trouble. He was flying in manual reversion. I remembered how the A-10 tech manual warned against trying to land in manual reversion, since the back-up flight control system is designed only to get the aircraft out of the threat area.

Just go to a secluded spot and punch out of the damn thing, I thought. Don't take a chance on landing an aircraft that's shot up. There were plenty of helicopters to pick him up. They would probably be there waiting for him.

I willed that pilot to hear my thoughts.

We landed right in front of him. As we taxied into our parking spot, I looked down the ramp where he was coming in. He seemed to be lined up with the runway, but moving excessively left and right, up and down, too much motion for a smooth landing. I watched as his airplane hit the runway, slid to one side, bounced up into the air, and then veered to the right. The nose wheel collapsed and the nose of the aircraft plowed into the soft sand, cartwheeling the jet over on its back. His ordnance started to cook off, and then the jet blew up. There was very little chance for a pilot to survive that kind of explosion.

He didn't. And a couple of ground personnel in the area got hurt trying to save him. God save that guy right there, I thought, as I watched a crew chief dash toward the flames. Anger welled up in me. This guy was a FAC from my old squadron, and I wondered if he was somebody I knew.

What a waste. All that pilot had to do was eject out of the airplane and chances are he would have lived. But that's a hard decision to make. What's worse, he was probably set up because earlier on somebody else had landed an A-10 that was all shot up, and that guy became a hero.

This young lieutenant was probably thinking he could do the same thing, he could go home a hero, too. Instead he went home dead.

Half an hour later, as we taxied out to take off again, the carcass of his charred jet lay skewed in the sand off to my right. I could see the pilot's body still in the cockpit, all black and stiff from the fire. On the other side of the taxiway, the other badly shot up A-10 that the "hero" had landed was getting loaded onto a flatbed to be shipped back to the U.S. Both airplanes were class A, totaled. Only one killed a pilot and the other didn't.

I felt pissed and angry and wanted to go kill somebody and get these lousy Iraqis and just bomb the shit out of them and end this thing.

The war may have been close to ending, but it wasn't over yet, and we hadn't won yet. We were to lose yet another aircraft before we could say we had lived to tell the story.

We called him Psycho for a reason. The only pilot in our squadron to be shot down during the war, Bill "Psycho" Andrews was doubly unlucky: he was shot down on February 28, 1991, the last day of combat. His initials were BA, short for Bad Attitude, and that attitude showed in whatever he did. When we played Crud, Psycho was more aggressive than most others. For him, Crud was a contact sport.

The evening of February 27, Psycho and I were sitting together in the briefing room looking at his HUD videotape from that day's mission. We reviewed the section of his tape when he had taken his wingman, young

Joey Booher, call sign Boo Boo, down pretty low beneath a deck of weather to see if they could find a target. Triple A and small arms fire peppered the sky all around his aircraft, and Psycho's voice on the tape told the story of his brush with disaster.

"You know, Psycho," I told him, "we're kicking the shit out of these guys. The Army's running all over them. There's no sense going down that low." It wasn't like me to give another pilot advice. I learned a long time ago not to judge what someone else does in a single seat airplane.

But this was so dangerous that I felt moved to say something. Plus, there's a very fine line between bravery and stupidity, and Psycho was teetering on the edge. I was worried about the guy and especially about young Boo Boo. It clearly wasn't a very smart idea to be poking around down low right over the top of a bunch of pissed-off Iraqis, especially if there wasn't some dire need like troops in contact or a search and rescue mission.

Psycho stroked the large, unkempt mustache he had sprouted and cocked an eyebrow at me. I got the sense that, as usual, Psycho wasn't taking me too seriously. He squinted his brown eyes at me, his face lit with that familiar irreverence that seemed to dictate his every move.

Like many of us, Psycho had taken advantage of the relaxed regulations that governed personal grooming during the war to grow some facial hair. Psycho's mustache contributed to his reputation as a slightly unpredictable pilot; while his head was helmeted with light brown hair, the mustache looked like it belonged on some swarthy Mediterranean type, like my Uncles Guido and Pat. I could see that he relished the odd picture his mismatched hirsute appearance presented.

We finished up our session and headed back out into the night, Psycho ducking his head under the door as he slapped me on the back. "Thanks for the advice, D. See ya."

I wouldn't catch sight of that long, lanky frame again during this war, because apparently my advice didn't sink in. The very next day he took Boo Boo back down underneath a bad section of weather again, looking for targets.

Most of us were already back at the base when we got word to gather in the camouflage-covered patio we had built next to our hooch. Julio, squadron commander, and Woody, operations officer, followed the stragglers in and then turned to face us.

They didn't need to call for quiet. We could tell from their faces that the news was not good.

"I have some bad news, gentlemen," Julio began, scanning the group of pilots standing nervously before him. "About an hour and a half ago, Bill Andrews got shot down." None of us dared look at anyone else. Psycho's loss was a defeat we could only take personally, collectively. I felt a surge of feeling connect us, linking us in our powerlessness and rage.

"We have audio of Bill going down," Woody continued. "He managed to pull out his hand-held radio on his way down. It doesn't look good. His leg is broken, and they were shooting at him in his chute." We exchanged glances, knowing glances. It sounded very bad indeed. I doubted I would ever see Psycho Andrews again.

"I know you're angry. We all are. But there's nothing any of us can do," Julio told us. "And by the way, all of the sorties are on hold for tomorrow."

They had gotten word the war might be over, news that meant two different things: the war might be over, but Psycho Andrews was down behind enemy lines, most likely dead or dying, and if not already dead on the ground, most likely a prisoner of war.

> A helicopter with five people on board is shot down by triple A. All are assumed dead trying to get Psycho out. Radio contact is lost. We assume he is a POW or dead.

The squadron is silent and we file over to the O Club to drink a toast to Psycho. No one can sleep that night.

When Boo Boo got back to base that night, he brought his HUD tape. We headed over to a briefing room to watch the tape and see what we could learn about what had happened.

Boo Boo was just 23. Tall and slim, with sandy hair, blue eyes and the smooth complexion of the boy he still was. He slumped into the room, the crowd of anxious pilots crowding him, welcoming him back into the brotherhood. None of us blamed him for Psycho's downing. One of those rites common to athletes and pilots, we wanted to console our comrade with our silent presence. This was a collective loss, no one's fault.

Boo Boo was clearly dejected, shaken by the day's events. He talked excitedly, his nervousness apparent in his restless gestures and darting eyes. I didn't know if he felt guilty that Psycho went down, but it was obvious to me that he was relieved to be back in the squadron.

He plugged the tape into the VCR, and we settled in to watch the downing of our comrade. Mostly what we watched was a grey landscape, striated greyish sky and the HUD record from Boo Boo's flight.

The HUD symbology comprises fluorescent green markings projected onto the clear window that protrudes over the cockpit. The HUD window contains all the data the pilot needs to fly the aircraft and employ the munitions: air speed, altitude, dive or climb attitude, heading, and fight or fly mode. With the quick flip of switches on the throttle and control stick, the pilot can select different modes and quickly shift from navigation mode to air-to-air mode or to air-to-ground mode. Each connotes a different symbology set, guiding the pilot in his flight and battle.

While the war raged on in living color, HUD videotapes were muted records of the destruction on the ground, and the black and white account of Psycho's downing cast a sinister light on the scene we watched. The sky rocked from side to side, up and down, the symbology lines snaking, the clouds incongruous grey puffs, the SAM and triple A fire looking deceptively innocent on the screen.

"Here's where it got really hairy," Boo Boo told us. "Right here." He stopped the tape, backed it up to the point where Psycho punched out. We had to listen twice to make out his words through all the radio traffic, the crackles of interference.

"I got hit!" Psycho screamed. "I got hit!" We could barely hear his voice, already as distant as Mars.

"I'm over his position and I've got the lat-longs," Boo Boo reported, his voice high, panicked. A kid in deep trouble.

After Psycho got hit, Boo Boo lit his after burner and zoomed up through the clouds, triple A tracers chasing him skyward.

"All right. Don't pass the lat-longs," Ivan Thomas called out. Ivan was flying number three in the same four-ship. He and Abner McCaffrey, his wingman, had stayed up over the weather when Psycho and Boo Boo went down underneath to look for targets.

"Reference steer point five, reference steer point five." Ivan spoke with alarming calmness, enunciating every word like it was his last chance to send a message home. "Standby on the location. It will be a reference off Randolph." The radio ticked with alarm.

"Once you get the location marked, give a bearing and range to it. We're coming down now!" Ivan again. He didn't want Boo Boo to announce the lat-longs over the radio in the event the Iraqis were listening in. The last thing they wanted was to give Psycho's position away before they had to.

Meanwhile, Psycho was hanging in his chute, floating down over enemy territory, suspended in time, but not forever, screaming into his hand-held radio.

"This is Mutt four one!"

I could not imagine what he must have felt, falling from the sky, watching the ground approach, knowing there was no way out but down, and down was not a good place to be.

"I'm going down! I'm due east from the burning . . . There's a large fire west of me. It's probably my jet!"

Ivan shouted his plan into the mike. "Ok, Mutt four four, hang on. I'm going down underneath."

"I've got vehicles to the northwest of me! It looks like they're moving toward me! That's northwest of me. I'm between a . . ."

Interference ended Psycho's transmission. We heard the rat-a-tat of machine gun fire in the background, the popcorn staccato of death on the prowl, as Psycho shouted his location.

Then an aggressive beeping filled the tape, a sound like Morse code, a SAM radar warning lighting up Boo Boo's jet. The voices, interference, Boo Boo's labored breathing, his occasional moans of frustration, Psycho's broken screams, all of this noise ran together, a symphony of fear echoing the crescendo of panic and chaos in the air.

"Four two, this is four three," Ivan shouted. "Say his position off of steer point 12. I'm down around 10,000 feet. Where are you?"

"I'm visual on you," Abner answered.

"Come down with me!"

"Standby, I'm coming through the clouds. I'm right above you." Abner and Ivan were trying to locate Psycho, braving the triple A fire, the SAM warning, trying to protect Psycho from the Iraqi ground troops. If they couldn't do that, at least they could get a good fix on his location so the search and rescue team could go in and pick him up later.

Boo Boo interjected with Psycho's location. "Okay, he is approximately . . . from steer point 12, he is approximately the three-two-zero at 200 miles. There is an east-west running highway." A steer point is a set of coordinates on the ground. Psycho was 320 degrees from steer point 12. If someone drew a compass on the ground and went along the 320 azimuth, his approximate location would be at about 200 miles.

The SAM radar warning blared again, cutting off a fractured shout from Psycho.

"Mutt two, this is Mutt four three. Reference steer point five and give a bearing and range from *on Guard*," Ivan ordered.

"Guard" is the emergency radio frequency, "guarded" by all aircraft all the time. Up until this point, they had been communicating on their prearranged strike freq. A common frequency accessible to any and all, Ivan wanted to switch to Guard so that other friendly aircraft in the area would hear Psycho's location. For all they knew, a search and rescue mission was already underway. Forward air control needed to know as well.

Of course, switching to Guard also meant the enemy might learn Psycho's location. But the enemy wouldn't know what steer point five meant. And besides, they needed to locate their fellow pilot. From Psycho's reports, it sounded as if the Iraqis were already forming a welcoming party anyway.

"You want me to start working on getting some helicopters up?" Abner asked Ivan.

"That's what I'm trying to do," Ivan answered impatiently. "I want to get a bearing and range off Randolph from number two now. Okay, we're going underneath. Now!" They dove and headed under the cloud cover, toward Boo Boo's heading.

"Mutt four two, this is Mutt four three. When able, say his position from this berm."

"From the berm he is on the east-west road. Take the factory two miles to the east," Boo Boo answered, trying to mimic Ivan's calm, his diction a map of his barely controlled panic.

"They're shooting at me!" Psycho cried. "They're shooting at me!" He sounded very far away, the hand-held distorting his voice through the squawk of radio chatter.

Then another country was heard from.

"This is Islamic Republic of Iran transmitting on channel guard. You are coming near to Iranian boundaries," a man with a French–Middle Eastern drawl warned.

Just what they needed. The goddamn Iranians interfering with their frantic efforts to find Psycho. If it really was the Iranians.

We could hear Psycho screaming something into his radio, but the Iranian stepped on him, corrupting his transmission. Now Boo Boo's breathing sounded almost hysterical. He was working hard to hold it together, to do the right thing and hang in there until Ivan and Abner arrived on the scene.

"On Guard, this is Mutt two. We're approximately from Randolph zero-eight-zero for 30 miles." Steer point five was Randolph. Boo Boo was letting the world know his bearing and distance, where they could find Psycho.

"Psycho, where are you, buddy?" Ivan's worried voice came over the radio. He and Abner were down under the cloud deck, searching, looking for some sign of a chute in the air, of a burning jet on the ground.

Meanwhile, Psycho was already on the ground. "My leg is broken!" he screamed, "my leg is broken! They're shooting at me! My leg is broken. I can't move!"

Boo Boo stopped the tape. "It doesn't sound real good, does it?" He looked around at us for some consolation, some word of hope. We had none to offer. We couldn't meet his eyes.

"Let's see the rest of it," someone said quietly. Boo Boo restarted the tape.

"Mutt four three, this is Mutt four two." Boo Boo again.

"He's on the east-west road. Take the factory two miles to the east. Do you copy that?" Boo Boo trying to steer Ivan and Abner.

"The guards!" Bill again. "The guards . . . I just saw a big explosion! Two miles from a big explosion! There are alarms, explosions, a burning fire!"

"Goddamn it! Where the fuck is he?" Abner.

"We're getting lots of triple A, buddy. Heads up!" Ivan warned Abner. "Missile right three o'clock! Flares! Flares!"

"Goddamn it!" Abner wanted to find Psycho. Bad. And Psycho could see them. The Iraqis were onto them, though. Chasing them around the sky with triple A and SAMs, rabid dogs snapping dangerously at their heels, taunting them from their safe vantage point on the ground.

As we sat in that briefing room, listening to Psycho scream, alone, lost to this enemy we all despised, my fingers itched with angry frustration. I felt my eyes water with fury. The Iraqis were playing with Ivan and Abner, Boo Boo and Psycho. How I hated them for having us at their mercy.

The record of the loss of Psycho Andrews was still running.

"Break right! Break right! Flares! Flares!" Psycho shouted from somewhere on the ground. Apparently he was taking in the entire scene. "I am two miles to the southwest. I have soldiers attacking me!"

"Goddamn it!" Abner bellowed.

And there the tape ended.

Part IV

The Wings of Icarus

When at last the work was done, Daedalus the artist, waving his wings, found himself buoyed upward, and hung suspended, poising himself on the beaten air. He next equipped his son in the same manner and taught him how to fly, as a bird tempts her young ones from the lofty nest into the air.

When all was prepared for flight he said, "Icarus, my son, I charge you to keep at a moderate height, for if you fly too low the damp will clog your wings, and if too high the heat will melt them. Keep near me and you will be safe." While he gave these instructions and fitted the wings on his shoulders, the face of the father was wet with tears, and his hands trembled. He kissed the boy, not knowing it was for the last time. Then rising on his wings, he flew off, encouraging him to follow, and looked back from his own flight to see how his son managed his wings.

As they flew the ploughman stopped his work to gaze, and the shepherd leaned on his staff to watch them, astonished at the sight, and thinking they were gods who could thus cleave the air.

Bulfinch's Mythology

I enlisted in the Air Force with the promise that I would see the world, and see the world I did. I buzzed the treed mountains of France and the bright, craggy peaks of Turkey. I looped over Belgian fields of flax, sliced orderly German river valleys. I autographed the skies of Spain, and of course, the entire Middle East. But in all my travels, as exotic and thrilling as those flights were, none prepared me for the trip I now make.

I have traveled to another place, one not advertised on those recruiting posters. I have traveled to a country far from home, uninhabited, unpilgrimed. This is not the land of the living or the dead. This is the land of the sick. And while there are many others who are also as sick as I, none of us recognizes one another here, for we each inhabit our own individual island nation of illness.

From a foggy distance I recognize my family and their valiant efforts to help. Sad, but they don't realize they are powerless to reach me now. I have gone over, and while I can still see, touch and smell them, we may as well be speaking different languages, be natives of two foreign cultures whose ways are simply too different for bridges to exist between.

For a while after I first became ill, my family was my new nation. I retreated in bewildered disappointment from the country to which I had committed my life. If they would not listen to me, a highly decorated major with 15 years of service, with 44 combat missions over Iraq, then they would listen to no one. It was as if suddenly the features of my country's face had shifted before my eyes, and instead of the noble mask of liberty and truth, a truer identity revealed itself. I cannot say what I saw, because I do not have a name for it. All I know is the ideal to which I had wedded my very soul was a false one.

I allowed myself to rest for a time in the shelter of my family's loyalty. At least I knew I could trust them. Our efforts to unearth the truth about what happened in the war, to force an acknowledgment, as my father said, to get the "lying bastards" to tell the truth, became my new protocol. Here was a battle truly worth fighting. Here was a battle for truth in the most literal sense of the word.

Now, although that battle is still important to me, I see it from afar. My soul is with me here on my island of isolation, where all the bad things that you ever imagined might happen have come true. This is my nation now, and while it is lonely and often sad, no one can reach me here. It is a safe place, where my God will be my final and only visitor.

No Joy

All those years ago, I entered OTS at Lackland. Now I have returned to Lackland, this time not to learn to fly but to learn why I am no longer allowed to fly. I have come full circle in 15 years, from young, would-be pilot, eager to prove himself, to a man who has flown into combat and survived, returning to the institution that formed him, looking for answers to his body's unseasonal questions.

Wilford Hall at Lackland Air Force Base is actually a whole set of buildings, dominated by an 11-story poured concrete complex that looms just inside the gate. The tallest building in the area, Wilford Hall serves as the major Air Force medical center for all of the western United States. It's comparable to the Army's Walter Reed Hospital near Washington, D.C.

For a pilot, Wilford Hall is the worst possible place to be sent. They send you to Wilford, you never know what they're going to find. The word is, though, you walk in for tests and they'll find some way to ground you. Once you're there, you may as well resign yourself to never flying again, even if you're perfectly healthy. A place to avoid at all costs, and while I have tried to avoid it, my trip here seems inevitable.

This is my second visit. I came down in February for an EMG—electromyogram. The first of a long series of unpleasant, uncomfortable tests I would undergo, the EMG is its own special kind of torture.

I lay on a padded table while a technician taped diodes that connected my thigh to my heel, my upper arm to my hand. Then, she took her position with the doctor at an ancient, evil-looking machine off to my left.

"We're going to test your right thigh now, Major Donnelly." She spoke from behind the machine. The first time, I braced myself against the table, not knowing what to expect. An electrical shock like lightning on a desert mesa traveled down my thigh, a rivulet of pain that robbed me of my breath.

The technician repeated this over and over, testing each thigh/heel reaction, each upper arm/hand reaction, to measure how quickly the sensation traveled to my nerve endings. I stared up at the ceiling, the first of many hospital ceilings I would come to know intimately, and gritted my teeth. I was new to the adventure, so I hadn't yet developed my resistance techniques, hadn't yet learned how to vacate my body.

Turns out the electrical test was only the overture, though. The technician removed the diodes from my skin, ripping the shreds of white tape off in short jerks that tore small clumps of hair from my thigh, my arm. Then the doctor spoke.

"We're going to perform the second part of the test now, Major Donnelly," she said, her face still obscured by the arm of the machine. "You may experience some discomfort."

At the time, I was still such an initiate I didn't yet understand that "some discomfort" is medical talk for extreme pain.

The technician was young, perhaps in her early twenties. Too young or too coarse to empathize with yet another middle-aged man strapped to her EMG table. Her actions were businesslike, her round, shiny face intent on the task at hand. I imagined that this is how all medical professionals must become in time. Immovable, distant, unfeeling. Do they steel themselves from so much suffering to survive, or is that they really don't care?

I could not remove my eyes from the woman's manicured fingernails, from the perfectly formed gleaming spears of red that tipped each finger. How she got away with that manicure in a hospital setting was a mystery, but it gave me something to think about other than my pain.

She was exceedingly proud of those nails; I could tell by the way she plunged and twisted each wired needle into my limbs—thigh, bicep, calf, forearm. I kept my eyes, now swimming in the brine of agony, fixed on those fingernails, as if their methodical movements could decipher these telegraphs of pain into some intelligible message.

First the left side, from upper body to lower body she worked. Then the right, twisting the needles in my flesh while the doctor monitored some screen on the glowing instrument in the corner as it spewed sheets onto which the signals my muscles sent to my nerves were inscribed in undecipherable code. The doctor was listening for abnormalities in the messages my motor neurons received.

I've always hated needles, for one thing, and doctors for another. How odd, I thought, that I should put all my fighter pilot training, all those prisoner of war techniques, to use in surviving a medical test while prone on a table at Lackland Air Force Base. That it would be a young woman's fingernails, like the legs of some pernicious spider preparing its prey, to spin the web of pain that would entrap me.

That was in February. For my second trip to this medical amusement park, I drive down on a Wednesday in March. The intervening month I've spent grounded, slogging through desk work, undergoing MRIs, CT scans, X-rays, and more blood work than I thought I had blood. All the while, I watched the T-38s taking off and landing, the sweet smell of JP-4, good old jet fuel, still perfuming my days. The flight surgeon at Sheppard is a new guy, too timid to come right out with the ALS diagnosis. I can tell he doesn't want to be the one to make the final call, so he sends me down to San Antonio again.

I can still drive pretty well. While my right leg is ever less predictable, I am not concerned about making the six-hour trek in the standard transmission Saab we brought back from Germany. How soon, I wondered, before I come to treasure the simple act of driving a car? How soon before I become a permanent passenger, unable to locomote at all? I try not to think in these terms, but the worries take wing in my mind, a legion of bandits intent on their target, which is me.

Most of the drive is straight highway, so I let my misbehaving leg rest idly while I speed south. My appointment is for 1300 hours. I haven't slept much the night before, that's how nervous I am about what I might find out today. That's how successful I've been at keeping those errant thoughts from staking a claim in my mind.

The guard waves me through the gate no problem.

San Antonio is home to hundreds of thousands of military retirees, and they all come to Wilford Hall for their medical care, so parking here is like finding a spot at a Cowboys game. You get a space far enough from the facility and you might have to take a bus to the door, or else you can walk the two miles. I get lucky today, though, and I nose the Saab into a narrow slot between two sport utility vehicles. At least the car will be shaded.

The hospital itself is a maze of corridors and elevators. I head toward the last bank and take the elevator up to the neurology ward on the ninth floor. Being here makes me think of first grade in elementary school. The place has the antiseptic odor of a 1950s institution, one constructed not to reassure but to terrify. It is working just fine on me.

On the ninth floor, I head off to the right, past the closed door I saw on my last visit. "Gulf War Room," it reads. This time I stop and try the handle. It's locked. The engraved plastic sign is relatively new: the crooks of the white letters aren't yet filled with grime the way the other signs are. There are no hours posted, though, so I figure it's hit or miss for the Gulf War Room.

"You just have a seat right over there, honey," the blue-haired receptionist tells me. "Dr. Stevens will be with you in just no time at all. Is that your paperwork there?" She reaches to lift the file away from me. "Why don't you let me take that and we'll see if there's anything else we need you to do today?" I hand over my X-rays, MRI reports and lab tests, a file fattened on the story of my illness.

I find my way to the blue and mustard-yellow vinyl-clad waiting area and settle into a well-intentioned seat cushion that has held far too many military backsides. I get to enjoy this particular cushion for no more than fifteen minutes before Dr. Stevens herself comes out to the waiting area.

"Major Donnelly?" She scans the room until her eyes locate me in my vinyl nest. I wonder what she has in mind for me this time.

Dr. Stevens is an Air Force major. Of medium height, with dark hair that frames her square, blank face. Her personality is unsettling. Maybe it's her small stature, maybe it comes from being a woman in a man's world, but she has perfected the major-doctor demeanor, a disconcerting blend of distance, arrogance and peevishness.

The good doctor escorts me into the examining room, which also serves as her office. There we are greeted by a tall young man looking awkward in his white coat. Dr. Stevens introduces him, and while his name escapes me as soon as she utters it, I get the impression he is an intern, along for the ride and in for one hell of a training session.

I change into the blue paper robe, opening in the back, as Dr. Stevens pulls the curtain around the examining area and they wait for me to undress. Meanwhile, she and Mr. X review my files together. I can hear their conversation, a low rumble of worry that fills the small space.

"Now try to relax, Major Donnelly," Dr. Stevens orders, her eyes on my twitching foot muscles. One of the symptoms of ALS is what they call fasciculations: a cluster of nerve and muscle cells that twitch uncontrollably. My foot has been twitching like this for months now.

She performs another physical exam, her rubber hammer tapping my knees, the undersides of my feet. She grabs my right foot between her cold hands and instructs me to resist her pressure. The intern stands off to the side, watching, his face blank with studied disinterest, although I can tell he is excited. Only later will I find out why.

"Do you feel this? Does it feel sharp or dull?" She pulls a straight pin from her lapel and runs it gently enough across my toes. I get the impression my answers are both the right ones and the wrong ones, although she doesn't react when I say "sharp" or "dull." Then comes the tuning fork, which she slaps against her thigh and holds to my big toe. "Tell me when the vibrations stop," she orders, her dark hair a veil over her face, obscuring her eyes.

I have this catechism memorized by now, and I will have many opportunities to show off my knowledge in the months to come. If only I got credit for it, a reprieve. Very good, Major Donnelly, we're granting you an extra three years of life because you've learned the neurological exam better than any of our previous patients.

Now Dr. Stevens launches into what I come to think of as the neurologist's theme song. Do I have tingling in my fingers and toes? Am I experiencing any numbness? Is there pain in my extremities? Is my vision blurry, double?

When she finishes, she still betrays no emotion whatsoever, no hint of what might come next. "Why don't you change back into your flight suit and join us in my office?" she says, pulling the curtain shut behind her.

By now, I have been through months of tests, months of intermittent terror when I am sure I have ALS, although it has only been mentioned as one possibility. The last few weeks, especially, have been filled with a new kind of fear. My parents have started to research what is known as Gulf War syndrome and are gradually hooked into a whole underground network of people—doctors, veterans, veterans' families, well-intentioned crazies looking for a new cause, even fringe militia members searching for one more reason to bring down the government.

My parents have spent hours on the phone with people who tell them their own stories of sudden, inexplicable illness, stories of veterans dying of bizarre cancers. Of veterans who have undergone years of surgery, tests, more surgery, more tests, only to be told they have no real illness at all, that their symptoms are stress related. They feed me information, by mail, over the phone. My Dad even faxes me articles at work, although I have to ask him to stop. I can't imagine my commanding officer looking kindly on Gulf War syndrome faxes peeling off the machine.

While my parents are now convinced that my symptoms are Gulf War related, I am not. I don't have the rashes, the digestive disorders, the other symptoms that more than 50,000 veterans claim to be suffering from. I haven't heard of any pilots being sick, so I figure it is only a ground troop problem. Besides, I reason with myself, why would the government try to hide something? They would have no cause to do that, I am sure. Especially not with me.

I am a major, after all, a highly decorated fighter pilot marked for speedy promotion up the ladder. Before all this happened, I was on the lieutenant colonel track. Why would they lie to me? In print, the Pentagon is insisting with the unassailable certainty of true authority that no veterans were exposed to any injurious level of chemical or biological weapons. Up until now, I believe them.

I believe them until I learn about Don Klein, a former F-15 pilot, a lieutenant colonel who remembered flying home through a spume of fallout after a bombing mission, who later died of ALS. I believe them until I glimpse the vastness of the problem, the tens of thousands of veterans suffering not just from rashes and digestive disorders but from fatal heart conditions, from pancreatic cancer and brain lupus, from cancer of the spine and optic nerve, from pseudotumor cerebrae. I believe them until the truth about my own illness hits home, a freight train running full speed into the brick wall of my denial. I believe them until that meeting with Dr. Stevens.

"Major Donnelly, I'm afraid I have bad news for you," Dr. Stevens announces, her voice flat, toneless. "We've performed all of these tests because we wanted to be sure of ourselves before we had this conversation with you. We are now fairly certain that you are suffering from amyotrophic lateral sclerosis, or ALS. It's also known as Lou Gehrig's disease. I believe your flight surgeon at Sheppard mentioned this to you as a possibility?"

The question is the first time she looks at me. Here is a woman, a doctor, telling a patient that he is suffering from one of the most horrible of illnesses, and she hasn't looked at me the whole time. Not in the eyes. And I don't get the impression it is because she is sorry for me. It is more that she seems to feel nothing at all. She is a void, empty. She has successfully achieved that separation of self and profession I will detect in most of the doctors I encounter. Her soul is not present in the room. It couldn't be, given what she does next.

"There is no treatment for ALS, Major Donnelly," she continues. "The only hope we can offer patients such as yourself is a drug which is thought to slow the progression of the disease, although studies so far are inconclusive."

Here she turns to the intern, who raises himself up off his stool to enter his moment in the spotlight. Now I understand why he is so excited. Dr. Stevens continues. "A representative from the pharmaceuticals company is here. I asked him to be here today so that he could tell you about the medication. We'd like to get you on it as soon as possible."

She turns the floor over to the pharmaceutical representative, who hands me a pamphlet, his card, and then suddenly seems to deflate. Here it is, his chance, and he loses his ability to speak.

"Why don't you take a look at this and give me a call if you have any questions, Major Donnelly."

I finger the pamphlet, read the cover. "The first agent that extends tracheotomy-free survival in ALS patients!" I read. I feel my self fall away, leaving me rudderless in this room, surrounded by people whose motives I cannot divine, whose essence I cannot fathom. I turn the pamphlet over. I look up at Dr. Stevens, scrape myself from the ceiling.

At this point, I decide I have nothing left to lose.

"As you can probably imagine," my voice is choked, and I fight to control it, "I've been doing a lot of research myself." I look to Dr. Stevens for acknowledgment, but she offers none. "I couldn't help but notice the Gulf War Room down the hall. You know I served in the Gulf War, and you've probably heard about all the vets who are sick now."

She doesn't let me finish. The familiar change occurs. Her jaw muscles start to work. Her face tightens into a knot, and she gives me "the line." She sieves the words through teeth so tight you'd think she has sudden-onset lockjaw.

"Major Donnelly," she says, "there has never been any evidence showing any link between any illness and service in the Gulf War."

This is her opening salvo in what becomes an angry ten-minute tirade. A doctor who has just condemned me to certain death chooses this as the appropriate time to berate me about the studies that she claims support her own and the government's position.

The whole time she's talking to me, I'm staring up at her, trying to look into her eyes, trying to find something in there on which to anchor my floundering awareness. But I find nothing. Nothing at all. Meanwhile, Mr. "Pharmaceutical" slumps on his stool, by now probably very sorry he has allowed himself to be invited to this particular Tupperware party.

Dr. Stevens concludes her speech with a line she has clearly used before. "People just get sick, Major Donnelly."

If I weren't shell-shocked from the news I have just received, I would find a way to tell her where to put her self-righteous smugness.

Instead, I decide not to argue the point with her. I realize I have other, far graver problems now, and it is obvious I'm not going to get anywhere with this particular version of the Air Force's idea of a doctor. But I wonder why I'm not automatically put into some kind of registry or put through some special regimen of tests that other sick Gulf War vets might be put through, just to prove their point if nothing else. I may not be a doctor, but it seems to me this would be the best way to corroborate their theory and shut us all up for good, if they're right.

No special regimen is offered. No further discussion is allowed. Mr. "Pharmaceutical" has made his sales pitch, courtesy of the United States Air Force. Dr. Stevens has said her piece, and it is time for me to leave.

More than anything else, I am overwhelmed by confusion. I don't know what to believe, where to turn for help. The Gulf War illness theories are legion. The newly minted authorities too numerous to count. The wall of denial and skepticism erected by the Pentagon thick, impenetrable. All the while, my body continues to deteriorate, heedless of the possible causes of its slow degeneration.

Some say it is the PB—pyridostigmine bromide—the lethal little pill we were all ordered to take before the war. The PB was supposed to bind with cholinesterase, an enzyme, and thus inoculate us against the effects of nerve gas. The FDA has only approved PB for use against myasthenia gravis, but granted the Pentagon a waiver, in the interests of national security. Turns out, though, that the Pentagon was supposed to distribute warnings about the drug's potential side effects. Turns out the Pentagon did no such thing. Turns out PB is a dangerous drug known to cause cancer in humans when administered without a partner drug, atropine, which protects against PB's deadly side effects.

Turns out the Pentagon knew all of this, but ordered us to take the PB anyway—under threat of court martial, absent any warning about possible memory loss, rashes, muscle weakness, incontinence, absent the atropine. Most ironically of all, it turns out that in the presence of low doses of chemical weapons, when combined with adrenaline, PB actually impedes the production of another enzyme that neutralizes those same toxins.

In 1994, a U.S. Senate hearing on Gulf War illnesses concluded that when it ordered soldiers to take PB and failed to provide the appropriate warnings about potential side effects, the Department of Defense violated the Declaration of Helsinki, the Nuremberg Code and the U.S. Common Rule on the use of experimental drugs by federal agencies. Does that make certain individuals in the Department of Defense war criminals? If so, where is the trial? The outcry? Where are the indictments? Where in hell is the press?

So much for truth, justice and the American way. I'm finally coming to understand that the American way is not what I thought it was. That the American way is actually something much more sinister and tragic. A dark shadow of the light ideal we all prefer to take for granted.

I remember taking PB. It was actually a series of doses over a couple of days. I remember wondering what it was, and we were all a little suspicious. I remember swallowing the pills, washing them down with bottled water in my hooch right before I suited up to fly.

But after the first few days, when we realized that the war would be over quickly, we stopped taking it. None of us liked swallowing a drug when we didn't know what it was or what it could do. By then, though, the damage must have already been done.

Now experts are claiming that Hussein knew exactly what he was doing when he dosed us with low levels of nerve agents, so that his poison would go undetected by the chemical detection field kits that just weren't sensitive enough to pick up low amounts of sarin and VX in the air.

Turns out the CIA knew that Hussein had learned the technique and the efficacy of low doses from his friends, the Russians.

But the Pentagon continues to claim you can't get sick from low-dose exposures. They're adamant that even if Hussein used low doses of chemical or biological weapons against us, our illnesses could not result from that. We would have all dropped dead in the field, they claim. The birds would have fallen from the sky. Dr. Steven Joseph, formerly DOD's Assistant Secretary for Health Affairs, testified before Congress that "the current body of research proves that low level exposures cannot cause health effects."

Despite my experiences, I had been inclined to believe the Pentagon. It kind of made sense, given the little I knew about those weapons, that we would have all gotten sick sooner. And besides, there was no proof that low-dose exposures could make you sick.

Read any veteran's testimony before the President's Special Commission, though, and you learn that the birds did fall from the sky. Troops came upon camels lying dead and decaying in the desert, whole packs of them, just fallen over in their tracks. Dogs and rodents and other small animals died, suddenly, inexplicably, shortly after those tens of thousands of "false" chemical weapons alarms rang out. The alarms were so common, some commanders even ordered their troops to disable or disregard them, since no obvious symptoms appeared immediately after they sounded.

Maybe it was the 15 years of training or the depth of conviction that led me to this place, but I had been inclined to believe the Pentagon despite the veterans' testimony. Maybe it was because I didn't want to believe the alternative.

I believed the Pentagon until we discovered that there was indeed proof that low-dose exposures could make you sick. Until I read the news release my Dad faxed me one day in June 1996.

On the cover sheet, he wrote, "This breaks my heart. Dad."

The release described a study the Pentagon had conducted on primates at Brooks Air Force Base, in which they subjected the primates to low doses of sa-

rin over a period of just a few days, not weeks. All of them suffered severe neurological damage, lost the use of their legs, then their arms. And then they died. The Air Force conducted that study in 1991. The year the war ended.

Solo

June 1996

By now, I am frantic, as are my parents, my siblings, my wife. We spend hours on the Internet, searching for information, following the links that lead from ALS to Gulf War syndrome to multiple chemical sensitivity and back, a vicious cybercircle. We spend hours, days on the phone, talking to strangers all over the country who tell us our own stories back at us about their husbands, sons, daughters, fathers, mothers. My parents' phone bill approaches $500, $600 a month.

We are not alone, but we are truly on our own. We cannot find a doctor who will take the lead and show us the way, tell us what to do next, what we can expect. On the one hand, we have the military doctors insisting that I have ALS, people get sick, end of story, there is no connection to service in the Gulf, and so on. On the other hand, we find scores of other veterans suffering from similar symptoms, as well as other doctors, researchers and alternative practitioners who are certain my illness is somehow related to my service in the Gulf War.

We don't know what to think about any of this. There are so many people involved, the network of Gulf War illness-related organizations and individuals is far-reaching, each group fervently convinced that its own interpretation of the phenomenon is *the* explanation.

Meanwhile, I continue to deteriorate. I am limping badly and have started to use an old bentwood cane we had in the garage. For a time, my mother spends hours talking with Joyce Riley in Texas, a former military nurse who served in the Gulf and then formed a Gulf War illness information clearinghouse when she got sick.

Joyce is very kind to my parents, consoling them, sending them huge packets of information, videotapes of Gulf War veterans' meetings, newspaper clippings. She believes the Pentagon knows very well what happened to us over there and is intentionally withholding information. We prefer not to believe this, but by now aren't sure what to think. About anyone. We remain on Joyce's radar screen until we finally figure Joyce Riley probably can't help us much, nor we her.

Then there is the woman, also in Texas, who is convinced that Gulf War illness resulted from our ingesting large amounts of aspartame. According to her, when aspartame is heated above a certain temperature, it breaks down into its component chemical parts, one of which is formaldehyde. And since we drank huge amounts of diet soda and chewed sugar free gum in great quantities over there in the desert, she concluded that we are all suffering from aspartame poisoning. We dutifully clear the diet soda out of the house, scour our shelves for anything containing aspartame, hoping that this is all it is, aspartame poisoning, and we wait for the symptoms to abate.

It's not that I seriously believe these people have the answer, or that any of us believe it. It's just that we are frantic and at least they are looking for some explanation, while the people who are responsible for providing my medical care clearly are not.

Then, *Newsweek* publishes a story about Dr. Robert Haley, a researcher out of University of Texas who has just completed a study funded by Ross Perot. Haley proves, contrary to the Pentagon's assertions, that pyridostigmine bromide, when combined with exposure to large doses of pesticides, which we used in great quantities, causes chickens to suffer neurological symptoms similar to those of which veterans are complaining.

Dr. Haley calls the condition organophosphate-induced delayed neuropathy—OPIDN.

That story sends my parents to the University of Connecticut medical library, where they comb dense medical texts for information on organophosphate poisoning. I can just picture them there, fumbling around the stacks, the object of puzzled stares from librarians and annoyed looks from doctors in training.

The thing is, we have located a connection: the symptoms of OPIDN match exactly the symptoms I experienced when I was exposed to malathion back at Sheppard during my late night jogs around the base. But there is more. A lot more. So much more that it terrifies us. We may have a clue, but it's not the clue we wanted to find.

The clue is this: The basis for nerve agents, poison gases like sarin and soman, gases the Iraqis were known to possess, gases manufactured in the U.S. and sold to the Iraqis, the basis for these agents is organophosphate. This is the very same poison in the pesticide malathion, the poison they were spraying in Wichita Falls in August 1995. The clouds I passed through, like a ghost in a bad dream, were clouds of nerve agent.

Then we learn of a study published in a U.S. medical journal by a Dr. Jamal about British Gulf War veterans suffering from neurological damage. He corroborates Dr. Haley's findings: the veterans he studied had likely been exposed to organophosphate poison, to nerve gas, and are suffering from its effects.

The Pentagon, meanwhile, continues to insist that no chemical weapons were used during the war. That the hundreds of chemical weapons alarms that sounded were all false alarms, misfirings. That the chemical weapons battle logs that mysteriously disappeared were not really important anyway. Nothing to worry about folks. You can all go home now. Everything is under control.

As much as we would prefer to believe this story, our research, and my symptoms, tell us otherwise. We have discovered the link, and the link is the poison. I am slowly dying the way a cockroach dies, from the extremities inward. The poison is gradually killing each of my nerve cells, one at a time, to deprive me first of my limbs, my movement, to paralyze me, and finally, to rob me of my breath, my life. Who would choose to believe this? And who would choose to believe that his own government, the one to which he dedicated his career, his life, would lie about such a thing?

But we have found something to work on, a thread to pull. And while I want to unravel the whole tangled mess, to find out the truth about what really happened to me over there, I must first focus on my health.

Then we find Dr. Frazer.

His Center in Dallas draws patients from around the world, people who have tried every other course of medical treatment and who turn to Dr. Frazer's clinic out of desperation. Dr. Frazer is a pioneer in the area of multiple chemical sensitivity and environmental exposure. Depending on whom you ask, the man is either a genius or a charlatan. If you ask the patients he cures, he is a genius. If you ask the traditional medical community, who do not even recognize environmental exposures as a true condition, he is a fraud. Maybe a well-intentioned fraud, maybe not. He is only one of many such individuals we will encounter on our medical odyssey.

"You're free to go and try it," my neurologist tells me. "It certainly won't hurt you. Well, it will hurt your wallet," he chuckles. "The trouble with these people is that they create hope where there is none. I'm sorry to tell you that there is no such thing as multiple chemical sensitivity. In my professional opinion, it's a waste of your time, Major Donnelly. But go ahead and try it if that's what you feel you need to do."

It's what I feel I need to do, and I somehow can't help but think the neurologist would feel the need to do the same if he were in my place.

My family goes back East for the summer, for the six weeks I am to spend in Dallas. It's not that I don't want to be with them. But my days will be so tightly scheduled, so packed with treatment, that it doesn't make much sense for us all to try to stay together in Dallas. Anyway, I want to be able to focus my entire being on getting better, so that when I rejoin them, it will be as the father and husband they remember, a whole man.

Goodbyes are common in the military, so we are all somehow used to them. This time is different, though. We part at the house at Sheppard. Sue is driving the van back to Connecticut, because they'll be there all summer and will need a way to get around on their own. We can't afford to have all three of them fly out and rent a car for the summer.

"Bye, Daddy." Erin hugs me as I lean against the side of the van. "We'll miss you. Hope you feel better soon." She jumps into the back seat and settles Jingles the stuffed bear on her lap. Jingles waves to me from his perch.

"Daddy," Bubba asks, drawing out the Dad-dy so that it sounds like four syllables, "are you coming with us?" His sweet, open face is the most painful sight I have ever beheld.

We've called him Bubba since he was born. I had just gotten back from the war, and we were living in a furnished apartment near McDill Air Force Base in Tampa while we looked for a house. His bassinet was a basket, and we were making believe we were locals. It was kind of a joke at first, but now he's stuck with it, poor kid. It fits him, though. Besides, down south, every third person is called Bubba. Nobody looks twice when we call "Bubba!" in the grocery store.

"No, Bub," I answer, turning my head away, "I have work to do." I brace myself and lean inside to kiss him. He curls his old, yellow blankie on his lap, wraps his arms around my neck and hugs me goodbye. "Bye, Daddy," he whispers. "Maybe you'll be better when we come home?"

"Maybe, Bub," I tell him. "Maybe."

I don't see them again for two months.

All told, the treatment will cost me $10,000, but there is no price I won't pay to regain my health. At least it is something I can do, something constructive. At least I won't be sitting at home waiting to die. Meantime, I'm still active duty. My wing commander continues to be understanding, as much as the regs allow him to be. I have the time to go to Dallas, but if I don't return a well man, he will have run out of ways to keep me on.

I rent a ground floor apartment in a complex two blocks from the clinic, sort of a strange arrangement. Former or ongoing patients own these apartments and rent them out to new patients. Anyway, they put me on the ground floor because by now I am getting around with difficulty, even with the cane.

A barren cave of a place, the apartment has been stripped of every shred of fabric, because fabric might be treated with a poison like formaldehyde or resin. There is no carpeting, no wallpaper, no curtains. Only the bare cement floor, the white cinder block walls, and vertical metal blinds on the slider that lead out to a miniature square of grass where I never venture because it is always so hot. The air conditioning echoing in that lonely, hollow room is better than the wall of torpid air that greets me when I open the door.

The Center sits in the corner of a park-like office complex in northeastern Dallas on a trim lawn shaded by the occasional, well-placed tree. It is an upscale complex sided in an understated, stained wood. Inside, the Center takes up the entire top floor of one wing. The whole place is very plain, like the apartment I'm renting. Tile floors, wood furniture, enamel walls. An air purifier sits in the hallway and runs constantly. Resins, chemical finishes, these are given no quarter at the Center. It is a poison-free zone.

Reaction testing is performed in a large unadorned room. Outside, along the corridor, metal folding chairs are arranged, white cotton towels folded on the seats the only comfort they offer. Comfort is not the defining principle here.

In the testing room, two medical technicians sit next to a desk stacked high with trays of vials and bins of allergy needles. Here they test for reactions to any number of foods, chemicals, molds, and bacteria. Of the six weeks I was there, I spent four days in the reaction testing room, together with 15 other patients also being tested.

They injected tiny amounts of each substance into our arms, from the shoulder to the elbow. Each time they inject you, they circle the area with a black ink pen so that by the end of the day, you may have 20 or 30 black circles up and down your arm. For someone who hates needles, this was needle hell.

Reactions range from a slight swelling or redness in the injection site to loss of breath to unconsciousness. I don't believe in much of this when I arrive, but I find myself becoming a convert when I start to have headaches, swelling in my throat and dizziness. When I see people who are deathly ill get healed before my eyes.

I learn I am sensitive to a number of chemicals, including benzine, a byproduct of burning jet fuel, cigarette smoke, and formaldehyde, which is used in the manufacture of almost anything you can think of, from furniture to wallpaper, from carpets to clothing and building materials. I get up early, maybe seven or eight, and head over to the clinic every morning but Sunday. I would go on Sunday, too, if they were open. Each day starts with 40 minutes on a stationary bike, stairstepper, rowing machine or treadmill, followed by a 30-minute sauna. Then on to a shower and a lymphatic massage. Then I repeat the whole process up to three times each day, for six weeks. It is exhausting, draining, but I figure that's the whole point.

Over the course of almost two months, I spend 40 hours in the sauna. That's a lot of time to reflect, a lot of time to look back over your life and wonder what you might do differently, what you might do again, given the chance. Time to think about people, about turning points, about the bittersweet and the bitter. About how I got to this point at all.

A lot of the other patients are talkers, and the sauna is their favorite place to catch you up on their latest symptoms. I always look for the emptier of the two saunas, and there, dressed in running shorts and a t-shirt, I lie back on the hot plank bench, close my eyes and watch the reruns of my life, the early years, when flying was still a new sensation, when I savored every take-off and landing, when time opened up before me, ever generous, ever renewing. When I believed that if I were to die young, at least it would be mercifully quick, a short, violent explosion on impact, and then nothing. Not this protracted decline in which my mind remains ever vigilant as it witnesses the slow corrosion of life.

*   *   *

Poisons like organophosphate collect in fatty tissues called lipids, where they accumulate and remain unless somehow dislodged. The theory is that you have to sweat out the poison, that once you get your system pumping at a certain rate, the culprit will leak out with your sweat, released from your cells like so much blood from a stone.

Dr. Frazer's therapy requires that I eat a low fat, macrobiotic organic diet, so most of my groceries I buy at the Whole Foods store about two miles away. Shopping is an almost daily event because I can't carry much to the car, what with the cane and the trip from the store to car, from car to apartment. And each time I have to buy a two-liter glass bottle of Arkansas spring water.

One lesson the Air Force taught me is to apply my whole self to anything I do. I apply myself to Dr. Frazer's program with the very will to survive that beats in every cell in my body. To my mind, there are enough reasons to believe that Dr. Frazer can help me as there are reasons to believe the Pentagon is lying. Truth is no longer a fixed, immutable point in space for me.

Like a pilot in a spin, I have lost track of what is up and what is down, and I cannot remember my spin recovery procedures. I rely on instinct now. Instinct doesn't lie.

My instinct speaks to me at night, when I am alone in my garden apartment, eating a dinner of steamed organic squash, millet and catfish. My instinct tells me that something is very, very wrong with this picture.

*   *   *

July 1996

I can't really tell how I am feeling. Better, but I am afraid that is just wishful thinking. Besides, who wouldn't feel better after six weeks of organic, low fat food plus hours of exercise, sauna and massage each day? I am certainly leaner. I've lost 15 pounds, and I am not so sure this is a good thing.

Also, I've fallen twice in the past week. Once at an indoor flea market, where I had gone to try to sell my 1972 Cadillac El Dorado convertible. My fall was quite graceful, actually. Winding my way between the irregular aisles of knick knacks and china, leaning heavily on my cane, I suddenly felt my balance give out from under me. I managed to tilt sideways and back, thus avoiding the wall of bric-a-brac behind me. "If you break it, mark it sold." I had no intention of hauling a trunk full of shards back to that apartment.

The second fall was worse. Outside an organic food restaurant, I was stepping from the sidewalk to the parking lot after a meal. I'd just finished eating with some of the other patients—this was one of the only places we could go, an organic Mexican place with great homemade salsa—when I lost my balance and fell over backwards onto the pavement. I really smacked my back on that one, saw stars. Luckily, I was able to tuck my chin and avoid hitting my head on the curb. That would have been ugly indeed. My friends had to help me up, once I got my feet reorganized beneath me.

My last week in Dallas, Dad comes down to visit. He takes a cab from the airport to the apartment and meets me one morning, early. We have an appointment with Dr. Frazer. We want to ask him point blank: can he help me or not? I don't seem to be getting much better, and my time is almost up. He's not sure, he answers. Not sure at all.

It seems I am not to be one of the people Dr. Frazer can help. I have watched other desperately ill individuals arrive here, unable to walk from car to clinic door. I have watched them slowly improve, their bodies regain strength and health. I have watched what look to be medical miracles occur before my eyes. My own body, meanwhile, refuses to remember health. It travels a path that seems to point in only one direction.

I will move on, then. If Dr. Frazer cannot help me, there must be someone who can. I am still healthy enough that I believe more in health and life than I do in sickness and death.

My Dad and I plan our next deployment. I will go to Los Angeles to see three doctors whose names we've gotten from the Gulf War network. Doctors who say they can help.

I am not sorry to leave Dallas. I am only sorry to be sitting in the passenger's seat of my own car as we drive away. We don't talk much on the trip back to Wichita Falls. What is there to say? Dad drives, I look out the window at the flat Texas terrain. Miles of alfalfa and wheat fields, fenced acres of cattle ranchland, dotted with thousands of cattle grazing in the mundane sun, once in a while, a cluster of them huddling under the occasional locust tree. What a different landscape from my childhood, from the green suburbs, from the rolling hills, from the wooded acres of towering deciduous trees. From the orchard, the hills, the New England twilights. I may as well be on another planet.

In two weeks I will be off to Los Angeles, city of my birth, where oranges once bloomed and rooted behind a small house on a dead-end street in Orange, California. Where we celebrated birthdays at Knotts Berry Farm and rode Dumbo at Disneyland, before there was such a thing as Disneyworld.

Maybe, I think, the city of angels will yield the answer that saves my life.

Of the more than 110,000 now reported to be ill, we know of three other pilots with ALS, counting Don Klein, who died four years ago. Plus there's Tom Oliver, a crew chief who worked on the jets when they returned from their missions. That's five, including me.

Plus there's Jeff Tack and Randy Hebert. Jeff was an infantry sergeant, a member of the Seventh Corps, the troops who led the attack from the west.

Randy, a Marine major, part of the force that breached the berms in Kuwait during the ground offensive. That's seven.

Then there's Kevin Wright, who served as General Schwarzkopf's bodyguard. Kevin stood outside the general's underground bunker as the chemical weapons alarms sounded, while the general planned the war from three stories underground. Kevin has been under evaluation for ALS for the past eight months. He would have made eight cases of ALS, but after 26 spinal taps courtesy of the VA, they finally diagnosed him with spinal AVM, arteriovenous malformation, a life-threatening disease that at the very least will likely leave him paralyzed from the chest down and bedridden for life.

Of course the general himself got sick immediately after the war, with prostate cancer. Made the cover of Newsweek. The conquering general conquers cancer. There's no way anyone can tie his cancer to his service in the Gulf. Just one more of those irritating little coincidences you don't quite know what to do with, I guess.

Then there's Rob Booker, in his late 20s, who was with the Alabama national guard. He was diagnosed with ALS only about six months ago. Then just last night, my parents were talking to Tatianna Oliver, Tom's wife. She told them of three ALS cases at Keesler Air Force Base in Mississippi, where her husband was stationed before he got sick. And she knows of ten possible cases at Patrick Air Force Base in Coco Beach, Florida. So if they turn out to be true, that makes more than 20.

What the hell is going on here?

How many more are out there, looking for us, waiting to die, or waiting still to get sick, as we look for them?

We're not sure if any of the people we know of are among the nine ALS cases the Pentagon will officially acknowledge. I know I am not among them. I never subjected myself to the Gulf War physical.

The Pentagon has the names and the numbers, if anyone has them, and they're just not telling. Protecting our privacy, they claim. Not that they've asked, but I would willingly waive all my privacy rights to find out the truth, to find out how many of us are dying from this disease.

We have plenty of reasons to believe there are many more cases than nine. Good reasons. There are all the cases we keep hearing about. And there's the General Accounting Office study of the Pentagon's handling of Gulf War illnesses. Just this week we learned that the Pentagon has officially acknowledged 200 cases of cancer among Gulf War veterans. In its study, the GAO has so far found 9,000 cancers. And they haven't finished counting.

So if there are 45 times more cancer cases than they will admit to, how many more cases of ALS are there? If the Pentagon were to concede that there *are actually 50 cases of ALS, or 35, or 123, what would that mean? That we are suffering from an epidemic of ALS? That they've been lying? That we don't really know how many more will get sick? And what in hell made us sick?*

Like me, Jeff Tack and Randy Hebert returned home from the Gulf War to lead fairly normal lives. They considered themselves relatively healthy, although, also like me, both suffered from repeated bouts of what seemed like the flu. Then Jeff's kids came home from school with lice, and his wife washed everyone's hair with lindane. The next week, Jeff first started to get the weird symptoms that later blossomed into ALS.

Randy, too, got sick years later, after an exposure to dursban. Randy remembers a specific event when he must have been exposed. It was after a chemical weapons alarm sounded and a SCUD hit nearby. The windshield of his vehicle misted with an odd spray of something liquid, and he felt a tingling on the skin of his arm. But they gave the all-clear signal, so Randy figured it was nothing. After the war, he and Kim and the kids were living at Camp LeJeune in North Carolina, the exterminator came in to fumigate the base housing with dursban. Standard procedure. And that's when Randy got sick, three years after the end of the war.

Like malathion, the pesticide I was exposed to at Sheppard Air Base in Texas, like the poison gases sarin and VX, lindane and dursban are organophosphate-based poisons.

Bogeys

August 1996

I was born in Orange, California, on 3 February 1959. They named me Michael, after the Archangel, defender of heaven, soldier of God, leader of the heavenly host, the mightiest angel of all, whose great wings sheltered the other angels when Satan rebelled against God.

Michael the Archangel is also the special protector of the Jewish nation. It is he who escorts the souls of all the departed into heaven. Angels are either good or evil, and they are sometimes sent from heaven as messengers of divine vengeance, to punish the sins of men. They can destroy cities and nations. At least that's what I've read.

My sister Denise meets me at the airport in Dallas, and we fly to the city of angels together.

Before I leave, I sign the papers to initiate my medical retirement. I have not returned from Dallas a healthy man, and there is nothing more my wing commander can do to protect my job. When the flight surgeon calls me this time, it's at home, where I am spending most of my days since Dallas.

"Major Donnelly," he says, his voice stiff, ready to return any volley of resistance I might offer, "we have the paperwork ready for your medical retirement. When would you like to come in and get this rolling?"

It's more of an order than a question, I know, but I decide to buy some time. I have an important decision to make. Will I fight them and claim that my illness is related to the Gulf War? Or should I take the path of least resistance, retire without a fight?

Upon reflection, I realize that the choice is a simple one.

The Air Force medical system is not about to help me look for answers. That much is clear. If I claim that my illness is combat-related, my retirement will be delayed by a protracted, unwinnable battle. Our lives, already disrupted by my illness, will be put on hold for years.

I sign the papers and take off for California.

Stop number one: Dr. David Schultz's temporary office in the Tarzana Medical Center in Sherman Oaks. And right away I am wondering if we should have come.

The first clue that something is awry is our Saturday morning appointment. Not your typical doctor's office hours. Then, the way the nameplate on the door that reads "Dr. David Shultz, MD" is awkwardly taped over the nameplate for the pediatrician who occupies this office on weekdays.

The door is locked. While I wait outside, wondering exactly who this Dr. Shultz is, Denise rushes downstairs to call him from the lobby pay phone so he can let us in. Finally, the doctor himself opens the door. His appearance does little to inspire confidence: he looks the mad scientist part, his head fringed with slightly greasy, wavy steel grey hair, each eye with a mind of its own, the pupils working to locate spots on opposite walls in the corridor.

The doctor ushers us into the waiting area, a dark, wood-paneled room decorated with prints of ducklings and their mommies, beat-up toys and old issues of *Highlights* magazine.

"I'll be with you in just a minute," he informs us breathlessly, those eyes everywhere at once as he dashes down the corridor. We later hear him escort what we take to be another veteran out a side door. Then he is back.

"Why don't you just walk this way, Major Donnelly."

I can't help but think of Dr. Frankensteen. Walk this way.

Shultz walks backwards down the corridor in front of me, his wayward eyes on my legs as I hobble down the hall, one hand braced on the wall for support, one hand on my cane.

"Absolutely no doubt about it. Absolutely no doubt!" He is grinning, triumphant, his eyes misting through thick eyeglasses. "There is *absolutely* no way you have ALS. You are clearly suffering from organophosphate-induced brainstem encephalopathy." We are still in the corridor.

There is it again, though. Organophosphate poisons. I feel as if I am collecting the pieces to a hugely complicated puzzle, that they are strewn about me on the floor, millions of pieces. But this is not just any jigsaw. My life depends on finding the way they fit together. Trouble is, I'm a fighter pilot, not a doctor. I know how to fly jets and win wars. I know nothing about collating the clues to a medical mystery.

How Schultz can make this diagnosis from a distance of ten feet without having examined me or my medical records, I don't know. But I am glad that he is glad. The fact that he too is talking about organophosphates seems significant to me. And I am very glad to hear a neurologist insist I don't have ALS. The man should know. A Veterans' Administration doctor who is conducting research on Gulf War veterans on his own time, I figure I should be able to trust him.

He leads us into the office, a bright room oddly empty of any personal effects, even any doctor's paraphernalia. Just some manuals strewn around and Dr. Shultz's fat briefcase open on the desk.

"I'm a renegade, you know," he tells us as we sit. "They'd love to find a reason to get rid of me. But so far, no luck. That's because they know *I'm right.* They know I'm on to something here. I'm the only one who's really *helping* you guys." He pauses, perhaps for us to congratulate him.

"I had one guy, went out in the sun, almost died. I told him not to. Don't go out in the sun, I told him. You're photosensitive." He pauses. "Let me see your files." Denise hands him the fat stack of lab reports, X-rays, MRIs.

He is excited, grateful for the receptive audience. He flips through my records, his eyes scan the reports busily as he speaks. "Then I treated him with intravenous immunoglobulins, and now he's better than he was, but he'll never be the same. In a wheelchair forever. That's one of the classic symptoms, you know. Are you photosensitive?" Another grin.

"Yes," I answer, trying not to get too excited. This seems a good sign. "I get dizzy in the sun. I can't even open my eyes. I need sunglasses just to walk out the door, even on a cloudy day." Photosensitivity is not associated with ALS, and none of the neurologists has had a good answer as to why this symptom has accompanied my disease.

"Good, good," he murmurs, holding an X-ray up to the tinted window. He squints. "That's good."

He performs the standard neurology tests, the pin pricks, tuning fork, reflex reactions. His conclusions remain the same throughout. "You don't have ALS. I'm sure of it," he says over and over. I want to believe him. Why don't I?

"I'm going to set you up for some IVIGs," he announces an hour and a half later, after he's finished his exam and shown me on my MRI where the little white dots in my brainstem reveal encephalopathy. "Let me call over to the hospital now." He picks up the phone. "Are you free? Can you go over there now?"

Of course we are free. We have come thousands of miles for this. I want to know more about IVIGs and how they are supposed to help, but I am thrilled to be getting such rush treatment.

"They'll see you in an hour." He hangs up the phone looking a little pensive, his animated pace slowed by something he has heard during the phone conversation.

"Intravenous immunoglobulins are extracted from donated blood," he explains. "They are the naturally occurring disease fighters everyone has in their bloodstreams. The trouble is, your blood has been compromised by exposure to the organophosphate poison, so the opportunistic viruses we all carry take control. And you get sick."

It all seems to make sense.

"What we need to do," he continues, "is resupply your blood with those natural disease fighters. So we pump you up with IVIGs. I *know* this will cure you. This is very good news, Major Donnelly. *Very* good news."

Why am I not happier to hear this? Something bothers me about this guy. The long-distance diagnosis, the speedy cure, the mad scientist behavior. Plus, it all seems too good to be true.

"Can these IVIGs hurt him?" Denise asks. The natural question, I think.

"Absolutely not. No side effects at all. Nothing to worry about." He grimaces at her, as if he wished her absent.

Even aspirin has side effects, I think. How can there be no side effects to pumping gallons of someone else's plasma into my veins? Denise is busy scribbling notes in her notebook, recording every word of the conversation.

After a confused goodbye, in which we promise to call him on Sunday morning, we cross the parking area and make our way to admissions. And this is when the fun begins.

Two hours of paper shuffling, phone calling and general confusion yield little. "Well, we have a little problem," the admitting clerk tells us at last. She is a kind woman and has let us use the office WATS line to call home during the long wait.

"Our little problem is that Dr. Shultz doesn't have admitting privileges here." She looks at us apologetically. "So, we called the hospital administrator at home to see if we could get you in anyway, and, well, he refused." Here she blushes. "I guess Dr. Shultz never renewed his privileges after they were, well, expired."

Here is a brick wall if ever I met one. We start to wonder if we should be doing this IVIG thing at all. What do we know about it? And what is the big hurry, anyway? We call Dr. Shultz at home. By now it is late, evening.

His alarm and surprise seem genuine enough. Almost like he had forgotten that he had forgotten to renew his admitting privileges. Or maybe he thought they wouldn't notice? He negotiates with the clerk.

Finally, they strike a deal. I am to be admitted, but not until later this evening, when a hematologist will be on duty. I head up to the room to wait, while Denise runs out for dinner. We spend the time chewing on deli sandwiches, watching reruns of the Simpsons, waiting for someone to appear to inject me. Finally, around 9:30, a nurse shows up to tell us that they are looking for the hematologist who is to oversee the entire procedure.

"Procedure?" we ask together. "What procedure?" We thought they would inject some sort of relatively quick IV and then we could go back to the hotel and wait for the results.

"Oh, no," the nurse answers. "These things take up to six hours to administer. And you have to be watched the whole time for adverse reactions. Some people get very sick."

Aside from the high grades we give her for bedside manner, we are grateful for the information. In our uninformed opinion, it doesn't make much sense to rush into this or to start it late at night. I am not exactly the picture of health, after all, and at this point I am exhausted.

We leave the hospital and decide to start the IVIG earlier the next day. We also plan to do a little research in the meantime. On IVIGs. On Dr. Shultz.

He has promised to call us at the Carriage Inn to tell us when we can go to the hospital. When he finally does call, late Sunday afternoon, he informs us that we will have to go to some doctor's office on Monday morning. It seems the Tarzana Medical Center is having nothing more to do with Dr. Shultz. And he has no admitting privileges, at any hospital, anywhere. By now, red flags are flying across the LA skies.

My gut tells me this Shultz is a quack, probably a well-intentioned quack, and I am running out of false hopes. I am wondering what happens when I have no more alternative treatments to chase. No more chances for salvation, however thin. What then?

I am limp with disappointment. I try not to let Denise know, because she is making such an effort to put it all in the best light. "Maybe these IVIGs will help after all, Mike," she offers. She's trying to make me feel better. I don't look up from the pre-season game. Dallas versus the Vikings. I don't want to talk about it, not now.

"Want me to go out and get some Mexican?" she offers.

"Yeah, and bring me back a beer."

I had asked Shultz if I could drink beer. "One a day," he'd answered. "No more."

"Bring me back the biggest single you can find," I say. She laughs.

Denise leaves me alone in our room at the Carriage Inn. Air conditioner humming against the late afternoon heat. Plaid coverlets on the beds, grey carpeting, plaid curtains closed against the southern California sun and the parking lot. We are on the first floor.

I sit with my feet propped up on a chair, to keep the fluid from collecting in my now useless feet. My eyes are on the game, but my mind is not on football. Instead, I work at keeping the tears from leaking out of my eyes. I am afraid my soul will crack if they do. Once I start to cry, I know I will never stop.

I wonder what I will tell Susan. What I will say to Erin and Sean, who have observed my deterioration with the fearful, mute detachment of children. Occasionally they find ways to ask me when I will get better. Sean is easier with the questions because he is still too young to understand that adults lie to children to hide things they themselves would prefer not to face. With Erin, it's more difficult. She knows too much for me to pretend.

Like the day before I left for LA. We were in the bedroom, Sue and I, packing up my suit bag.

"I don't need much," I tell her. "Just some shorts and t-shirts. Maybe one pair of pants. I need to travel light, since Denise is going to be carrying everything."

Sue pulls some underwear out of the dresser. I am sitting on the bed, my back up against the brass headboard, my feet propped by a pair of pillows.

"I'm just going to run into the kitchen to get your other shorts out of the dryer," she says, her face turned away. She hasn't looked at me all morning. After 12 years of marriage, I know this means Sue is angry. Angry and hurting, but not able to talk about it. Who can blame her and what comfort can I offer, anyway? We are both of us afraid to talk about it. If we talk, we may find our own fears realized in one another's words. Or speak our hopes, only to have them crushed, again.

Erin wanders in from outdoors. Her brown eyes wide under the shelter of her dark bangs, she looks up at me, sideways.

"Daddy?" she asks.

"Yeah, honey," I answer. I know I haven't talked to her enough about what's happening. I don't know what to say because I don't know what's happening. At least that's what I tell myself.

"Carrie said her Daddy said we have to move." She is snapping my suit bag clips open and shut, not looking at me now. "Do we have to move, Daddy? Because I really like it here. I like my friends and Mrs. Frost. And everything. We don't have to move, do we?"

What do I tell this child? My mind spins. I pull her onto my lap, trying to buy time to think of something to say. I wrap my arms around her, pull her close.

"I like it here, too, honey," I finally answer, which is in itself not quite the truth. "I hope we don't have to move, either. But if we do, we'll move back to be with Grandma Rae and Grandma Pat, Grandpa E.J. and Grandpa Tom. You'd like that, wouldn't you?" I stroke her hair.

She is crying, that silent, desperate weeping of children who know too much. "I guess so, Daddy," she answers.

I am lost here on this bed, my eight-year-old daughter anchored on my lap. We are both too young for this, I think, for me to have become the child and she the parent, trying to comfort her failing father with brave words.

We rock from side to side, her head up underneath my chin. I have always been the tall, strong man who could do anything. Her father. Who rode her on his shoulders so she could touch the ceiling. Who took her out camping in the desert, sang songs around the campfire, launched the boat into wide, flat Texas lakes for daylong picnics. When she was just three she would point up at airplanes in the sky and tell anyone who would listen, "That's my Daddy."

Sue finds us here when she comes in from the kitchen, looks away, stows the shorts in the suit bag, and goes back out into the kitchen to start dinner.

Denise comes back with the food and a 20-ounce bottle of Old Milwaukee and saves me from this memory. I will worry about what to tell my family later, after the beer.

Next morning, when we find the appointed doctor's office, we do not even get out of our rented Grand Am. Instead, we park next to the dilapidated building in a run-down section of LA, out beyond Studio City, where the streets are paved not with gold but with the anguish of poverty, crime and drugs. I am not about to open my veins in this place.

I have tried to brace myself for this letdown from the time I left home on this trip. Last night, I prepared myself again. Under the hum of the air conditioner, as Denise slept in the next bed, I lectured myself to be prepared. Even so, I am crushed. I wanted to believe there was an easy answer. I wanted to believe that it would only take a few quarts of someone else's blood to cure me.

We leave LA that night, ahead of schedule, the hope that brought us to California now transformed to dust by the grim alchemy of disappointment. Next stop, San Diego, a place governed even less by the rules of reality than its sister city up the coast.

Cy Richardson is an energetic, cheerful man, and when we meet him in his Del Rey office, he is dressed in expensive-looking linen shorts, a print short-sleeved shirt and elegant leather sandals. A naturopath, he is one of those alternative practitioners who dispenses all kinds of remedies, from herbs to homeopathic drops. He prescribes a combination of both for me, and while I also would like to believe him, my faith is running short against the odds by now. Denise carries the package of drops and herb tea as we make our way out of the office. I wait at the door while she gets the car, and then we drive across town to our last stop.

Dr. Gates, osteopath, practices in a warren of rooms in the lower level of a shopping center office building. To start, his assistant asks us to sign a form saying we won't sue the doctor. The tired red flags give a half-hearted flutter. I sign, but I feel like leaving. Before I can manage, Dr. Gates shows his kindly face, and he spends a full hour with me.

His theory is familiar, although different from Shultz's. He believes that many serious illnesses are linked back to the polio vaccine we received as children, when vaccines were still grown on live monkey tissue. My illness, like AIDS, he claims, is a trans-species disease. His recommendations are less concrete than his theory, and we leave wondering exactly what he has said.

I fall twice in California, once in the Tarzana Medical Center emergency entrance, once outside a taco stand in San Diego. A young skateboarder, looking puzzled and a little worried that I might be contagious, helps me up from the taco stand pavement. At the hospital, a hefty guard gets me to my feet again and worriedly loads me into the car, asking if I'm sure I don't want to stop at the emergency room. What I can't tell him is that no one in his emergency room can help me.

Denise brings Dr. Shultz's bill back to my parents. He wants $1,300 for something, I'm not sure what. This is my bill for false hope? I'm a good guy, on your side, here's my bill? We never send him a penny, and while he calls a few times to ask how I'm doing, he never asks about the bill. Dr. Richardson we pay when services are rendered, as the sign in his office requires: $500—office visit, herbs and homeopathic drops included. Dr. Gates sends a bill for $680, which my parents pay.

No one sends a consolation notice, a card inscribed with sincere regrets at our lack of success.

I feel like such a dupe. All this time, as I've chased around the country looking for answers under rocks that are perhaps better left unturned, I am waiting for the Department of Defense, or at least the Air Force, to come clean. I am waiting for the headlines, "PENTAGON TO OPEN ITS FILES TO GULF WAR VETERANS." I am waiting for someone to have a conscience.

Why do I expect someone in the Pentagon to do the right thing? What is it in me that won't let that particular hope die? I am your comrade-in-arms, I think. A brother soldier. Do not betray me.

I'm at the point where I enjoy what they call "semi-independent" living. I need help with eating, drinking, brushing my teeth, getting dressed. But I can still manipulate the switch on my electric wheelchair enough to move about the house. I can still hook my crooked hands onto the bars over the toilet, hoist my-self up and pee. And despite all of this, I have not given up hope. I will not give up hope.

Every level is a new loss, every phase a new frontier in mourning the pass-ing of a self I never really thought I would lose. It doesn't matter how much reading I do, how much I educate myself, how many questions I ask. Nothing prepares me for what comes next, nothing eases the passing.

Usually I prefer not to talk about it. Maybe that's the fighter pilot training. Just grit your teeth and tough it out. They weren't big on expressing your feel-ings in the Air Force. Not the kind of thing that gets jets flown or bombs dropped. I put that training to use every day now, though not in the way I planned.

In survival school, where we learned prisoner-of-war endurance tech-niques, they taught us to resist at every opportunity. If the enemy wants to know what you know, he can and will torture it out of you, they taught us, but resist as much as you can. Because everyone has a breaking point, and eventu-ally you will hit yours. You don't want to give in, though, you don't want to give him something you don't want him to have. Resist, they taught us. That way, you have the mental superiority of knowing you did not relent until you reached your breaking point.

They gave us a realistic picture of what it would be like to be a prisoner of war based on the real life experiences of those who survived imprisonment. They also covered all the different interrogation techniques we might encoun-ter: good cop–bad cop, phony Red Cross worker, coercion, and so on. Unfor-tunately, they never taught us how to handle the insidious invasion of a delayed-action neurological agent. That technique I am teaching to myself.

Now I am a prisoner of war, and I resist at every opportunity. I fight the dis-ease. I fight the very people who taught me to resist. I have not reached my breaking point, and so I maintain mental superiority, just as they taught me to do. While I suffer losses, the skirmishes are real, and although I lose a lot of them, I am glad to fight.

I fight, therefore I live. Today I am the luckiest man on the face of the earth.

Near Miss

When I get back to Sheppard, the medical evaluation board has the discharge papers ready for me to sign. Guess somebody is in a hurry. Turns out they aren't feeling too generous, either. For while the Air Force is more than willing to diagnose me with a fatal illness, they are only willing to grant me 50% temporary medical retirement. In English, this means that I will receive 50% of a full pension, and I will have to reapply next year for a review of my pension and status. Meanwhile, I am, in their medical estimation, 100% likely to die within two years.

I have the option of rejecting the MEB offer and requesting a formal hearing to argue my case for 100% disability retirement. I figure if they're going to tell me I'm 100% sick, I'll put my cards on that bet.

"I'm going to reject that offer," I tell the processing sergeant at the hospital. "I'm going to go for a formal hearing in San Antonio."

The sergeant, a plump man whose ruddy face is highlighted by the thick black rims of his Air Force–issue spectacles, is stunned.

"Most people are lucky to get 50%, Major Donnelly."

I guess he figures I'm making a bad move.

"I have to warn you that very few ever change the board's decision." In his mind, I suppose, since I am still able to walk with a cane, I must be nuts to pass up their offer.

"I'll take my chances," I say. "Where do I sign?" I scrawl my signature on the form where it reads, "I reject the MEB offer and wish to request a formal review before the board."

With that signature, I flick the magic switch. The Air Force bureaucracy swings into action, if action you can call it. They begin to do what they do best, which is to thwart the efforts of anyone who dares to question their authority.

They review every medical record that exists, dating back to 1981 and my induction, records which by now document my treatment outside the military medical system and my conviction that my illness is combat related. Obviously, I must be a troublemaker looking to make more trouble.

"They'll call you when they set a hearing date, Major Donnelly. Good luck."

I am looking forward to that hearing. In my mind, I am daring them to deny me this compensation.

Of course, they cannot know who they are up against, namely, my family. My Dad is already on the phone with every elected representative we can think of who might be sympathetic to my situation. My sister Denise makes almost daily visits to Senator Kerry's Boston office to solicit his help. And while Kerry will later disappoint us greatly when it comes time for him to take a stand, before three weeks have passed, he and more than a dozen of his colleagues have sent letters of congressional consternation. I am definitely looking forward to my day in court.

In the meantime, my parents have not rested in their search for help. They call doctors at random at all of the best hospitals—the Mayo Clinic, Johns Hopkins, Columbia Presbyterian. Through the Gulf War veterans' network, they hear of a Dr. James Tolland in the D.C. area.

"If his illness is the result of exposure to a poison," Dr. Tolland says during the only phone conversation he allows us, "I can tell you."

Then he puts us through to his office manager.

"I'm sorry," she answers in response to our request for an appointment, "but Dr. Tolland can't set up an appointment with you until we receive a retainer."

Silence. I am on the phone from Texas, my Mom from home, my Dad from the office, where he has set up this conference call.

"A retainer?" I finally ask. "How much?"

"Dr. Tolland requires a minimum of $5,000."

"$5,000! Just to set up an appointment?" My Dad. "You gotta be baggin' me! Excuse my French." He has reacted before he's had a chance to think.

"Tom!" My mother, the peacemaker. "Why does he need a retainer in advance?" she asks. "We'll be happy to pay when we come. We've just never heard of a doctor asking for a retainer before."

"Could you get the doctor on the phone again, please?" My father. I can hear him thinking. You wanna play hardball, he's thinking.

"I'm sorry, but he's in with a patient right now."

"Then have him call me at his earliest convenience."

We hang up.

We are desperate. Dr. James Tolland is banking on it. My Dad talks him down to $2,500 and sends the check. Only then are we permitted to make an appointment for early September.

I fly alone to Washington Airport, where my parents meet me with a wheelchair, for which I am grateful. They have driven down from Connecticut. Two round-trip airline tickets and a rental car are out of the question, what with Dr. Tolland's retainer. My own flight has been difficult because by now the cane is not enough. I walk slowly through the airport, through the jet, down the jetway, bracing myself between the cane and any wall I can find.

We check in to the Holiday Inn directly across from the Watergate. Later, we order Chinese and eat in my parents' room, the television tuned to CNN. Mom orders enough to feed the entire Chinese army, but we do our best.

I sleep fitfully. I am thinking about what Dr. Tolland will find. I am wondering if he will be worth my parents' money. I am no longer able to hope, at least not consciously. Mostly I am storing my emotions in a bunker buried deep within, an underground cave I prefer not to visit.

The next morning is cool, overcast, rainy. First stop, Dr. Tolland's office. We find our way through the maze of Washington streets, searching for the address. It takes us a while, especially since Dad won't stop for directions.

"Tom, why don't you just stop and ask someone? Here. Here's a gas station. Just pull in and ask the man." My mother has been reciting this incantation to "the man" since before I was born. And my father has been answering her in the same way ever since. They must take comfort in the familiarity of the argument.

"Rae, for Christ's sake, will you just let me drive? I know where it is. If you'd just let me drive, maybe we'd get there." I watch wistfully as we sail past the gas station.

Finally, we find the doctor's office, an old brownstone surrounded by an antique wrought-iron fence, on a street filled with brownstones, all of which seem to be doctors' offices associated with the hospital. Dad pulls into the narrow driveway that leads around to the back.

The receptionist takes our name and we find a seat in the small waiting room. We wait. And then we wait some more. I'm getting used to waiting. I think maybe I should write a treatise on the art of waiting in doctors' offices. It must be a class they teach in medical school. "How to Impress Your Patients with Your Own Importance."

At last we are led into a small conference room where we shake hands with Dr. Tolland himself. My $2,500 handshake, I think. It feels expensive.

Dr. Tolland is a middle-aged man, his grey-speckled brown hair combed over a rather large bald spot, just like the before pictures on the television hair-replacement ads. I wonder why he hasn't had implants if the bald spot bothers him so much. Finances shouldn't be an issue.

He has a slight accent, but I can't tell where he's from. I think maybe Germany or Switzerland, but then again maybe not. His face is tanned, and this is not a tanning salon tan. This is a Caribbean tan. He sits at the head of the conference table facing us. We talk and he listens closely, his neatly manicured hands folded across his starched white labcoat. The words "Dr. Tolland" are embroidered in red loops across his right breast pocket.

We tell him the whole history, from the malathion exposure to the first symptoms, from the ALS diagnosis to the Dr. Frazer episode to the California trip.

Mom, Dad and I split different parts of the story, each of us eager to fill him in on the details. When I finish the Dr. Frazer piece, he asks me, "Honestly, Mr. Donnelly, do you think that guy is a quack?"

"I'm no medical professional," I answer. I look at him. "I'm a pilot. But I spent almost two months there, and I saw people getting well. I just wasn't one of them. Unfortunately."

"You know," he answers, "I heard a story about a guy who claimed that he and his family were made sick by the gear he'd sent home from the war. Now how could that happen? From his gear?" He looks at us for agreement, as if we will concur that the very notion is preposterous.

Right away we suspect that this guy is not going to be any help after all. What he doesn't know is that we have met the very soldier he is referring to, and we don't think it's odd at all that his family could have become ill from his gear, not after hearing the story from Larry and Susan Landers, who live in Connecticut.

The Army shipped some of Larry's gear directly from the battlefield to Susan in Germany, where they were stationed before the war started. Susan stored the gear in the baby's room. Three weeks later, the baby, 21 months, developed gangrene.

At the same time, Susan and the twins got asthma. Suddenly. To this day, the entire family continues to endure a bizarre range of illnesses and symptoms. Larry suffers from pseudotumor cerebrae—which means he's going blind—intercranial pressure, precancerous lesions in his esophagus, tachycardia, an enlarged liver and spleen. Susan also suffers from an enlarged spleen and is being tested for lymphoma and connective tissue disease. The twins have recently been diagnosed with the same pseudotumor cerebrae their father has. It is only a matter of time before they both lose their sight. They are 11 years old.

When the military forced the Landers family to enter the Gulf War evaluation network it set up after years of pressure from veterans, they determined that both Larry and Susan are suffering from somatoform disorder: in other words, the military told the Landers, their years of symptoms and illness were all stress-induced.

By now, the entire family has been sick since the end of the war—seven years. That's a lot of stress.

Interestingly, what Dr. Tolland also must not know is that almost every other soldier evaluated under the special Gulf War network is diagnosed with somatoform disorder or PTSD, post-traumatic stress disorder. Funny what stress can do to a person, I guess.

Dr. Tolland clearly finds the soldier's claim spurious, and if he isn't open to the notion that some kind of agent may have adhered to Larry's gear, then he certainly isn't going to listen to my story.

"Have you seen any of the recent news releases about Gulf War illnesses, like in the *New York Times*?" my Mom asks. "Dr. Robert Haley of the University of Texas recently released a report of a study he did where he gave pyridostigmine bromide to chickens and then exposed them to pesticides. It made the chickens' legs stop working."

Dr. Tolland is having a hard time controlling his expression.

"No," he says, "I don't usually read the newspaper. I read mostly medical journals."

I am not sure if he is trying to impress us, again, or if he is just stupid. We exchange worried glances.

"And besides," he adds, "what possible reason would the government have for hiding this?" At this point, I know we are wasting our time and our money. Why didn't he say any of this on the phone? Oh, the retainer. That's why. I want to scream. I don't.

I remain seated in Dr. Tolland's conference room. I look out the window at the grey Washington day. I think about my family back in Texas, waiting for me to return home with good news. Waiting for me to get better. I am not getting better, and I do not think I will be bringing home good news. I feel my entire will straining against the backs of my eyeballs as I scan the Washington skyline. I am afraid my eyes will explode from the pressure, that all the anger, fear, and frustration will blast out of my brain. Sometimes, it seems that such an end would be a relief from the agony of hoping.

"I will now examine you," Dr. Tolland proclaims, and I feel as if he is instructing me to be grateful. I can practically perform the exam myself at this point. I think of leaving. I know what he is going to do, what he is going to say, and what he is going to conclude.

I let him examine me, though, because my parents have paid $2,500 for the privilege of a visit with the man, and I don't want to waste their money. I also want to let them hope for a little longer. It doesn't occur to me that their motives for continuing with this charade might be identical to my own, that the backs of their own eyes may ache with the same torment of misplaced hope.

While we're in the examining room, I ask him all the questions I can think of. I figure I may as well try to get something out of this. "What causes this disease?" I ask.

"We don't know," he answers. I am beginning to think that most doctors are absolutely useless. Expensive, but useless.

"What about the effects of environmental exposures?" I ask. "And how about organophosphate poisoning?"

"In the studies of the Japanese exposure to the nerve agent sarin in the subway incident, there were no cases of ALS," he states.

"That just happened recently," I counter. "Are they sure it isn't a longer-term problem? That maybe people might develop ALS and other diseases later, after a subsequent exposure to another poison?"

After all, I didn't get sick until four years after the end of the war. The other vets we know who have ALS also got sick some time after the war's end. It took years and the subsequent exposure to a pesticide to put us over.

"I don't know," he answers. He seems satisfied with not knowing.

I continue to pump him for answers about motor-neuron disease and motor neuropathy. The former is ALS, the latter a less severe affliction that mimics ALS in some of its earlier symptoms, but is not fatal.

"I'm fairly certain that the diagnosis of ALS is correct," he states. He is clearly a member of the fraternity of doctors who believe that bluntness is best, bedside manner an indulgence.

"How are you going to tell my parents?" I ask him. I am trying not to cry. Not because I don't want to cry, but because I don't want to cry in front of this man. I will show him no vulnerability. He already owns too much of me. I hate that he is healthy and that I am not. I hate his smugness, his white lab coat, his neat hands. I hate his bald spot, his tan, his complacency.

"I'll be very direct with them," he answers, "just as I must be with you. It's time to face facts, Mr. Donnelly." Why do I feel he's enjoying this? Am I being unfair to him? He seems to be a man who lives to tell other people to face facts.

"You have ALS. Your prognosis is poor. I give you two to three years, on the outside. You can expect a gradual but permanent deterioration. Usually, in cases where the disease first presents itself in the lower limbs, the fasciculations progress to the upper limbs, then to the face and mouth, and then to the lungs. Every case is different. We don't know how quickly or slowly you might progress."

I am not looking at him. I am looking out the window. I am in Washington, D.C. The very people who sent me to war are here, in this city. The people who ordered me to take pyridostigmine bromide are here, in this city. The people who know what chemicals I was exposed to during that war are also here, in this city. Even the people who condoned the illicit sale of chemical weapons to Iraq are here.

I feel I am in the presence of great evil. I cannot breathe. My chest feels like it is enclosed in a vise, that the vise is tightening. I gasp for air. I begin to feel faint. I want to get out of this room, out of this place. I want to be away. Somewhere away.

"Death usually occurs as a result of asphyxiation." He is still speaking. I wonder how much I have missed. "Of course, you will need to go on a feeding tube at some point. And you will likely have to decide, while you are still able, how long you wish to prolong your life on a respirator and feeding tube. When the time comes."

I look at him, finally. Is he evil, I wonder, or is he just a fool? I don't really care.

I look around inside myself for speech. It is missing. I look at him, but he is blurred. He has fallen away, and I see him from a great distance, through a wall of water, it seems. Words come to me, at last.

"Is it possible," I ask, "that my illness is the result of some incident in the Gulf War?"

"I can't tell you that, Mr. Donnelly, and in a way, it doesn't really matter anymore, does it? You have other things to think about now."

We are nearing the end of my $2,500 adventure, I sense. He stands.

"Why don't you get dressed and I'll meet you and your parents back in the conference room." He leaves me.

I look out the window at the greyness. This is what evil looks like, I think, my eyes wet with the injustice of it all. I force myself to breathe. At last I pull my clothes on, slowly, watching my hands as they button my shirt, as they zip up my fly. I love my fingers, I think. I love my arms. I love to breathe.

Somehow, I find myself sitting at the conference table. My parents are seated here, too, although I don't remember them coming in. Dr. Tolland starts to explain the disease to them. They are weeping. I am weeping. Dr. Tolland is delivering a lecture on the progression of ALS. This cannot be easy for him, day after day, I grant him that. Maybe he has just become a jerk as a defense. I am grateful to feel something for him. I don't want him to be a monster.

"Tell me, doctor," my Dad asks, "is there any way to ascertain that this is indeed what Michael has? It seems like we're just collecting opinions, that no one can say for certain."

I already know the answer to this question before the doctor starts to speak.

"There are no definitive tests for ALS," he states. "It is a diagnosis by exception. We rule out all the other possibilities, for which there are definitive tests. And when these prove to be dead ends, well, then, we are left with ALS as the only possibility." I think I detect a smirk on his face, but maybe I am imagining it.

Dr. Tolland scans through my thick medical file searching the lists of tests for anything that he might be missing.

"I see you never had a spinal tap," he says. My heart takes a jump. I hate doctors. Yet a new way to torture me.

"No," I answer reluctantly, "but I have the feeling you're about to change that."

"I can suggest that we check Michael into the hospital overnight. We can perform a spinal tap and another EMG and have him seen by one of our specialists." Oh goody, I think, more needles.

We drive over to the hospital. Dad pulls up to the front door and when I step out of the car, I trip over a crack in the sidewalk and fall. I don't hurt myself, at least not physically. A huge man wearing a uniform helps me up, and with his arm around my waist and my arm around his neck, he escorts me into the admitting office.

We make an arrival, a four-legged creature lumbering into the crowded room. The guard maneuvers me into a seat and then leaves. We do the usual hospital admitting dance, only it turns out that Dr. Tolland does have admitting privileges here. I am spared the drama of Los Angeles, as well as the false hope.

Eventually, a steward appears with a wheelchair and escorts me and my parents up to my room. I hate hospitals even more than I hate doctors.

The smells, the sights, the nearness of so much illness and death. I do not want to be here. But here is where I am. At least for tonight.

I do not sleep at all. It is a night in hell, complete with the devil, who appears in the form of a nurse who interrogates me as if I am in an insane asylum. My very own Nurse Ratchett.

"What's your name?" she demands. "What day is it? How do you feel? Who is the president? Squeeze my fingers. Wiggle your toes. Now I'm going to take your blood pressure." This last sounds more like a threat, like she's going to take it and keep it. I wonder if she has a secret collection at home.

About 10:30 or 11:00, Dr. Tolland wanders in, a phantom in a white coat. He appears in my doorway, the bright corridor light casting an ominous silhouette.

"I've spoken with my colleague," he states. "And he has agreed to see you. He should be around some time in the morning. I just want to make sure you understand this really is nothing more than a formality. We're certain of this diagnosis."

I feel like reassuring him that I am adequately depressed, thank you very much. I get the message. No false hopes, not to worry. We chat about inconsequential things, but my mind is not on the weather or Dr. Tolland's BMW. I am glad when he leaves. I do not like him, and I think he prefers it that way.

About an hour later a young man enters. "I am Dr. Pelligro, " he announces in an Italian accent.

He looks to be an intern and starts to ask me questions. It is by now midnight and I am wondering what another late-night interrogation will contribute to my well-being, but my well-being doesn't seem to be on anyone's mind but my own. Mostly the people I encounter are preoccupied with making sure I have no false hopes and that I do not do anything so ill-advised as sleep.

Dr. Pelligro wants to examine me, but he's come to the wrong carnival. I use a POW technique. I resist. I convince him that I am just too exhausted. I just want him to leave so I can be alone in this nightmare. All this company is crowding my personal hell.

Finally, Dr. Pelligro gets the hint.

When morning breaks, I am glad, even though I know the day will bring new and more inventive tortures than those I've already sampled. My parents arrive at 7:00. I can see they haven't spent the night sleeping, either.

Eventually another young doctor appears. "I am here to perform your spinal tap, Mr. Donnelly," he proclaims. Should I applaud? I wonder. Congratulate him?

Oh goody, I think again. At last. A needle in my spine. I haven't had one of those yet.

My parents leave, and the doctor asks me to lie on the edge of the bed, curled on my side so that my spine is curved. My mind walks out the door as I assume the position. I am not going to participate in this event. He can have my body, and notify me when he's finished.

This young man may be about to insert a needle into my spine, but he cannot know that I have trained for this. More than once, and in more than one way.

And while I haven't exactly volunteered for this procedure, I am here all the same, and the pain does not allow me to be absent for long. It is intense, enormous. It resists my resistance. It fills my mind to the farthest reaches, even finds me where I am playing in the Washington woods, chases me to my hideout in my underground bunker.

Thankfully, it is over fast. Once the intern removes the needle from my vertebra, the pain subsides instantly.

"Now roll over onto your back. You won't want to move your head too much, and you may experience a severe headache some time in the next 24 hours. That's normal. And that's it, Mr. Donnelly. We're all set."

Oh we are, are we? I realize that I am not in an apple orchard in Washington State. I am not buried in a tiger cage in some field. I am staring up at a hospital ceiling like many other hospital ceilings I have known, the rectangular white tiles slivered with silver flecks, punctured at regular intervals by the meanest-looking sprinkler heads I have ever seen.

I return to the room, arrive through the door and greet myself as I enter. Maybe Nurse Ratchett was right. Maybe this is an insane asylum. Maybe this is where I belong.

Dr. Tolland's specialist soon appears, with eight interns in tow. He has thoughtfully brought along an audience for the ALS patient show. And now, ladies and gentlemen, before your very eyes, the ALS patient. His knees are hyperflexic! His leg muscles fasciculate! And, believe it or not, he thinks his illness is due to service in the Gulf War!

The specialist conducts a cursory exam as I lie on the bed. I am on display, not a person at all but some kind of medical doll the doctor is using to make his points. Mostly he addresses his audience, none of whom looks me in the eye. Finally he addresses me, but only to tell me they have arranged for my EMG in a couple of hours, in the building directly across the street.

He gives me the time and room number and tells me someone will be along with a wheelchair to escort me. Then he and his entourage depart.

Mom and Dad reappear, and we sit in the room and wait. We try to make conversation, but our hearts are elsewhere. We look out the window across the city, the wedding cake white of the capitol building dome mocking us from a distance. Over there is where justice is supposed to live, I think. Over there is where they decide these things. Things like who will know what information. Things like whether acknowledging that Hussein or even the United States used chemical weapons during the war would threaten national security. Or whatever rationale they tell themselves and the world.

The appointed time approaches, but our escort doesn't show. Dad walks down the hall, reappears pushing a wheelchair. "Get in," he tells me. "We're going over there."

I already know the EMG game. They rotate the needles in my flesh just as they did in San Antonio. If this is all just a formality, I wonder, why am I allowing it? But mostly I retreat to my bunker.

Pain has its own script, and it doesn't allow you to rewrite the outcome no matter what your training. As much as I try, I feel the needles twisting in my muscles. I try to think about Erin and Sean, about flying my jet out over the desert. About the hunting trip I took last winter with Puck. I picture the ocean, the sky streaked with contrails, the lacy wake of my motorboat in a brown Texas lake. I conjure up the smell of JP-4. I taste my grandmother's lasagna. I am glad she is not alive to witness this.

At last we leave this place and head back to the hotel. I am just glad to get the hell out of there and am ready to get the hell out of D.C.

The next day, I board an airplane for home. I am fine until we are sitting in the airport, waiting to take off. Suddenly, I cannot move. I just want to lie down here, on the carpet. My head is throbbing, I feel nauseous. I am chewing aspirin like they're chicklets. And of course, I am seated next to a couple with a baby who cries incessantly the entire three-hour flight.

I recline my seat and keep my eyes closed the whole way. When I get to Dallas, there is someone waiting for me with a wheelchair. Dad had called ahead and arranged it. I am thankful.

The skycap wheels me out to the sidewalk, where the van service I have reserved is waiting. I stretch out on the seat, relieved that the van isn't full, and sleep the whole two hours to Wichita Falls.

I am home, at last. I say nothing as I stumble through the front door on Sue's arm. Sean is out playing with his friends. Erin rushes from her room to hug me.

"Daddy!" she shouts. "Daddy! You're home." She doesn't look me in the eyes, nor I her.

I don't have a plan for what happens next.

I have a recurring dream, one I first had in Dallas. It comes to me in fragments, my dream, shards of white light fracturing my sleep. Afterwards, I lie awake and try to splice the bits together, try to capture the meaning. More like a vision than a dream at times, it came to me several times in that cold, hollow apartment in Dallas, halfway through my time there. Then again back in Wichita Falls.

I have made the dream my own and I visit it often during my waking hours. I visited it in that hospital room in Washington. I certainly couldn't stay there. Now it comes to me again, as pain hounds me into sleep.

In the dream I am walking up a path. It's a beautiful sunny day. The sky is clear, with just some small very white puffy clouds dotting the sky. I am in some rolling hills that lead into the mountains. It's warm, even though I'm high up near the mountains. There's a light breeze, but I'm not uncomfortable. The path cuts upward and diagonally toward the top of the ridge. It's about four feet wide, paved with hard-packed crushed rock. I notice that the path seems to be unused, although it's perfectly formed, as if it is meant just for me.

The grass on the right leading up the hill toward the top of the ridge and also on the left is deep, deep green, punctuated with brilliant yellow, red and blue wildflowers. As I'm making my way up the hill, I'm having trouble walking, but I walk on. And as I near the top of the ridge, the path forks. To the left, it goes downhill, and as I look downhill, it seems to enter a valley located between two steep mountains. The valley is completely in shadow, even though the sun is straight overhead. And from where I am I can see the trees in the valley, and they look like dead trees, with no leaves, just gnarled cold bare branches.

The path to the right goes straight up over the ridge, and it occurs to me that the left-hand fork would be much easier, downhill. The right-hand path that goes straight over the hill, that's the one I choose, although it's the harder walk. As I come over the crest of the hill, I see the most wondrous, beautiful sight nestled down in the open hollow below the ridge. There's a crystal clear lake. The water is blue and shimmering in the sun, the light breeze barely moving the water, the ripples reflecting like diamonds.

I can see that the path leads down along the left side of the lake. The grass surrounds it with gentle hills rolling to the left and right. On the opposite side of the lake, the forest begins and beyond that, a mountain rises up, its caps domed white with snow. I can see that the path leads into the forest and on to the mountain.

And I walk down the path feeling warm. At the foot of the ridge, right before the lake, I see a man. As I get closer, I begin to notice that the way the man stands he seems perfectly relaxed, comfortable. He fits perfectly into the world around him. As I walk closer to him, I notice that he is smiling. Not a grin, not a big smile, but a whole face smile. He looks to be smiling at me.

There is an aura around him. And as I get closer, I notice he's about my size, with longish brown hair. He is dressed, obviously, but I don't notice what he's wearing, except to say this his clothes are plain. But he looks very comfortable. As I get closer still, I see that he is about my age. I see that he is facing me now, looking directly at me, and I notice that somehow it is much easier for me to walk.

"Hello," I say to him.

"Hello," he answers.

Somehow I sense there's no need for small talk. I look directly at him and he at me. And I ask, "Can I walk with you for a while?"

"Certainly," he says. "It's your path."

I give him a quizzical look but say nothing, and we start down the path. We walk next to each other for a while towards the left side of the lake, neither one of us talking. I feel perfectly comfortable, effortless and relaxed walking next to this man.

"What did you mean, this is my path?" I finally ask.

"Everyone has their own path," he answers. And we continue walking.

At this point, I notice something strange. Birds on the path don't fly away when we pass. Ground squirrels playing in the grass don't hide. Later, we walk down to the lake.

"The water is beautiful," I say. "Don't you ever wonder what goes on underneath?"

"Why don't you look?" he asks.

"Because I'll get wet and cold."

"As long as you walk with me, you won't be uncomfortable."

So I walk into the water and submerge my face. I see a whole other world. And when I walk out, he's right. I don't feel wet or cold. We return to the path and walk on.

A short time later, we come to a crevasse, about eight or ten feet wide. To the left, it continues all the way up the hill. And to the right, it continues all the way into the lake.

"What shall we do?" I ask.

"I've seen others do all kinds of things," he answers. "It's actually up to you. I've seen people spend lifetimes building intricate bridges. And I've seen others jump across. You decide."

"I think that I would like to see what's farther down the path," I answer. I look around and see three or four logs the right length. I put them over the crevasse and we walk across, single file. And we continue walking.

Finally, we get to the place where the path leads into the woods. I look ahead down the path. I look at my companion. I look back at the beautiful, sunlit lake.

"I want to go around the lake again," I say to him.

He looks at me and smiles. "Why don't you come up on the mountain with me?"

And then I wake up.

Lost Wingman

September 1996

I survive the $2,500 adventure with Dr. Tolland and the trip to Washington, although I return home with the worst headache I've ever had in my life. It takes me days to recover. I lie in bed with my head very still, not moving, because when I move even the slightest bit, I feel my brain slosh against the sides of my skull, the soft, wet matter knocking up against hard bone. I even feel the smallest blood vessels throbbing against the backs of my eyes.

My medical evaluation-board review date is set for 27 September, which gives me two weeks to prepare. Dad has already hired a lawyer and sent him my medical records and other information. He has told us it would be best if we could get a doctor to testify, better yet an Air Force doctor.

I call Dr. Stevens. It takes me several tries to get through to her, tries in which I leave urgent messages. She never does call me back. I think she finally talks to me because I am so relentless.

I give her the date and the time of the board and ask her to come. She is noncommittal, but I persist. She may be a doctor, but I am a fighter pilot, even if I don't fly jets anymore. And I have more at stake. I need to provide for my family. She's just annoyed about the disruption in her schedule.

"That's my clinic day," she says, "and I can't allow that much time away from my clinic patients." She pauses. Am I not a patient, I think. "But I'll try to be there."

Dad flies into Dallas, takes the transport van up to Wichita Falls, and we drive down to San Antonio in the minivan, the wheelchair folded up in the back. By now, we are using a wheelchair anytime I have to walk at all.

I have arranged for a room in the family quarters at Lackland for me and Dad, although this was a project in itself. I had to get a special letter from the Sheppard Air Force Base Hospital to get Dad into the building. Usually, only dependents are allowed to stay in family quarters. Just one more piece of paper to chase around to make them happy.

We arrive in San Antonio early the day before the board because we want to meet with the lawyer. But first we check into our room at the quarters. Naturally, they give us a room with only one bed. Dad will sleep on the pullout couch. We dump our things, stay only long enough to call Dr. Stevens' office to confirm the hearing time.

It's just your basic, plain motel room with a soft, narrow single bed covered with a worn plaid bedspread, nondescript prints on the wall, some kind of Texan theme.

The room is so small, the bed fills it almost completely. Two square formica dressers crowd the foot, and a beaten up café table and chair are squeezed up against the window. The pullout couch is in a small entry way, and when Dad pulls it out, it blocks the bathroom door. Once we're in, we'll have to fold up the wheelchair and pry it into the far corner so we can maneuver about the room. We don't plan to spend much time here, but what do you want for $21?

Dad wheels me out of the musty quarters into the bright San Antonio morning. Our meeting isn't until early afternoon, so we have time to get lost in the city. We drive around, locate the lawyer's office and then head out for a quick lunch at the Taco Cabana, tex-mex at its best. I order the enchilada platter, extra spicy salsa. By now, I have pretty much given up trying to maintain my Dallas macrobiotic organic food diet. It's just too hard to find the right foods in Wichita Falls, and it doesn't seem to have helped me, anyway. I figure I may as well enjoy what I want to eat.

Attorney Thomas Grady's offices are in downtown San Antonio. We had gotten his name from a law registry. An ex-Air Force officer, he turns out to be a pretty nice guy. Much to our relief. He has been through this whole appeal process numerous times before, seems to know the ropes.

"I know a couple of the officers who will sit on this board," he says. "They won't be friendly or tip their hand. But I think they're the kind to do the right thing. If our case looks good enough to them, I think we can get them to move up from the 50%."

We review our plan, all the information we will present, including the recent trip to Washington, D.C. He also has copies of the letters of support from all the senators and congresspeople.

"These letters won't hurt," Grady says. "They're not likely to be moved by the political pressure." He flips through the letters, ten of them. Raises his eyebrows. "Rockefeller. That's very good. Heads up the Senate Armed Services Committee. Can't hurt."

I look at Dad. We are by this time afraid to hope for anything. Something has to go right sooner or later, I think. But then I beat back even that thought, as if it might jinx our chances.

"You have a good case, Major Donnelly," Grady continues, stroking his smooth hair back over his head. "But I also don't want you to be too disappointed if they don't give you 100%. 100% is extremely rare. I myself have only seen it once."

He looks at Dad. He's realized he shouldn't finish his thought aloud.

"When was that?" my Dad asks, as reluctant as I am to hear the answer. I feel sorry for the attorney. He clearly isn't used to getting himself into such muddles of emotion.

Then he seems to think better of his hesitation and plunges ahead. "That, Mr. Donnelly, was in the case of a young captain with a brain tumor. He was given six months to live."

My father looks away. I glance at Attorney Grady. I am actually grateful he has been direct because he has thus granted me a reason to hope. I have been given two years to live. Perhaps that will also make me worth a 100% disability retirement.

Grady opens a drawer and pulls out a chart, which he has mounted on a backing. He holds the chart up for us to see.

"This is the Air Force's matrix showing how much a hand, foot, two hands, or an eye, or any combination of limbs and senses is worth in terms of disability payment," he explains. "Since they originally rated you 50% disabled, that means according to their chart, your particular combination of disabilities added up to 50% of your base pay." His finger finds the spot on the grid where 50% appears.

"Tomorrow, we have to convince those three colonels that your disability actually adds up to 100%." He shows us 100%. I follow the grid across and read "quadriplegia, loss of use of all four limbs."

For months now I have felt that I have been living my life in two spheres. There is the sphere we can all see, where I lived completely until only months ago, where a lawyer points to words on a chart, or a doctor bounces a rubber hammer against my knee. And then there's that other place, the one only I can see, although I know that everyone else knows I have traveled here, and they have not.

This is the plane of departure, and with their charts and tests, they are telegraphing a farewell message to me. I am meant to be reading behind the letters that spell quadriplegia, behind the words that sound like "Your prognosis is poor, Major Donnelly." I am meant to understand that they are staying and I am leaving. Some gloat, while others are kind, but still relieved that it is I who linger here on this other plane, while they speak to me from the safe, comfortable haven of health.

The lawyer is still talking. I shake my head, try to listen. It is important that I listen, that I hear both levels of this message.

"Also," he continues, and I wonder how much I have missed, "we have to prove why you should be permanently retired, not just temporarily. The original offer is for temporary retirement, which means that you would have to come back before the board in a year to reclaim your benefits and prove that you still need them."

I think, but do not say, that I have other plans.

"Not only that," he adds, his eyes puzzling out my expression, "but you might actually have to come back to San Antonio, or else to the military medical facility closest to where you'll be living. I've checked into it, Major Donnelly. There are none near Connecticut.

"Finally," he continues, "the question of whether your illness is service-connected is important, and as you probably know, service connection is different from a combat-related disability."

I nod. A service-connected disability is an injury or illness that occurs because of your duties while you are on active duty, as opposed to negligence on your own part. A combat-related disability is injury sustained in combat or as a result of combat. Combat-related status doesn't mean you get more money, but it does mean you get the recognition from your government that you sustained your injury while defending your country. It's a matter of pride, of principle.

They give you a medal for combat-related injury. It's called the Purple Heart.

I know I have no chance of getting a Purple Heart. But I need to get the service-connected status. It's very important. It opens the door to a lot of help from the Veterans' Affairs Department. Help I know Sue and I and the kids will need. College education, medical benefits.

We decide after some discussion that it would be more prudent not to bring up our theory that my illness is related to my service in the Gulf War. I have decided that it is more critical to get my family taken care of than to try to fight the Pentagon, the most powerful enemy in the world, after all. I will do that after I have my benefits, the benefits I earned when I served my country.

"We have no hard evidence, Major Donnelly," Grady is saying. "And I'm fairly certain it will ruin your case if you do bring it up. It will just give them an excuse not to grant you the 100% permanent retirement disability."

"Let's just go for the 100% rating and move on," I say. "They're not about to grant me combat-related. I know that. You know that. I don't need to fight that battle now."

"I think you're making the right decision, Major Donnelly. I really do. We'll make a pitch for service connection, but not combat connection." He collects the papers from his desk, shuffles them back into my file.

Dad says nothing. He is staring out the window at the San Antonio skyline.

After our meeting, we drive around a little more, see some of the sights from the minivan. It isn't exactly fun, though, because our thoughts are clouded by memories of San Antonio and the trip Dad made here with Sue when I got my wings back in 1982.

We decide to head over to the Lackland Air Force Base annex, where I went through OTS 15 years ago this month. OTS is no longer conducted at Lackland. They moved it to Alabama several years ago during the base closures. But all the buildings look exactly the same. It is a ghost town now, which seems appropriate given the reason I am here. I even see a few tumbleweeds rolling down an empty street. Showdown tomorrow at noon, I think.

We drive by the chow hall, and in my mind I see and hear Kevin Denton again, practicing his routine in the dark. "Good morning, Mr. Mess Checker, *sir!*"

I hear the Liberty Bell March blaring through the speakers. I see my young self tumble off the bus, push my long hair out of my eyes and gawk up at the buildings.

I see myself as I was then, a newbee, eager to prove I had the right stuff. It was directly before undergraduate pilot training and OTS that they sent us on to FSPOT, flight school pilot officer training. And it was in FSPOT that I piloted an aircraft for the first time.

They issued us our first flight suits and flying boots, then loaded us onto a bus every day, hauled us an hour away to a place called Hondo, Texas, southwest of San Antonio, a godforsaken outpost that had been a World War II bomber base. The Air Force converted it into a pilot training center and hired civilian instructors to teach recruits to fly Cessna 172s, or what the Air Force calls the T-41 Mescalero.

The apprehensions were many. I had never flown before, so I didn't know whether I would make it. I remembered a story an officer told me when I was interviewing to go into the Air Force, about a young pilot in training. Every time this young pilot flew, he got sick in the airplane and in his mask. But this young man really wanted to pass pilot training, so he tried to ignore it. He just decided that the next time he got sick, he would keep his mouth shut. After his next flight, the instructor said, "You didn't get sick this time. How's that?"

The young trainee answered proudly, "Well, it wasn't so bad coming up, but the big chunks were kind of tough going back down." I laughed out loud.

I figured the recruiter told me this story to test my reaction, because one of the things everyone talked about at FSPOT was air sickness. In September the air in Hondo, Texas, is still hot and turbulent, so there is always the fear that air sickness will wash you out. Every day we saw another brigade of big, tough-talking jocks returning from the flight line, their faces white, sweat dripping from their noses, as they sheepishly toted little white bags that swayed full and heavy from their fingertips.

The first time I got in the plane with the instructor and we took off, it was exhilarating, watching the earth fall away beneath me, and though the ride was hot and bumpy, I took to it naturally. It was fun. I was a little queasy at the end of that first flight, but I never got sick from flying. In fact, in all my years in the Air Force, I never got sick on an airplane. Ever.

FSPOT was only 13 flights in all. The 10th flight was solo, the first time I ever flew an airplane alone. As I took off, I thought, "Either I get this thing back on the ground or it's all over anyway." Obviously, I got the Cessna back on the ground.

Flight 13 was the check run, a flight with an instructor who tested to see whether you flew the airplane according to regulations, gave you emergency situations to handle. If you passed that check ride, you proceeded to OTS and pilot training. If not, you had to choose another career path, one that might not include the Air Force.

Once we were airborne, my flight 13 instructor pushed the throttle in and announced, "Okay, you've lost your engine. What are you going to do now?" I went through all the procedures correctly—throttle idle, carb heat off, fuel switch centered, establish correct glide speed, look for suitable landing spot. I passed with flying colors, even brought the airplane down to a perfect on-speed landing.

But I am no longer a young recruit, full of idealism and promise. I am a man at the end of his Air Force career, a man prematurely old, not ready to retire because, after all, I am still young. I still want to fly. I want to do it all again. My face is still unlined, my hair still blond. I do not want this to be happening.

I start to weep. The images are too real, the memories too powerful. My father helps me into the minivan, stows the wheelchair in back, and we leave.

That night, we go to Landry's, a seafood restaurant, and eat fish, because Mom told Dad to make sure we eat well and that fish will be good for me. She also said that she had been looking into the IVIG therapy and had found a doctor at Columbia Presbyterian Hospital in New York who might be willing to treat me. We eat our meal pretending to one another to feel a renewed sense of hope. And as much as I try to control my hope, I can't help but feel that as long as we still have more things to try, I can secretly nurture that hope, and we can face each day with a new possibility blotting out the future we don't want to see.

Later, we cram ourselves into our $21 room and pretend to sleep. I am grateful for the morning, because I can at least stop pretending and move around. Dad is up at 5:00, shaved and dressed and ready to leave by 5:30.

For breakfast, we go to the Burger King on base. I have the french toast and coffee. Dad just has coffee, lots of it, black. Then it is time to make our way over to the building where my hearing will take place.

We arrive a half hour early. I recognize the name tag on the sergeant at the front desk. I have talked to him numerous times during this whole ordeal.

"You must know a lot of people, Major Donnelly," he says, and I can't tell if he means this kindly or not. "I think we've gotten letters from practically every senator on the Armed Services Committee." Good, I think. Let them take note.

I ask him a few questions about the paperwork, and then he shows us to a waiting room off the hearing chamber, a room that could have been any room on any Air Force base in the world. The same upholstered office chairs, the same laminated wood table, a matching desk, a phone.

We call the hospital to make sure that Dr. Stevens is going to be here. Her assistant is peevish, tells me that Dr. Stevens has said she will do her best.

"I can't make any promises for the doctor, Major Donnelly," she says, her voice ringing with an imperiousness she could only have learned from the doctor herself.

"Well, let me just make sure she has the correct building and time," I answer in my most charming drawl. I need Dr. Stevens. Without her, I think my chances are minimal. I am counting on Dr. Stevens to be the sullen, unpleasant and pessimistic technician who examined me. She owes me, I think. I have not forgotten the drug sales pitch she allowed to occur when she diagnosed me with a fatal disease.

Our attorney arrives, we shake hands, and he sits down at the desk and starts to review the files.

"Where's the doctor?" he asks, his face worried.

"She should be here," I answer. "I think she'll be here." I don't tell him how worried I am she will stand me up.

We then review how the board will proceed. Grady goes over the questions he will ask me and how I will answer. They're not hard questions to remember. They're just hard to say aloud.

Just as the clerk announces that the board is ready for us, Dr. Stevens walks in, looking harried and annoyed and casting me a glance that tells me I should be very grateful she is here at all. While the attorney reviews what he's going to ask her, she performs a cursory exam on me, testing for hyperflexia, fasciculations, the usual. It seems I am sufficiently symptomatic. She nods and looks at Grady.

The attorney enters the hearing room before we do, for a few minutes of administrative preparation with the board. He is concerned that the wheelchair might be seen as a prop, so I decide I will walk into the room. It is only eight feet from the door to my seat. When they call me, Dad pushes me up to the door, helps me stand. And I enter the chamber, my nervousness making it even harder for me to complete that short walk.

I have not brought my cane because I haven't been using it since we started with the chair. So I am on my own for eight feet of open floor between the door and my seat, where my attorney is waiting. I have no walls on which to brace myself, no furniture to lean on. I can't look up to acknowledge the board members because I am afraid I will lose my balance.

I think they see what we want them to see.

I am in full dress uniform, my chest a rainbow of medals. I salute the colonels once I arrive at my chair, bracing myself with my left hand on the table as I raise my right hand to my forehead. Then I fall back gratefully into the seat.

Dad waits to be called. For now, I am on my own.

The three colonels sit up front, all in their dress blues. Stern and straight-faced, just as Grady predicted, and they are not about to give anything away. They are here to judge, and they will judge in their own time, in their own way. Not in my presence.

The attorney asks me the prearranged questions, and I answer them.

"Major Donnelly," he asks, "when did you first notice that something was not quite right with your health?"

I tell the long, boring story. My words are measured. I feel like I am on trial. I am the defendant, and I am doing my best to act the part as my attorney has coached me to act.

Can these three colonels read my heart? Can they see that I want to scream, to cry, to beseech them for justice? This is wrong, I want to shout. My chest is bursting inside my uniform, which is odd because it is much too big for me since I've lost so much weight.

I sit, my face impassive but for the occasional trembling of my lower lip, a reaction I cannot control. All my emotion now lives in that lip. I am one of you, it shouts. Do not do this thing! Can't you understand, it quivers, if I had any other choice, I would choose to believe that this is not happening. I would choose to drive back to Sheppard Air Force Base and continue to oversee flight instructors. I would wing out over the brown Texas horizon and thank God for my health.

"What diagnosis have you received?" my lawyer asks.

I blink. "Doctors have told me I have ALS," I answer, "Lou Gehrig's disease." I am not going to cry in front of three colonels.

"And what have you been told to expect?" he asks. "About your health, I mean. What is your prognosis?"

My chest will surely crack in two, and then my heart will lie exposed for the three colonels to see.

"They tell me I have anywhere from between three and fifteen years," I say. "But most likely, two years. They don't know. They say I can expect a progressive degeneration, complete loss of the use of my legs, arms, death by asphyxiation."

I cannot breathe. I look up at the colonels. What are they thinking? My lip quivers like a child's, and I fear I will burst into tears. This is not how I imagined my career would end. We had planned to buy a bed and breakfast in Vermont. With lots of land. I would invite my friends up for hunting trips, maybe buy a Cessna. Sue would decorate the place—she is so gifted when it comes to interior design, as everyone who has ever visited our many homes can attest—bake muffins for the guests. The kids would love it. We would be close enough to family to see them at holidays, have them up for long New England weekends. I only needed another five years for full retirement.

The attorney calls Dr. Stevens, who scuttles into the room, the picture of impatience.

"I have to make this quick," she announces. Clearly, she is the most important person in the room, and we are all to be made aware of that. "I have patients waiting for me back at the clinic." Am I not a patient? I wonder again.

"Dr. Stevens," my attorney asks, "when did you first evaluate this patient?"

"Major Donnelly presented with symptoms consistent with amyotrophic lateral sclerosis in March of this year, when he was referred to my office for an EMG. He was subsequently referred to me in May for a final evaluation. It was in May that I diagnosed him with ALS." She looks very satisfied with her answer, with her command of the facts.

People just get sick, I think. Even so, my chest is not so tight now. I look down at my hands, regulate my breathing. Easy, I tell myself. Easy.

"And in your opinion, Dr. Stevens, is there any doubt about the diagnosis of ALS?" The attorney looks at Dr. Stevens. I think he may find her as unsettling as I do.

"Absolutely not."

"And what is the prognosis for Major Donnelly, doctor?"

She hauls her fleshy neck up and looks directly at the colonels. "Unfortunately, there is no effective treatment for this progressively degenerative neurological disease. Some patients progress rapidly and some go on for years. The average is three to five years from the date of onset."

I look up at Dr. Stevens, but her eyes are not on me.

"In your opinion, Dr. Stevens, is it at all necessary to make Major Donnelly come back here in a year to review his condition?"

"No." Well, at least she was good for something.

"What tests do you have to confirm this diagnosis?" one of the colonels asks her. They look at her in unison, three colonels stiff as mannequins in their pressed uniforms, their chests equally bedecked with multicolored ribbons attesting to their right to sit on the other side of the table.

"There is no definitive test for ALS," she answers, and I recite it with her in my head. "It is diagnosis by exception, and in Major Donnelly's case, we have performed every possible neurological test and ruled out all the other possibilities. He has ALS."

People just get sick, I think again. My Dad stifles a sob. I do not look at him. If I do, I will most certainly weep.

The board excuses Dr. Stevens. She leaves the room without looking at me again.

The attorney calls Dad.

"Mr. Donnelly, I understand that you recently took Major Donnelly to visit two leading neurologists in Washington, D.C. Is that correct?"

"Yes, sir," he answers. He is trying to be strong and brave for my sake, trying to be the Marine, the lawyer, the tough guy he has always thought himself to be.

"And what did they conclude?"

"They confirmed the ALS diagnosis." I can see that he is struggling not to cry in front of me, in front of the three colonels who are watching his face like it might be a map to their judgment. His lower lip wobbles, too. What a scene, I think. How did I come to this?

"Thank you, Mr. Donnelly."

He stays seated, waiting to help me out of the room.

"If you have no further input, Major Donnelly, you are dismissed. The board will make its recommendation." The same colonel. I am not going to try to guess what they will do with my fate.

I grab the table, hoist myself up and salute them. Then Dad helps me out of the room. The three colonels remain seated the entire time, watching me as I hobble toward the door, where relief waits in the form of a wheelchair.

We return to the waiting room.

"I think we presented an excellent case, Major Donnelly," Grady says, looking hopeful. "We couldn't have asked for a better witness than Dr. Stevens."

Dad and I do not look at one another, or at the lawyer. I am struggling for control. Dad too.

I feel strange. Trying to prove that I deserve 100% disability, that I have maybe two years to live. Here I am, trying to win a case by saying that I deserve this rating because I am desperately sick, when my whole career I've worked to stay healthy. My job depended on it. Now my family's livelihood depends on proving that I'm dying.

Not ten minutes pass before the clerk arrives.

The board has made its decision," he says. "You may come back into the chamber."

This time, Dad wheels me in. The three colonels are already seated. This time, their faces seem less rigid, but maybe I am imagining that.

"It is the opinion of this board," the only colonel who has spoken at all announces, "that Major Michael Donnelly has a progressive degenerative neurological disease that renders him 100% disabled. We hereby permanently retire him at the rank of major. This is obviously a tragic turn of events. We wish you and your family the very best, Major Donnelly."

My attorney and I thank the board for their judgment. They tell us the paperwork will only take 15 minutes. We are to wait next door. I find I am hyperventilating, and I work to control my breathing.

"I've never known the Air Force to do anything in 15 minutes," I say when we enter the room. "And certainly not anything that involves paperwork. Do you think this was a foregone conclusion?" I ask the attorney.

He shrugs. No one speaks. The finding is good news, but also bad news. They believed us.

The forms we are about to receive are critical. They open the doors to all the other benefits we will need to move back East. Now I can straighten out my pay, start my VA paperwork. I can leave the Air Force and begin the next phase of my life, although I cannot really imagine what that phase will be like, nor do I want to.

Once the sergeant delivers the papers, I sign, the attorney signs, and we return them. I am on my way. To what, I'm not sure. But at least the trip will be all-expenses paid.

We thank Attorney Grady. Dad writes him a check, and then we're back in the minivan, heading to Wichita Falls. Finally, I am coming home with good news, good news made possible by all the bad news of the previous months. At least my family will be cared for. I console myself with this thought all along the blank stretch of highway.

We call the kids into the living room that evening. They look shell shocked already, as if they have been waiting for this day, for the bad news they are finally about to hear.

"Come sit on Daddy's lap," I tell them. I pull Erin up on my right knee, Bubba up on my bad leg, the right.

"When can you come play outside with me, Daddy?" Bubba asks.

If my heart weren't shattered already, it would certainly break now. I look to Sue for help, but she cannot speak, I see that. Her eyes brim with confusion, pain. I look down at our son.

"Well, Bub," I answer, "I would love nothing better than to come outside and play with you again." My voice must sound strange to him, because he's giggling up at me. "And I promise I will just as soon as I get better again," I manage to finish.

"Why are you talking funny, Daddy?" he asks, pulling at my hair. He is four.

"Daddy has something important to tell you both."

Erin socks Bubba in the arm. "Quit it, Bubba!" she orders. "Daddy wants to talk to us."

Bubba looks subdued, fights the impulse to hit Erin back. Already he is growing up, too, understanding that there is something bigger than him that he must obey.

"We're going to be moving back to Connecticut," I tell them, looking from one to the other, "to live near Grandpa Tom and Grandma Rae, Grandma Pat and Grandpa E.J. You remember Connecticut, don't you, Bub?" I rub his crew cut. His resemblance to me is uncanny, right down to the rotten front tooth I had as a kid and the slightly mashed right ear.

"Nope," he answers. "And I'm not going. I'm staying here." He squirms off my lap, dashes outside. He loves it here. Has a gang of friends who adore him, the free run of the neighborhood.

"What about you, honey?" I ask Erin.

She shrugs, says nothing. Leans against me and begins, very quietly, to cry.

They say that in situations like this, it's not unusual for people to get divorced. That the stress of a major illness can be enough to drive a wedge of hate and anger between a husband and wife that kills the love in a marriage for good.

I don't know what to think, what to hope or expect for us.

"I'm so glad we took that anniversary trip to Hawaii," I tell the darkened room one night as we are lying in bed. "At least we had that."

We went to Oahu for our tenth wedding anniversary only last year. My folks came out to babysit, took the kids to Six Flags, where my mom tripped and hurt her ankle. They had to push her around the park in a wheelchair. A photo of the four of them, Mom in the wheelchair, Bub on her lap, Erin and Dad on either side, sits on our dresser. Next to it is a photo of me and Sue dancing at a luau. She is tanned, glowing, a white lei around her neck. I look over her shoulder at the camera, my cheeks golden, a proud wide smile on my face. Did we realize how lucky we were? I don't remember.

Sue doesn't answer. Ever since this started she has been angry. It was finally going to be her turn. After all the years of Air Force bullshit, dragging her life, her home, her children from one base to another, she was going to get to pick where we lived. The bed and breakfast idea was hers.

I can't blame her for being angry. But I am the one who's sick, I tell her. You think I wanted this to happen? She lies stony, unmoving in the night.

"You think you're the one who has problems?" I yell. "I should be so lucky."

"Be quiet, Michael," she answers. "You'll wake the kids." Her voice is even. It gives nothing away.

I roll away from her in the bed. I hate that I have no way to console her, that I am to be the burden. That she will have to be the strong one for me.

When finally I feel myself falling into an angry sleep hours later, I can tell she is still lying there, awake. She has not moved a finger.

Homecoming

October 1996

We leave Texas at 0-dark thirty, so we can get a good start on the highway before the sun gets too high. Tim has come down from Oregon to drive the Cadillac. Sue drives the minivan, packed to the ceiling with whatever we think we will need between the day we leave and the unnamed day we finally recall our belongings. Most of what we own—clothes, furniture, books, appliances, toys—is going into military storage in Oklahoma until we find a permanent home. A year's worth of that storage, plus the freight costs to move it East when we finally find a home, come courtesy of that important paperwork I signed the day the three colonels decided my fate.

In the meantime, we will live in my parents' house, while they move into a small apartment they've rented down the street.

We'd said our goodbyes the night before. The cars were already packed, and we slept in sheetless beds, rolled in old towels that we weren't bringing with us. Earlier, the kids had had dinner at their friends'. Sue, Tim and I sat around a bucket of the colonel's best in the hollow kitchen, halfheartedly gnawing at greasy chicken thighs.

As much as Sue and I are glad to leave Wichita Falls, Texas, the kids are not. There are lots of other kids their ages on base, packs of them roaming the neighborhood at will. We have always felt safe letting them run wild through the streets because there are no strangers here. Besides, we have lived here for three years, which to a nine- and five-year-old is almost forever.

Erin has already closed herself off, her anger as palpable as her mother's. For nights I have heard her crying in her bed, thinking either that we can't hear her or hoping that we will and thus be moved to stay, so that her life can continue as it was.

In the little backpack we are allowing each of them to bring on the trip, she has packed Jingles the bear, her fourth-grade class picture and her blankie. In the photo, she beams from the front row, her round cheeks red as polished apples, her intelligent eyes bright with achievement. Erin is a star pupil, loves her teacher, her classmates. Her backpack also holds a crumpled sheet of looseleaf, on which she has written her friends' addresses in childish pencil loops. This and a box of flowered stationery her best friend Carrie has given her, so she can write her letters on the trip.

What I cannot find a way to tell my daughter is that I would give anything in the world to make it all right again. That I want only to be her Daddy again as I was, whole and big and strong for her. I never meant for my children to have to be strong for me. I weep silently in my bed in the hollow room, in answer to her cries, but I do not go to her. It is too difficult in the dark, with the cane.

Bubba is different, though no less angry, I sense. He is a boy's boy, dashes around the house in scuffed cowboy boots, kicking at walls, leaping out of open windows to the driveway, punching Susan in the thigh. Until now Bubba has always been a good kid, cheerful, funny, obedient as you can expect a four-year-old to be.

He loves his Uncle Tim. "Pick me up again," he shouts, "Uncle Tim, pick me up! Twirl me around!"

He loves to be manhandled, and I watch from the kitchen as my brother swings my son through the air, holding one arm and leg, turning him in uneven circles. Bub screams in delight, his free arm and leg circling in the warm Texas evening. "I'm flying!" he shouts.

The caravan stops at Mickey D's on the way out of town for a quick breakfast, and then it's on the road for the Donnellys.

I had bought the Cadillac from Tim a few years back, after he decided he couldn't afford the luxury of a white convertible 1972 El Dorado sitting in the garage anymore. He had bought it about five years before that from the original owner, a widow who lived down the street from Mom and Dad. The car's a real beauty, mint condition. The rich thick paint still glistens on her broad flanks, the original red leather interior buckskin still glows soft and supple, and she still turns heads whenever we drive her, all the way from Texas to Connecticut, eight miles to the gallon notwithstanding.

The first day, we drive all the way to St. Louis, where we pass the night in a roadside motel, a good 12 hours of highway, Tim in the Caddy with the kids, Sue and me in the minivan. We switch off every other rest stop or so. It's long, boring driving up until St. Louis. Only the billboards punctuate the boredom. "FIREWORKS! FIFTEEN MILES! FIREWORKS! TEN MILES! FIREWORKS! FIVE MILES! YOU JUST PASSED THE FIREWORKS!" Or else they advertise the series of famous wooden bowl manufacturers or ceramic steer exhibits.

Already we are all exhausted. And we have another two days to go. We make up ways to keep the kids interested.

"Now I want you to keep your eyes on the woods for the dreaded Missouri redlegs," I warn them as we cross that long rolling state. I am in the Cadillac with Tim, giving Sue a little break. Erin and Bub are in the back seat, eyes glued to the windows. "Missouri redlegs are a famous pack of wild Missourians who hijack families." I look into the rearview mirror and see their eyes widen. Tim and I exchange a grin.

The kids keep a lookout for the redlegs all the way across Missouri. This works for almost the entire state, and when they aren't each transfixed to a window, eyes wide with terror, they are too afraid to whine.

In Indiana it is the Hoosiers, a roving band of mean farmers who are looking for out-of-state license plates. They make you pay a huge fine if they catch you, I tell them, my face serious. They keep watch for the Hoosiers as we speed across Indiana, scanning the miles of corn and soy for a pack of wild farmers.

In Pennsylvania, it is the Pennsylvania Jumanji, who are similar to Robin Williams' Jumanji. But the Pennsylvania Jumanji are big, black animals covered with fur, and they hang upside down from trees. When you drive under them, they drop down on you and grab your backpack, your food, your money. I see Erin feigning indifference, but we can tell she has one eye out the whole time, looking to spot the redlegs, the Hoosiers, a Pennsylvania Jumanji.

Sean fights for a window seat on the side closest to the road's edge, so he can dutifully keep watch, 100% sure he has seen that Jumanji hanging from a tree we have just passed. We stop at fast food places for meals, anything right off the highway and easy, especially if they have a playland, so the kids can run off some of their energy. Mostly we find ourselves at McDonald's, and by the time we get to Connecticut, I swear to myself I will never again ingest another soggy hamburger, greasy fry or plastic shake.

We make the drive in three days, close to 2,000 miles, and arrive in Connecticut midday of the third day, but our trip isn't over yet. Just west of home, we are slowed for a construction site in Hartford. Suddenly, what appears to be a very drunk young man driving a Nissan Stanza hits the car behind Tim, which slides into the Cadillac. And naturally the drunk driver is belligerent—and uninsured. Fortunately for us, all of this happens right in front of a state trooper, who is parked next to the construction workers.

The Cadillac, which is built like a battleship, sustains minimal damage, since no one was traveling very fast when the accident occurred. Plus, the driver of the Stanza is unlucky enough to have left his empties rolling around the floor. The Caddy is a couple of tons of good old American steel, and when the poor guy in the Chevy behind Tim got rammed into the Caddy, he may as well have slammed an empty Coke can into a concrete wall. Erin is riding in the Caddy with Tim, sleeping on the back seat. She never even wakes up, so slight is the impact.

We have a real story to tell when we finally get to my parents' house about a half hour later. Before anyone else can even unbuckle a seat belt, Sean is in the house screaming at the top of his lungs, "We had an accident! Uncle Timmy had an accident!"

Needless to say, our homecoming is dramatic. It takes several excited minutes to calm my mother down after she streaks out of the house to check to see that we have all arrived in one piece.

The Gulf War certainly seems to be the war that won't end. This is my third homecoming, and of all of them, it is the least joyous. Not that I'm not glad to be home. I am. At least now all the grandparents will be close by to help with the kids and with what everyone promises will become an increasingly difficult situation. But it's nothing like the day I came home from the war.

We stayed on base in the UAE for more than three months after Hussein's generals surrendered to Schwarzkopf in the desert. We were assigned to guard coalition army forces still stationed in southern Iraq for follow-up operations.

The place was barren, like a school in summer. Where only a few weeks ago pilots had strutted from the ops room to the flight line, all nerves and ego, now everything was quiet, the calm after the storm. You could practically hear your footsteps echo in the sand. Our daily missions broke up the monotony, but that was about all we had. After two false alarms when we went to bed at night thinking we'd be taking off for home the next day, just about everything on the base had been packed up and shipped home.

We found new and inventive ways to kill time then. We played pinochle and Risk. We measured time in "herms," named for pilot Todd Hermling.

Our complete and detailed explication on the subject of herms is a good indication of exactly how bored we were. A herm was 20 minutes of wasted time; 48 herms made up a day. The eight hours of sleep we were each allowed didn't count. Nothing productive could be accomplished during a herm, since a wasted herm was time well spent. And across the base, trained fighter pilots were seen herming their days away. If only CNN could see us now, we thought.

By mid-May, when we finally did leave, we were more than ready. We had spent a total of four and a half months in the desert, nothing compared to the eight months the Shaw people had endured, but our wait had taken place after the war was over. We survived the anticlimax.

The eight-hour return trip to Germany was a stark contrast to the night flight into war. During the flight home, we played radio battleship to make the time pass. Then, over Sicily, I noticed one of my wing tanks wasn't feeding properly. There was no way in hell I was going to divert and land any place other than home base. After going through the check list several times without result, somebody suggested I descend to a lower altitude in case the tank was frozen. Lo and behold, it worked! I counted the miles and calculated my fuel continuously, until I knew I could make it, even if the tanks stopped working again.

As soon as we got on frequency with the fucking French, though, they started hassling us about our airspace clearance to transit their country.

"This is the French military frequency one three one," we heard, just as we crossed over the Alps. "You have not clearance over French airspace. Repeat. You have not clearance over French airspace."

"Roger, this is the United States Air Force Tenth Tactical Fighter Squadron," the boss answered for us, sure that they would see reason. "We're en route to Hahn Air Base in Germany. Request clearance to bring these pilots home from the war."

A pause. What could there possibly be to think about?

"Repeat. This is French military frequency one three one. You have not clearance. You must circumnavigate French airspace. Permission denied."

I couldn't believe it! It was just like the French to give us a hard time, even on our way home from a war.

The boss didn't even bother to answer. Fuck 'em, we said, we're coming anyway. And if they wanted to stop us, they could launch their goddammed Mirages up here and take us on.

The French decided, wisely we thought, to let us pass. Not without a few well-chosen expletives. At least that's what we thought all those words might be that came spluttering out of the radio at us. Fortunately, none of us spoke French, so we decided to interpret the outburst as an enthusiastic compliment on our flying technique.

On 9 May 1991, at 1400 hours, we flew up in four-ships and pitched out to land at Hahn Air Base in western Germany, combat veterans and heroes, home for our heroes' welcome. By this time, Hahn was half empty due to the draw downs that had started while we were still cooling our heels in the Arabian desert. One of the other three original squadrons was already gone. The second was only half there. Those who remained came out to greet us.

I touched down on the strip at Hahn and taxied in off the runway, my heart crazed with excitement. I tried to keep my eyes on what I was doing, but all the time I was steering that $16 million jet, I was straining to pick out Sue and Erin in the crowds. As we taxied off the runway, olive green Volkswagen minivans, each with one pilot's name pasted in the window, escorted us past our squadron building, where the welcomers held up signs and waved flags and ribbons as we passed.

Then, each van led us to where we would park our aircraft. It was then that I saw Erin and Sue, both grinning hugely, in the minivan with the DONNELLY sign in the window. Erin was bouncing up and down on the front seat. She was four years old.

It seemed like it took me hours to park that jet. Finally, I set the throttle to "Off," raised the canopy, and scampered down the ladder as my family ran to me, arms outstretched. We hugged, all of us together. Sue was seven months pregnant and her belly bloomed huge between us. When I left in December, she wasn't showing at all. I put my hand on our child.

We made our way, the three of us together, my arm around Sue, Erin on my shoulders, to the front door of the squadron building. And who should I see standing outside there when we arrived but Bill Psycho Andrews. Alive. His leg was in a cast, and he was leaning on a cane, but he was alive, and he was grinning.

"Buddy!" he called, as cool as ever, as if he hadn't been shot down over Iraq, just happened to be hanging out at the squadron building when we showed up.

"We never thought we'd see you again, Psycho! You're alive!" I clapped him on the back, hugged him, and together we all rolled in to the welcoming reception together to hear his story, to greet our friends, to enjoy our first taste of home in four and one-half months.

I wanted to hear Psycho's story. I wanted to hear about how he had been captured, tortured, dragged blindfolded one night to Baghdad on a bus that turned out to be full of other blindfolded American POWs, but mostly I just wanted to go home.

We stayed at the reception as long as we thought we had to. Half an hour, long enough for the wing leaders to say a few words and thank us. And then, at last, we were free to go home.

Home.

I felt like I had been away for years, not months. Sue drove—our hands cradled in one another in the space between the seats—and the feeling of riding in the Saab, not a military vehicle, along the well-engineered German roads was such an odd, pleasant sensation, so soothing that I almost lost track of my wife and child.

My eyes were drawn to the wet fir trees lining the road, to the green meadows spanning the steep Hunsrück hillsides, the birds dotting the blue, blue sky. But Erin bounced on my lap, her arms draped around my neck, and didn't allow me to get too distracted. Sue talked about the house, about the other pilots' wives, about the draw down and how things had changed at Hahn. Erin just kept asking me one question.

"Are you staying home now, Daddy?" she asked me, again and again. "Are you finished with the war?"

What could I do but hold her in my arms, look into those round innocent eyes and nod?

"Yes, honey," I answered, "I'm staying home now, and I'm all done with the war."

I was wrong. I would never be done with the war. But I didn't know that then.

My second homecoming occurred when we finally got back to the U.S. in June, just a few weeks before Sean was born. We had been redeployed to Tampa, but we flew first into Connecticut.

Our families and friends greeted us at Bradley Field, then led us home to a grand patriotic bash at the Masons' Hall on Main Street. Red, white and blue bunting everywhere, yellow ribbons streaming from the trees and the telephone poles, people waving little American flags as we drove up. Even the food was red, white and blue: blueberry and strawberry shortcake, strawberry jello mold studded with fresh blueberries and topped with Cool Whip, a cake frosted with a flag and a giant yellow sugar ribbon, which Erin insisted on eating, and then of course hamburgers and hot dogs, chips, and three kegs of beer.

Homecoming number three, though, was something none of us could ever have predicted back in 1991. Not just that I'd be sick, or that we'd be coming home for me to be close to my family should I die, but that all the dusty little American flags, the bunting, the yellow ribbons that my mom still kept in the basement, would have become emblems of some very different nation, one we no longer knew. And that we ourselves would be-come people we couldn't recognize, a family bereft of a country, of ideals, of trust. It was a loss we couldn't discuss, but the elegy played behind every word, every look, every unspoken question.

I know my parents were convinced that the Pentagon knew exactly what had happened to me, up to and including the specific nerve gas to which I was exposed, where and when, and what effect the PB and pesti-cides had in conjunction with that exposure. And while I had every rea-son to believe my parents were right, something in me would not let go of the hope that they might be wrong. Maybe it wasn't a cover up, I thought, but massive inept bungling. Maybe the idiot bureaucrats in Washington weren't evil. Maybe they just didn't know how to make a bad situation right.

Trouble is, in the meantime, while they try to figure out which end is up, I'm dying. As far as I know, thousands of us are dying. And lots of the people we've learned about haven't been as lucky as I have, don't have the benefits I've gotten, or the family to support them, the parents to move out so that they and their family can move in. They got sick after they were discharged, most of these veterans, and since there is no proof of any connection between their illness and their service in the Gulf, the VA is denying them medical benefits, disability payments. They're living on welfare, our heroes, getting what medical care they can from Medicaid.

And none of the doctors who see them can explain what is wrong with them, why three of the six men standing one mile away when American troops detonated Kamisiyah on 4 March 1991 have MS, including Master Sergeant Steve Hegley. Or why Joy and John Chavez, whose romance blossomed in a wartime correspondence, and who married when John re-turned, have become so ill that their symptoms fill two pages, yet they still have no diagnosis.

People just get sick.

Or why Kyle Bittner, a strapping 31-year-old Marine with a chiseled chin and eyes that melt your soul, is dying of a cancer of the spine so rare it has only once before struck an individual of his age—and that was an ex-terminator. It was a civilian doctor who made the startling diagnosis. The VA told him he was perfectly healthy. And because he got sick after he was discharged, he has no disability income. He works as an arborist now, and says hanging from the trees in the braces actually helps his back. He is in constant pain—you can see it in those deep brown eyes. Has no health insurance, only the VA to fall back on, and as far as they're con-cerned, Kyle is a healthy man.

People just get sick.

As much as I want to believe the bunglers are simply bungling, it seems like someone should step up and take charge, speak out, tell the world that we can't have all these vets dying. That something is wrong with this picture. That we should straighten this out now, before any more damage is done. Because that would be the right thing to do, after all, and I'm still caught in the sticky web of idealism where I like to think that most people are motivated by a good conscience and a desire to see the right thing done. I still believe what they taught me about being an officer, about integrity and honesty in the face of adversity.

And I'm starting to think I've been a damn fool.

We set up the living arrangements. I can't visit the apartment Mom and Dad have rented because it's up a narrow flight of stairs up the back side of a house. The kids start calling it "the Cottage." Makes me half-glad I can't see what it looks like. All I know is that it's furnished in early K-Mart, complete with shag carpeting, waterbed and lacquered wall plaques of pastoral scenes ripped from magazines.

The kids do their best to settle in upstairs, Erin in the girls' room, Sean in the boys' room. While they have plenty of space, they are without most of their toys, and they miss their friends. And I am stuck on the first floor, dragging my cane across the wall-to-wall. I can't go up and kiss them good night, tuck them in, have a heart to heart.

At times I try to talk about what is happening to us, to me. But mostly I feel myself retreating. I have let them all down. In truth, I'd rather not talk about it, and I don't.

I can tell Sue is suffering, trying to find her own way through this nightmare. She has so much to shoulder, and I know her, I know she feels alone, lost, but cannot, will not talk about it. She is businesslike, brusque with me, with my parents, with her parents, with the kids, with herself, but this is simply her way.

She disappears for hours at a time. I think she goes shopping, but when she comes home with nothing, I'm not so sure. I understand her anger, but still I'm frustrated by it. I wish she would just talk, to me, to a counselor, to Father Jerome, anyone. But she walks around with her mouth sealed tight all the time, her lips a rigid colorless line in her face.

Still, I know that talking is not what will necessarily help her now. And I can see her point. What good will talking do in the end? What will it change?

I'm so sorry, I want to say. I wish I could undo this, I tell her in my head. But my heart is mute, buried. I say nothing, and Sue keeps her distance, nursing her fury like a hungry mother nursing her only child. We function, get through the days, for the kids. We want to get them settled, rooted, so whatever is going to happen will happen only after they have more stability in their lives. Sue is strong, and I admire her courage. She is a pillar, but she is mute.

Our first order of business is a trip to Columbia Presbyterian in New York to meet Dr. Nathan, a neurologist. My mom has found him through *Best Doctors in America,* just called him on the phone and somehow talked her way through his assistant. Once she gets a sympathetic listener, she's irresistible, my mom. Dr. Nathan succumbed to her pleas and bumped me to the top of his list to try IVIGs, the experimental treatment Dr. Shultz had recommended back in August.

Turns out there might be something to this theory, and we'll never know if we don't try. The IVIGs will only work, though, if what I have is not ALS but peripheral neuropathy, a deadening of the nerves due to some specific cause, in my case, maybe the organophosphates. Turns out it's also expensive: $30,000 for the entire treatment, which lasts about six weeks. Somehow, Mom has also talked the pharmaceutical company into trying this treatment on me for free. They are sincerely concerned about the number of Gulf War vets who are sick and they want to help. Also, I'm sure they think if they say they've found a treatment or a cure for Gulf War illness, they will have their claim to fame and a return on their $30,000 investment.

Dr. Nathan is sincere and compassionate, a welcome change from my recent encounters with members from the opposite end of the medical professional spectrum. He actually cares about what happens to me and wants to look at every possibility. He sees me gratis, the first doctor since Dr. Brown who does not see my hopelessness as a money-making opportunity, the first since Dr. Brown who does not trade on our desperation.

"We should know by Christmas whether this therapy will work," he tells us, his eyelids drooping kindly. Well, I think, as I'm sure we all do, that would be the best Christmas present ever.

As we leave his office, Mom on one side, Dad on the other, helping me along, I feel like crying with relief, not just because Dr. Nathan cares about what happens to me, but that doctors like this still exist. He helps to restore my faith in humanity just a little. I haven't willingly become this cynical.

The IVIG treatment is a little more complex than Dr. Shultz let on. Maybe he really didn't know what was involved, which wouldn't surprise me, given the three ring circus we encountered out there. A nurse comes to the house twice a week to administer the injections while I sit immobilized in one of my mother's dining room chairs that we've dragged into the family room. Because it has a stiff back, I can get in and out of this chair more easily than I could a comfortable overstuffed armchair.

Each session takes about three and a half hours. While the solution drips slowly into my bloodstream, the nurse monitors my blood pressure, heart rate, pupil dilation, pulse, to make sure the stuff isn't causing some strange allergic reaction, which it can do.

Sue and I spend all our free time looking for a house either here in South Windsor or in one of the surrounding towns. We enroll the kids at Pleasant Valley Elementary School, where I attended first grade, and which they hate. They hate it because it isn't Texas, because it isn't disciplined and because the kids are different.

"Everybody's so mean here," Erin complains, and I can see how she might feel that way. Back in Texas, people were just plain nice, even when you might have preferred a little edge. Even when you wanted them to leave you alone, they were nice. Here, people are always in a hurry, even the kids, and no one has time to be just plain nice. Not the teachers, not the people in the street or in the grocery store, not the kids in school.

"I know, sweetie," I answer. "But you'll get used to it. People are just different here. They don't think they're being mean. That's just how they are. Maybe it's all the cold weather and the snow."

"Well, I don't care," Erin pouts. "I hate it here. I want to go back to Texas."

"Me too," Bubba whines. He is not a whiner. "I miss Texas, Daddy." He crawls up onto my lap, which Erin has vacated. I look at Sue, who keeps her back to me. She is at the stove, my mother's stove, stirring something. Soup, I think.

"I know you do, Bub," I tell him. "I'm sorry."

I fear at times that the panic in my chest will overwhelm me. It's all so much. Sue, the kids, the house, the illness, the betrayal. Layers upon layers of complexity and worry.

My parents are always here. It's their house, after all, and most of their clothes are here, plus whatever other supplies they need for their routines. The Phillips-head screwdriver. A tablecloth for the card table in the Cottage kitchen. My Dad's shoe polish kit that he keeps in an old Marine shell case, which he's had since I was three. Every Sunday night he spit polishes his shoes as he sits on the floor, leaning up against the couch, watching *60 Minutes*. It's hard for someone who's 63 and used to his patterns to find them disrupted, as much as I know he would do anything to help.

They have no television at the Cottage, so Dad comes here to polish his shoes on Sunday nights. As Dad sits on the floor, Sean climbs on his shoulders, bounces in front of the television, shouts down Mike Wallace and Leslie Stahl, Steve Kroft and Ed Bradley.

"And I'm Goofy!" Bubba yells, dancing in front of the television.

Finally Dad loses his patience.

"Sean!" he shouts. "When I say quiet, I mean quiet!"

I have given up trying to discipline them. As has Sue. We are neither of us present anymore, not in any real way, and they are left to find their own way. Except when they encounter Dad's stern warnings.

"There's only two rules you need to remember in life, Sean," Dad warns him. "Rule 1: Grandpa is always right. Rule 2: when Grandpa is wrong, see Rule 1." Funny thing is, Bubba gets it. Not only that, he thinks it's hysterical. Dad can't stay mad at him for long because Bubba tells it back to him like a joke.

I can see that my mother is making Sue crazy. She's trying so hard to be understanding, to help, but she can't recognize that Sue just needs distance now. Mom is not the type to understand space, especially when she's frantic. Every other night she's here, cooking or cleaning.

"What are you making for dinner tonight, hon?" she asks Sue, and then answers before Sue has a chance to. "Why don't I bring some chicken parmesan down? It's all ready to bake. I'll just put it in the oven at 5:00 and then we can eat at 6:00."

Sue eats the meal my mother has cooked, her face leaden, sullen. Like a teenager. And like a brooding teenager, Sue stops caring. She lets the house go, which would be one thing if it were ours, but it's not and my mother has always been fanatically clean. It pains me to see her house so filthy, the scum in the toilets, the rotting food in the fridge.

Finally, Sue even stops taking care of the kids, and this is just not like her. One day there is no food for the kids when they get home from school, so I manage to hobble over to the kitchen to make Bub a peanut butter sandwich.

"Cut it sideways, Dad," he tells me. "That's how Mom always does it. It tastes better."

I can't cut his sandwich, but he doesn't understand this. I can barely manipulate the knife to scrape up the last of the peanut butter. "We're going to have them the way boys eat them," I tell him. "We're going to have foldover sandwiches."

Bubba is satisfied with this and we sit at the counter eating foldover peanut butter sandwiches and drinking some warm apple juice he has found in the back of the pantry.

When Sue gets home, we have a talk. "I'm sorry," I say. "I wish none of this were happening, but you have to be sure the kids have food."

"I know," she answers. "I'm really sorry," she says. "I'm trying to get a grip."

She doesn't look at me, but I can feel the anger, the hurt, the lost dreams welling up in her eyes.

This is good for none of us, but for now, it's all we can do.

One day we get a call from a Dr. Horace Petzel from Maryland. He has gotten my name from one of our Gulf War contacts, and is calling me to tell me about his discovery.

"All you have to do is try it, Major Donnelly," he insists. "I swear to you, Fen-Phen is the drug that is going to make you better. I've seen it work for hundreds of other vets I've treated." He pauses to catch his breath. He speaks like a fat man, always out of breath, not quite able to choke out his sentences. Maybe it is just his excitement at having found a treatment for Gulf War illness.

"But don't you think you should examine me first?" I ask. "Have you treated anyone else diagnosed with ALS?" I have seen this kind of enthusiasm before. It makes me nervous.

"Not specifically with ALS, but certainly other vets with neurological problems and symptoms. In fact, Fen-Phen is especially effective in such cases," he answers excitedly. "Why don't you give me your address? I'll ship some off to you right now."

What the heck is the hurry? Another doc in a big hurry. I figure he must have an agenda, something to prove. But I let him ship me the drugs. I'll look into his claims later.

I keep at him, though. "Have there been any studies proving that Fen-Phen will help people like me?" I ask. I've learned something over the past few months.

"Not specifically people like you, but the government doesn't want people to know about the powerful effects of this drug combination because then they won't be able to continue to make money off of their illnesses."

Hmm. Okay, I think. Another conspiracy theory.

I give him my address and let him ship me the drugs. He continues to call once a day for the next week. I receive the shipment in the mail, what looks like a lifetime supply of Fen-Phen.

"I want you to know that I'm concerned about what's happening to our vets, Major Donnelly," Dr. Petzel tells me, "and I'm offering to treat you pro bono. You did your part to defend this country and I feel it's the least I can do."

Well, I figure, if he isn't going to charge me, where's the harm?

It does strike me as strange that a medical doctor should be shipping drugs to another state and to a very ill patient he has never examined. He sends me a patient questionnaire in the same package as the drugs. I never get around to completing it, though. I feel I've answered enough questions.

Once when he calls, my mom talks while I listen in on the other phone.

"Mrs. Donnelly, I know I can help your son," he breathes, his voice wet sounding, messy. "It's just that right now my life is a little upside down. I'm calling from home because my wife left me and they've kicked me out of my medical practice, so I'm working out of my apartment right now. You know how it is when sometimes life doesn't go quite as you planned?"

We know.

She asks again what the Fen-Phen will do and whether there are any studies proving its effectiveness. Again he dodges the questions. But we have gotten his name from someone we trust, so we're not sure what to think of him. It does seem odd that he should be sharing his personal troubles with us.

"I just hope everything turns out all right for me, Mrs. Donnelly. I'm a little anxious, as you can imagine, what with my wife just taking off, no warning, and then losing my practice like that."

Those pesky red flags are flying across the room.

He calls the next day to connect me to a conference call and several other patients he is "treating," one other Gulf War vet, a couple of overweight women, and another patient with psychological problems. It is some sort of group treatment session, I realize after I've been on for a few minutes.

We are all on the phone together, and it sounds like we each have two bottles in front of us: one contains fenfluramine, the other phentermine. We have all, I assume, gotten our supply from Dr. Petzel.

"Go ahead and take one of each," he commands his weird little group. I can hardly believe I am part of this, but I take one of each of the pills, on the phone, together with my fellow lost souls. It is a strange sort of ritual that must fulfill a bizarre need in him and maybe even in some of us, his "patients." I feel a little like he is an aspiring cult leader and we are his disciples.

After a few minutes, he asks us each how we feel.

"I don't feel anything, doc," I say. "Should I?"

"Why don't we all hang up now," Dr. Petzel suggests, "and I will call each of you back by the end of the day for individual counseling." He pauses. "But first, I want to say congratulations to all of you! You're all now on your way to getting well!"

A short time later, I start to feel jittery and anxious, like I have just guzzled ten cups of coffee, extra strength. I worry that the side effects will intensify, that I will do myself some serious harm. My heart is thumping away, a racehorse trapped in my chest. By the time Dr. Petzel calls back, that afternoon, it is really racing, bad.

"I'm very uncomfortable," I say. "I think there's something wrong."

"Hmm," he replies. "That's not a typical reaction." I get the feeling my unexpected reaction is my fault, that I am disrupting his plans. "Go ahead and take another one of the orange pills. That will make you feel less jittery."

So I do. And it isn't until the next day that the feeling completely subsides. By now, my parents have talked to another Gulf War vet, a Marine colonel who has been diagnosed with brain lupus, who told us that he tried the Fen-Phen at Dr. Petzel's suggestion. It did him no good. He felt strung out on speed, on top of all his other problems. That is all I need to hear.

Dr. Petzel never calls me back. My next contact with him is in the form of a bill that I receive one month later for $877, for itemized services that would make me laugh if the situation weren't so sad.

I figure I know how to scare the shit out of him. I write him a letter. A real hardball letter.

Dear Dr. Petzel [I write], On or about the 13 of January I received a bill from your office for the amount of $877.00. The charges contained in this bill consisted of three individual items. These were:

Intake Fee-Admin/Educ. Supplies	$350.00
New Patient Comprehensive	$450.00
Psych Testing W/written Report	$ 77.00

[I copy these amounts and the itemized services directly from his so-called bill.]

You cannot imagine my dismay [I continue] at the sight of these numbers and then the total disgust I felt about this bill. Let me clue you in as to why.

I know I will never hear from him again. I am enjoying writing this letter. But I am also very angry. And tired. I am tired of fighting alleged medical professionals for validity and honesty. I am tired of fighting this battle on my own, without the help of the only people who have enough information to know what to do: the Pentagon.

I let Dr. Horace Petzel have it.

First [I tell him] *you* sought *me* out through people who know me due to my connection and involvement in the Gulf War. *You* offered *your* services *"pro bono"* as someone who was concerned about the poor health of many Gulf vets and was willing to help. You initiated phone conversations that you now contend are "treatment." Feeling uncomfortable about that, I contacted the Connecticut Department of Public Health. I think you would be very interested in the answer I received from them about such "treatment."

Second [I am angry, very angry now] your bill contains charges for items and services you never provided. For instance, you offered to fax me several items to increase my understanding of your theories. However, the fax did not work, and I doubt seriously whether two or three faxed pages of anything you have are worth $350. Also, I cannot call to mind you ever conducting any Psych Test or any other test, unless you refer to my being present during a conference call in which you were treating several people at one time, testing!

[I can just picture the fat man sweating, worrying on the phone to his next victim-patient that things are a little bumpy right now, you know how it is?]

Third, the "new patient comprehensive" has me a little befuddled. The unfortunate circumstance in which I now find myself has truly been an education. One of the most educational aspects is that I have seen doctors all over these United States, many of them in very prestigious schools and hospitals to include Columbia Presbyterian Hospital, University of Texas Southwest School of Medicine, and Massachusetts General Hospital. Many of these doctors are highly regarded, published members of the medical field. None of the bills I have received have even come close to your "comprehensive," and they all examined me *in person.*

Fourth [I cannot stop myself from writing more] in my own haste to find something to save myself from my present prognosis, I actually tried your prescribed medication. My reaction to it truly was a frightening experience, which I can only describe as one of extreme nervousness and heightened anxiety, from the effects of which it took me two full days to recover.

It was during that time I realized the foolishness of my desperation and recognized that I had gone too far and was now being unsafe. It has since struck me as curious as to why you never called back to check on the bad reaction I was having to your medication. You can then imagine my dismay at receiving your bill a month later.

For these reasons [I write] and several more which I currently am not able to put into civilized words, I am refusing to pay this bill as I consider it at the least ridiculous, and at most, outrageous, unethical and illegal.

Sincerely [I sign with the title that used to define me] MAJOR MICHAEL W. DONNELLY, USAF (RET.)

And just for good measure, I copied the world, including God, at least from a doctor's point of view.

> CC: Connecticut Attorney General
> Maryland Attorney General
> Connecticut Department of Public Health
> Maryland Department of Public Health

Dr. Petzel need not know that I never mailed copies to these august agencies.

My letter seems to work. I never hear from the illustrious Dr. Horace Petzel again. I do receive a subdued apology from his office manager who claims that the bill was sent "in error." I figure they decided it was an error because they didn't know who they were dealing with. I wonder about those other desperate people on that conference call and whether they all got bills "in error" too.

The trouble is, Dr. Petzel is a symptom. The real problem, those who really deserve to feel my anger are protected, insulated by the thick wall of professionally calibrated denial. Dr. Petzel would never have gained purchase on the likes of me had my country stood by me. If I felt I could trust the agents of my fate in Washington, I would never have lent my soul to the Dr. Horace Petzels of the world.

Most of all, I am angry at myself for falling victim to it all: for getting sick, for succumbing to the inevitable desperation of my plight, for believing the patriotic bullshit in the first place, for throwing my life away for nothing, for serving what has proved to be the most false of all gods—deceit masquerading as virtue.

But anger will get me nowhere now, I tell myself. I parse the problem. Just get through today. And when today is more than I can manage, I promise myself I can survive the next hour, the next five minutes. I will dose my life out this way until I reach the bottom of the jar, and then my problem will be solved for me. Won't it?

Meanwhile, the weeks pass. I continue my twice-weekly doses of IVIG and we pray for a Christmas miracle. I sit in my chair, my arm linked to the IV like it was dripping the elixir of life into my veins, and watch *CNN*, *Oprah, Maury,* the soaps. I am hopeful for the first time, not just because Christmas is coming and, at least in TV-land, that's when miracles happen, but because I have real faith in Dr. Nathan's sincerity.

In his experience, it is possible for someone to have a motor neuron neuropathy which closely mimics ALS. The only way to find out for sure is to do the IVIG and see if anything changes. He, like Dr. Brown, is very interested in the number of Gulf War vets with the ALS diagnosis. I'm sure in their minds they feel maybe we can identify some link that might lead to a better understanding and treatment for this disease, whatever it turns out to be.

By week four, worry is beginning to corrode my optimism, although I say nothing to anyone. My slow loss of hope, again, is my secret. I want them all to sustain the sad myth for as long as possible, before they know what my body makes clear to me by week five, week six.

I come to know that I will not be one of those cases where IVIGs will help. I let Christmas pass without telling my family. I don't know why I think I'm fooling anyone, though. I know we can read it in one another's eyes. But we all continue to pretend, even as I need help cutting up my roast pork at Christmas dinner. Even as I watch helplessly as Dad erects Bubba's racetrack, holds the seat as Bub wobbles his new bike down the driveway, inserts the batteries into his remote control tow truck.

Bubba looks up at me. "I wish you could do this, Dad," he says. "I remember when you used to put my batteries in."

"Let Grandpa do it," I tell him. "He knows how."

For the first time in two years, we are home for Christmas.

More and more, the external distractions that interrupt my inner life are technological. Just today Susan went up to the VA hospital in Newington to pick up my latest piece of equipment, a portable suction machine. Seems they're getting worried I might choke on my own saliva, which is one of the problems that occurs as ALS progresses and the esophagus muscles deteriorate. I have had some trouble with dysphagia: the muscles in my throat are reluctant to move these days, so swallowing is sometimes a challenge.

I am surrounded by technology, just as I was in the cockpit of my F-16. My new van is equipped with an elevator, so I can ride my electric wheelchair right onto the ramp and get lifted into the air. At first, this was almost as disconcerting as fighting G forces. I face not the van but the outdoors, ride up with my back to the entrance, then roll in backwards, trusting that the floor will be there.

The chair itself is remarkable, both for the freedom it allows me and for its poor ergonomic design. I may even write the manufacturer with my engineering suggestions one of these days. More than once I've torn the padding on the left armrest trying to maneuver through a door. Then the tilt/recline system broke only a month after I got it, with me in the fully reclined position. It took a phone call to my Dad to rush over and help get me out of the damn thing.

Next on my list of technological acquisitions is an onscreen keyboard for my computer that will enable me to use the mouse to type. Then adaptive thermostat equipment so I can manage the house's heat and air conditioning from my chair. I'll also be getting an electric door opener, so I can go in and out of the house by pressing a button on my chair controls. All of these devices are courtesy of the industry of rehabilitation engineering, a burgeoning field with its own specialists who consult on everything for the disabled from equipment to specially adapted clothing designed to work like magician's clothes: they're velcroed at the side seams, allowing an aide to slip you in and out by just ripping or smoothing the seam.

Much of this technology has come about since the end of the Cold War, when defense contractors were forced to retrofit their factories and their products to non-military purposes. And here I sit, not quite mute but not silent either, a defense-industry product, transformed by that very industry into a next generation consumer of their goods. Paints a funny picture, doesn't it?

As for those goods, I have yet to test the wonders of the suction machine and will put that day off for as long as I can manage. I wonder, though, if the same engineer who designed my portable suction machine also designed my jet's oxygen mask. I wonder about the controls on my chair, which resemble an F-16's control stick. And my onscreen keyboard looks a lot like the multi-function display in my cockpit. I wonder, too, if those engineers could ever imagine that the same individual would use both devices. It occurs to me that where I am now is really not so foreign to me after all. It is, in fact, disconcertingly familiar.

This battle is not over, and I am glad to recognize the weapons. The weapons of technology are my armaments against a world of doorknobs and steps, forks and spoons, a world which yesterday was normal and today has become my enemy. In my head, I resist this implacable, insidious disease as it corrodes my nerves, melts my muscle. And I have taken up the weapon of words against those I loved, my brothers in arms.

I am surrounded, and I rally my defenses. My enemies are legion, my friends few. I am outnumbered, but I am not alone. I am not sure if I am gaining ground on any front, and I am beginning to worry about defeat.

A Full 360

January 1997

We have been looking for a house since our return early last October. There isn't much on the market that will suit our needs—specifically, someplace that can be easily adapted to a wheelchair. In other words, we need to find a house that is almost completely on one floor, with extra-wide doorways and a wheel-in shower and toilet.

After four months of straight-out searching, calls to and from realtors, hours spent scanning the newspaper, we aren't having very much luck. Then my mother gives Dick Kelley a call. Kelley built their house 20 years ago. She tells him what we're looking for, just in case he knows of anything.

A few days later Dick Kelley pays me a visit. He is a handsome man of average size, in his mid-50s, with silver grey hair that he combs back over his head. As he sits with me at the kitchen counter, he leans forward, his face pleasant, kind.

"Michael," he says, "I'd like to build you a house. I'd make it so that everything is accessible to you."

I look at him. I'm not sure how to interpret his offer. We don't exactly have money to burn.

"Not everything has to make money," he adds, as if he can read my thoughts.

"I appreciate your offer, Mr. Kelley," I tell him. "I really do. But I don't want charity." I can feel my bruised pride purpling behind my eyes.

"No, and you don't need it," he answers. "But you can accept help. And by the way, call me Dick."

This is a good, decent man, I decide. I almost cry. It's been a long time since I've met a good, decent man. And I know I need help. I don't want to need it, but I do.

He tells me of several areas where he's building and lots that he owns around town.

"Think about it, Mike," he says as he pulls on his barn coat. He turns back to face me before heading out the door. "Let me know."

"I will," I answer. "Thanks." I stay seated at the counter. It's too much work for me to get up to see him out. But I mean to think about his offer.

A day later, Steve Callahan, who played on that winning Little League team all those years ago, calls to tell us there is a house in town that's in foreclosure, and it is handicapped accessible. We locate the advertisement in the *Journal Inquirer*: the open house is scheduled in just a few days.

The next time I talk to Dick Kelley, I tell him we appreciate his offer, but that we first want to look into this foreclosure deal.

"We just don't want to have to wait too long for a house to be built," I explain. "Not if we don't have to." The kids are living without all their things, without being settled in, without a real home of their own. They miss Texas fiercely, and it doesn't help not having a home. If we build, we'll have to wait until the ground thaws in the spring to get started.

By the time the open house takes place, we have driven by numerous times. It is a contemporary with a long slanting roof that dips almost to my height, a large yard, lots of windows. You can tell it was once a nice place. But the broken-down fence, the faded stain on the cedar shingles, the general disrepair tell the story of its neglect. We learn the chapter and verse of that neglect once we get inside.

Sue and I go alone. My parents have offered to come, but this is something we need to decide. And when we arrive, there are already 10 or 15 cars parked outside. Sue gets me into the wheelchair, and we make our way up the driveway, threading the cars.

I know that if the outside is any indication, the interior might not be in great condition. I am right. But nothing could have prepared us for the sight that meets our eyes when we walk in the front door.

Matted, filthy orange shag carpeting as far as the eye can see. The house is dark, the walls lined with dingy paneling. Heavy, rotting drapes obscure windows filmed with grease. All the light fixtures are black cast iron 1970s-style Mediterranean, fitted with yellow and orange plastic lenses, and everywhere the autumnal shadows they cast are cloudy from the patina of grime that films them. There is almost no furniture except in the den, where a 30-year-old couch and chair set fill the room, the orange, lime green and yellow velvet faded and torn, the stuffing exposed.

The hardwood floors in the master bedroom and den haven't been cleaned or waxed in God alone knows how long, and they are streaked grey and black. By the door in the den stands a four-foot-tall hoop on a post, and on the hoop sits a huge cockatoo who tilts his head and eyes us nervously as we enter. It looks as though the bird has had the run of the place for quite a while. The molding next to his perch is chipped and gnawed, the dark olive green paneling is caked with bird droppings.

In the kitchen, counters are piled high with dishes, pots and pans, all filthy with dried food from the ages. Old appliances crammed into corners are blackened with the ancient remains of past meals eaten in haste, and, apparently, over the sink. We choose not to look inside the refrigerator, at the realtor's warning. She has already made that mistake. Her face wrinkles in disgust at the memory.

On the good side, although the house spans three floors, the master bedroom is on the first, off the kitchen, there is a working elevator up to the second floor where two large bedrooms are located, and down to the basement, which is set up as some sort of hunter's den. Throughout, the halls are wide enough for me to pass, and off the master bedroom, a wide-doored bathroom reveals an open shower area into which I could easily wheel. I try to ignore the odor and look only at the structure.

Downstairs, more surprises greet us. Here the walls are grey barnboard, and the room is cut in two by a bar—bars were big in suburban houses in the '70s. A badly executed mural adorns each end of the bar area. In one, clumsy-looking mallards shoot up in alarm from a large swamplike lake, which springs from the rough-hewn paneling. In the other, frighteningly mutated Disney-like deer pose on an expanse of open meadow. The overall effect is more disconcerting than anything else. I feel like we have landed in someone else's nightmare.

It turns out we have.

A Vietnam vet had the house built after he returned from the war a paraplegic. I assume the VA paid for it. It's a lot tougher for them to deny you benefits when your limbs are blown off.

The guy lived here for years, and when he died, his brother continued to inhabit the house, alone. At some point, he borrowed against the equity, and he borrowed a lot. Unable to make the payments because of his own troubles—troubles that seem to have something to do with drugs—the brother is about to lose his home. Oddly, he is here, showing people around.

"What are you going to do when they evict you?" Susan asks him. We are worried about buying a house equipped with a tenant who has nowhere to go. We need a place to live, and we certainly don't want to be the reason this man goes homeless.

He looks like the house. Disheveled, unkempt, pathetic, in need of a good scrub and a new occupant.

He swipes his well-bitten fingers through his hair.

"Oh, I'm all set," he assures us, nodding to himself. "I'm going to be moving in with some friends."

Great, I think. I wonder if the friends know yet.

Despite its many problems, I like the house. Sue is convinced I have lost my mind, but I see potential. Beneath all of the debris, the caked detritus of years of misery, it is a solid structure, well built. And it is already modified. I have made arrangements to have it inspected while we are here, to make sure we aren't getting into something that requires more than just cosmetic repairs and renovations, however massive.

The inspector assures me it is sound.

In three weeks, the house goes to auction. I refuse to let my mother see it. I know what she will say about all the diseases undoubtedly festering in years of accreted bird excrement, the indescribably disgusting bathrooms.

Sue and I talk about it. I am working on getting her to come around. Meantime, we continue to look at other places. But I keep thinking about the house on Maple Avenue. Already I'm calling it "my house" in my head. It seems meant to be. I will live just a half mile from Benson Drive. My children will go to Orchard Hill Elementary and Timothy Edwards Middle School, right up the hill, just as I did. They will play in the orchards we roamed.

I know that house is mine. It completes the circle.

The auction takes place on 18 January. We show up with the requisite cashier's check for $20,000 that buys us a spot in the bidding.

There are three other couples present, and a man Dad points out who is probably from the bank. We are each given a piece of paper with a number printed on it. In the bare living room, heated only by the fire in the fireplace, we wait for the bidding to begin. I am freezing, sitting toward the back corner, without a view of the banker. Maybe it's the cold, but I am shaking a little. My bidding chit quivers slightly in my hand, where Dad has placed it.

I don't notice that Mr. Kelley has entered. Dad tells me after it's over that he was here, looked around, said not a word to anyone, then left when the bidding ended.

The attorney who's running the show walks up to the front of the room. "The bidding will be by $100 increments," he announces.

The first bidder opens with $100. The next two pass, and I pass also. I want to see where the bank starts.

"$115,000," says a deep voice that resonates from behind the half wall. The banker. They have already figured they've lost everything, so whatever they get for the house will be pure gain. Besides, the foreclosure appraisal valued it at $155,000. Neighboring houses go for $150,000 to $200,000.

After that, the others fall quiet. It's down to me and Mr. Bank.

"$115,100," I offer.

"$125,000," he answers.

This is unexpected. I didn't think he would go that high. At least not so soon, and not in such a big jump. But he is bidding with the bank's money. His pockets are deep.

"$125,100," I venture.

"$132,000." Not good. Mr. Bank isn't done yet. Is that a little edge I heard in his voice, though?

I turn to Dad. "How high you think this guy's gonna go?" I whisper. He knows my cutoff is $150,000. That's all I figure we can afford, what with all the closing costs and the major renovations we will need.

"Well," Dad whispers. "You said $150K, right?" I nod.

We have talked about the option of letting the bank buy it and then offering to buy it back from them. But they won't sell it for less than the appraised value, $155,000, so anything less than that is my gain.

I think for another few seconds, and then I bid again.

$132,500."

The voice from around the corner answers my prayers. "That's all I got," he says.

The lawyer turns to me. "You just bought yourself a house, sir. Congratulations."

I am excited. Everyone else, including Sue, is leery, to say the least. She has gone along with this, but begrudgingly. No one else can see what I see. I am sure I have just gotten myself the best buy in town. And I can once again feel I am providing for my family.

Now the real fun begins.

Next day, Dick Kelley calls me. "Congratulations on your house," he says. I'm worried he might be pissed that we didn't let him build for us. Was I ever wrong about that.

"Listen, Mike," he says. "That place is going to need a lot of work."

We laugh.

"I'd like to help with the renovations." I never expected this. I'm not sure what to say. I'm worried about money and Dick is not exactly your low-priced spread.

"I've just been crunching the numbers," I answer. "And you know, Dick, I'm going to have to nickel and dime this renovation. I'm working with our savings, and I'm not paying in that much from my retirement income."

"I just want to help," Dick Kelley answers. "All you have to say is 'thank you.'"

It turns out he has already talked to the South Windsor Rotary Club and gotten all of them fired up to help us renovate so we can move in as soon as possible. Dick Kelley has people coming from all over town, first to help clean the place out, and then to renovate.

Once we close and clear all the paperwork, a dumpster appears on the front lawn, and the pace picks up from there. By the time they take it away two weeks later, it is overflowing with debris, and the ghosts of another war are hauled off to the dump.

My life takes on a new shape. Every day, I sit in the cold, hollow living room, watching people I have never met gutting my house from basement to attic, working as if they are being paid to impress the boss. But they're not even getting paid, many of them. They are here just to help me and my family.

Some donate their time, and we put them to work spackling or priming, or doing yard work, or helping with the interior demolition bull work. Others help in their special field. Steve Wisneski installs all the plumbing for cost. Joe Martin brings his paint crew in and they paint the entire place in just three days. Dalene's Carpet Store sends a crew over to refinish all the hardwood floors, carpet the basement family room, tile the kitchen. Joe Fradiani shows up one day with a crew to seal the driveway.

Throughout the two months it takes to complete, Dick Kelley is my guardian angel, making sure people show up, arranging everything before we even realize what we need to have done next.

These are the people I went to war for, I think. People like Dick Kelley, Joe Martin, Steve Wisneski, Joe Fradiani. People who realize what it means to fight for your country, to risk your life for your ideals. These are people who know what it means to put your money where your mouth is.

As much as I would prefer to get up out of this chair and help them, my soul takes nourishment from their goodness as I watch them work. It is hard for me, at first, to accept their help. I never wanted charity; I still have my pride. But gradually I come to see how it gratifies them to do this thing, and I rest in the comfort of allowing them to help. It is all a funny, circular kind of gift we give one another: I accept their help; they are proud to do it; my misfortune is the agent of their satisfaction.

Sue is here every day, too. She works from early in the morning till very late at night. At last, she will have a home of her own, a home to fill with light and family. A home in which to nest her troubles, where the closets are capacious enough to receive all the months of anguish, and the walls are white, the color of nothing.

Sometimes nothing can be comforting, I know, especially when all around you chaos commands your every ounce of energy. White absorbs light, just as it absorbs the silent howls that stream from her pores, her eyes. I watch her spackle and paint, her forearms taut, her jaw tightened in a permanent clench.

Around us, a home begins to emerge. And I was right. It is beautiful. Open, bright. The hardwood floors have polished into a warm gleam, the windows, once cleaned and cleaned again, reveal soothing views out back, across a farm field, now overwintering, in which deer come to graze each evening. Once, at dusk, I see a proud six-point buck stalking the field's perimeter. At first, I can't make out his rack against the branches, but then he slowly turns his head as if to reveal his magnificent profile to me, and I count the tips. He is there for me, examining me from the safety of his field. He stands there for several minutes, and we just look at one another, counterparts, kindred souls.

We call the storage facility in Oklahoma. They cannot guarantee an exact date, but tell us our things should arrive within one week. We will just have to be ready to let them deliver when they call the night before to tell us they're in town. And when the day comes, the kids are thrilled. It is a second Christmas, only better, a coming home to belongings they forgot they had, but which offer the comfort of the familiar. Old toys look to them like old friends after the trauma they've been through, but those toys are more like anchors, holding them safe to good times now gone.

Erin unpacks her legendary Barbie collection and arrays them on her bed. Her stuffed animals, all 17 of them, crowd her pillows. Bubba rips his toys out of the boxes like a madman, flinging trucks and planes and stuffed animals over his shoulder, shrieking with delighted recognition.

"Look!" he shouts. "My tow truck! My matchboxes!" He streaks downstairs with each new discovery.

Unlike the kids, Sue unpacks the objects of her past individually, unwrapping each bowl, each plate as if it might hold the answer. Her reverence unnerves me, and once my computer is set up, I plant myself there, spend my days wondering what I will do now that this problem has been solved.

That's when my parents introduce me to Father Jerome.

*　　*　　*

He is an old-fashioned kind of priest. I don't just mean a 1940s Bing Crosby throwback. I mean he belongs in Robin Hood's merry band, wearing green tights and drinking ale, Friar Tuck personified. A hearty, rotund man who loves to eat, especially Italian, Father Jerome's ruddy complexion is testimony to his culinary interests. He is not your typical Catholic priest, a point on which I think he takes great pride.

An excellent cook, Father Jerome loves everything gourmet. He shelters his rather large girth in the traditional brown Franciscan cowled robe, bound at the waist with a cincture, knotted three times. According to Father Jerome, the three knots remind Franciscans of their vows of poverty, chastity and don't forget to pick up the dry cleaning.

No matter what the weather, like Franciscans the world over, his feet are shod in simple sandals. Unlike his feet, his face is not weathered. He looks to be about 45—although I've always had trouble telling priests' ages—and he wears a fashionable goatee, streaked with grey, just like the faded copper hair that hugs his head.

Father Jerome is the pastor of St. Patrick-St. Anthony in downtown Hartford, otherwise known as Pat and Tony's or the A & P. As is the case with most American Catholic parishes, the suburban churches around Hartford have been witnessing a drop in attendance. Pat and Tony's, on the other hand, has more than tripled in membership since Father Jerome took the helm.

We begin to meet weekly. Slowly at first, and then with the intimacy born of urgency, he becomes my friend, my counselor, my companion on this journey. Without Father Jerome to chortle with, to find the comic and absurd in this horror, I would be lost indeed. He berates me for not coming to Mass more often, although he doesn't warn me my soul will burn in hell for all eternity.

"Oh, Michael Donnelly!" he shouts for all to hear, on the rare occasions when I make it in to Mass. "I *think* I remember you. We're *honored* by your presence here today."

Only Father Jerome could pull this off. He should be on stage. Father Comedy. But he has heart, and his cajoling is affectionate.

After the first few months, though, my counseling visits become less regular. More like semimonthly rather than weekly. It's just becoming too hard to get me in and out of the minivan. At least that's what I tell myself.

I may have been raised a Catholic, but I've never been very good at the faith thing. Somehow it always seemed empty for me. When I tell Father Jerome how I feel, he has an answer.

"Obviously," he says, then pauses wryly, "you're not the only one."

I feel the need to explain.

"But I've always tried to figure out what is really important in life," I tell him, "and what is not. I've always tried to live my life the right way, do what's right. You know what I mean? Be a moral person."

"Uh-hmm," he says. He nods kindly, strokes his goatee.

"I'm not saying I've always been a saint," I continue. "I've sinned, just like anyone else."

"Well, that's what makes us all human," he answers.

I pause. There is something I've been wanting to talk about. Something dark that visits me at night when I'm lying in bed, when self-pity stalks its easy prey and I wonder what I did to deserve this fate.

"In fact," I tell him, "I'm fairly certain I have taken human life." I have never talked about this before, not in this way. "To tell you the truth," I say, "it never really bothered me. I mean, they were certainly trying hard to take mine."

He pauses. He looks at me, and then at his hands, his big, copper-haired hands, which are neatly folded in his robed lap. And when he speaks, I get the feeling he has known where this conversation was going before I even said a word.

"This illness is not a punishment, you know." His voice is mellow, aged by wisdom, or pain, or, more likely, both.

I look up at him, and I feel the familiar tears flood my eyes, the tears of gratitude. I look back down at my inert hands. I am afraid for what I have done. But his simple expiation has an instant effect. I feel the guilt lift from my shoulders. I know I will never be free of this burden, but somehow I feel lighter.

"Why don't you think about it," Father Jerome continues after I've recovered a little, "and next time we meet, I'll hear your confession. By the way," he asks, a smile teasing the corners of his mouth, "how long has it been?"

I knew he was going to ask me this. And I can't exactly lie to a priest.

"Umm. Years," I answer sheepishly. I find a sudden fascination for the pattern in the carpeting.

"Only a few?" he asks, testing me, daring me to look him in the eye.

"Well," I pause. I look at him and then away. I'm more intimidated by my priest than I was by my commanding officer.

May as well get this over with, I think.

"More like 20," I tell him finally.

"*Years?*" he practically shrieks. "20 *years* since your last confession?" Father Jerome is trying to control himself. He is a priest after all. He's seen and heard everything, right?

"Well, don't worry about it," he manages to recover, and he's starting to smile again. "Just come and tell me what's on your mind."

I nod and say I will. But I plan to put that day off a bit. Maybe not 20 years. I don't have that much time. But just a little while longer. Until I get my thoughts straight. Until I have no last treatments to try. Until I reach the end of that tapering path of hope I've been traveling.

Until I get back from Germany.

*　　*　　*

We hear about Dr. Wilhelm Geiger through some other ALS patients he has treated. Geiger draws patients from around the world to his clinic in Hannover, Germany, just like Dr. Frazer in Dallas. And like the patients in Dallas, those who come here are on a final mission, before they surrender all hope and, either willingly or reluctantly, look the future full in the face.

Unlike Dr. Frazer, Dr. Geiger is not an environmental health specialist. His treatment has more to do with preserving the nerve cells that are still alive.

In phone conversations with Geiger's staff, we learn that he has been partially successful in stopping the disease's progression about 50% of the time. However, he does not know which cases are most amenable to his treatment, and there are no tests to tell us if it will be effective for me.

I talk to a man who was diagnosed with ALS 13 years ago, and after seeing and being treated by Geiger, his disease has not progressed at all. I decide I want to be able to tell the same story 13 years from now.

The only thing to do is to go there and try it.

We are all apprehensive. We can find no independent studies showing the effectiveness of calcium EAP, Dr. Geiger's treatment. Traditional physicians tell us it is a waste of time and a waste of hope. Either they have never heard of him, or they tell us there is no clinical evidence showing any effective treatment of ALS, anywhere in the world.

We already know this, of course. But they seem unable to grasp what seems to me to be such a simple point: it doesn't matter, because there is nothing I won't do or won't try if there's even a chance it might save my life. As long as I am able to get there and back I will go.

We make reservations for Sue and me. The kids will stay with her parents. We take off out of Boston on 1 February.

When we arrive in Frankfurt, they carry me off in a special wheelchair that fits in the aisle, but there is no such device to get me on the plane to Hannover. I must be carried bodily on board, and then down again when we arrive. I am not looking forward to the return trip. But that is two weeks away, and I have other worries to occupy me until then.

Our hotel is located just across the street from Geiger's office. Nice by German standards: modern and well kept, and we have a second floor room right over the lobby entrance. We look out over the main intersections in town. It's all right, though, because we have the famous German triple-paned windows to mute the city sounds just one story below us. And because it is a corner room, it is actually fairly big. I can use the wheelchair to maneuver around, for which I am grateful.

We visit the doctor every day for two weeks. Day one, he examines me, takes some blood samples, performs some other tests. He sends Sue down to the pharmacy with a list of prescriptions. He explains his theory and the treatment he has devised, but I am not interested in trying to understand. I let the details slip past me. Either it will work or it won't.

When the weather is cold, we stay in our room and Sue goes to the Bahnhof to buy us something for dinner, usually sandwiches, bratwurst and rolls, french fries. There is a McDonald's close by, where we often eat, since it is cheap and easy. Sue just has to order zwei Big Macs, zwei fries und zwei cokes. So much for my promise never to touch the stuff again.

When the weather allows, we venture out to one of the surrounding restaurants. The two years we spent in Germany come in handy. We know what to order and are able to get around.

I loved flying in Germany. Actually, I loved living in Germany. This time, though, I won't be touring wine cellars along the Mosel river valley, or driving out to shop at the French commissary or tour the Roman ruins in Tübingen. When you travel in a circle, you don't always end up in the same place.

Every day Dr. Geiger injects me with liquid calcium EAP, and he is none too gentle with the needle. He complains about the size of my veins, which are apparently too small for his taste. Eventually, he just picks one out on the back of my hand and jabs it. It hurts like hell, but I feel I am not supposed to show that I am in pain.

I am in Germany, the land where you grimace and bear it.

Dr. Geiger looks like a hobbit. He is short and round, with wet eyes that bulge behind gleaming wire spectacles. His white hair recedes all the way to the back of his head, creating a longish white halo that rings his shiny pate. We ask him questions and he answers them as best he is able. He likes me. He likes the fact that I was a fighter pilot. He knows right away why I am sick when I tell him I was in the Gulf War.

"You have been poisoned, young man," he says to me. "You know this?"

Yes, I nod. I know this.

I continue the treatment he recommends for three months after we return. Apparently, I am not among the 50% of cases who benefit from calcium EAP.

Somehow, I am not surprised. Just sorry.

Before the war, Powell and Schwarzkopf professed to the world that we had the smartest, best-trained, most-motivated professional all-volunteer fighting force ever assembled. When we got to the Persian Gulf, they pumped us full of patriotism with remarks like, "We must take care of our troops," and, "We're going to get it right this time."

And we believed them. We didn't just believe them, we were proud to fight, proud to serve, proud to risk our lives, even if we knew it was at least partly about oil.

Now, though, they're singing a different tune. Now those of us who fought feel like we weren't the smartest force ever assembled. We were the most gullible.

I have a lot of questions, and the longer I sit here in my house, in my wheelchair, and stare at my computer screen, the longer those questions brew, the angrier I get. I do not want to die an angry man. I do not want to die a bitter man. I do not want to die at all. But if I must, I want truth to be my companion on that journey, not regret.

Combat logs go missing, but only the pages that relate to the chemical weapons alarms. The military is meticulous about keeping records, especially combat logs. How could these pages just disappear? Why do they expect us to believe that? More importantly, why do they have so much power that they can tell such transparent falsehoods and get away with it? Where is the outrage? The press?

The chemical weapons alarms were all false, they claim. How could every one of the tens of thousands of these alarms that sounded during the war have been false? Is the detection equipment we spend millions of dollars on completely useless? Then why bother with it? And why are we sending our troops into battle with it? "Have we asked for our money back yet?" asked Bernie Sanders, Member of Congress from Vermont, during a Congressional hearing on the subject.

Why are we so concerned about getting weapons inspectors into Iraq? What are we afraid of? If Hussein has the capacity now, after seven years of embargo, inspections and sanctions, to produce enough chemical and biological weapons to worry us, what did he have at his disposal at the start of the Persian Gulf War?

And why would the VA pressure doctors who are trying to get to the root of these illnesses? Why are they either fired or pressured to stop their research? What possible reasons could there be to cover this up? And why would more than 110,000 veterans invent serious illnesses? Or fall victim to stress after we launched the least stressful, most successful tactical campaign in the history of time?

Why didn't the DOD warn us that the depleted uranium in some of the weapon heads was harmful once those weapons had detonated? There are memos and other documents that indicate the DOD knew of this danger before the war. Why didn't they warn those who worked on and around spent weapons that there was a strong likelihood DU dust covered everything? That they'd likely inhale live radioactive particles? That they should use protective gear in dealing with these materials? Why?

Why didn't they warn us that Hussein might have been using the oil fires to mask his secretive dispersal of chemical weapons in the smoke, when they knew in January 1991, on the eve of the invasion, of the threat of these fires, of the serious health threat these fires would pose? Why didn't they tell us what the U.S. Army Intelligence Agency knew: that the potential for petroleum fires was high, and that these fires would pose a grave health risk?

I have a lot of time on my hands. Time to conjure up all sorts of theories about what happened. To read every document posted to the Internet about what the Pentagon did and when. Time to read all the testimony to the Presidential Advisory Commission. To read all the congressional hearing findings.

To read and reread Patrick Eddington's book, Gassed in the Gulf. *A former CIA analyst responsible for the Persian Gulf region during and after the war, Eddington left the CIA in 1996 in protest over the lies and cover up. He documents everything: that the U.S. command knew in advance about the chemical weapons stored at Khamisiyah, the Iraqi depot nine football fields across that we detonated on 4 March and 10 March 1991. That the Pentagon and CIA have thousands of documents showing that same command knew about the chemical weapons danger and exposure during the war and after.*

Did we lie about Iraq using chemical and biological weapons during the war to keep the coalition together? To prevent widespread panic? To keep the 700,000 Americans assembled in the world's most massive build-up of troops on foreign soil from wondering if their own government could send them into battle inadequately protected? What if we had known, during the war, that Hussein was using chemical and biological weapons and that our shoddy, outdated gear would do little to protect us?

Iraq's chemical warfare capability was known to the U.S. government before the war. A month before it began, then CIA director William Webster estimated that Iraq possessed 1,000 tons of poisonous chemical agents, much of it capable of being loaded into two types of missiles: the FROG (Free Rocket Over Ground) and the SCUD B(SS-1). What was in those SCUDs that fell like hail day after day?

As for the biological agents, U.S. companies manufactured them, illegally, and then sold them to Iraq, illegally, in the years before the war. Most chilling of all, the Commerce Department has the documents to prove it. Why would they lay the groundwork for genocide in the first place, and why document it as they did it?

The Commerce Department documents reads like Satan's shopping list.

> Date: August 31, 1987
> Sent to: Iraq Atomic Energy Commission
> Materials Shipped:
>   1. Escherichia coli (ATCC 23846)
>   Batch # 07-29-83 (1 each)
>   2. Escherichia coli (ATCC 33694)
>   Batch # 05-87 (1 each)
> Date: September 29, 1988
> Sent to: Ministry of Trade
> Materials Shipped:
>   1. Bacillus anthracis (ATCC 240)
>   Batch # 05-14-63 (3 each)
>   Class III pathogen
>   2. Bacillus anthracis (ATCC 938)
>   Batch # 1963 (3 each)
>   Class III pathogen
> Date: May 2, 1986
> Sent to: Ministry of Higher Education
> Materials Shipped:
>   1. Bacillus Anthracis Cohn (ATCC 10)
>   Batch # 08-20-82 (2 each)

Class III pathogen
2. Bacillus Subtilis (Ehrenberg) Cohn (ATCC 82)
   Batch # 06-20-84 (2 each)
3. Clostridium botulinum Type A (ATCC 3502)
   Batch # 07-07-81 (3 each)
   Class III pathogen
4. Bacillus subtilis (ATCC 6051)
   Batch # 12-06-84 (2 each)
5. Clostridium tetani (ATCC 9441)
   Batch # 03-84 (3 each)
   Highly toxigenic

Allegedly, both Presidents Reagan and Bush gave their tacit approval to these transactions. It was their creative way of buying a friend in the Middle Eastern equation.

Are the Pentagon and the CIA covering up to protect those who made millions of dollars on those sales? Individuals who served the very government that sent us into war?

Am I crazy to imagine that it's a conflict of interest for members of my own government to serve on the boards of defense contractors? Individuals like John Deutsch, former CIA director and William Perry, former Secretary of Defense, both of whom were on the board of directors of a company called SAIC—Scientific Applications International Corporation. Between them, they made more than $1 million for their services.

SAIC is the company the DOD hired to research whether troops would be exposed to chemical weapons fallout. When SAIC modeled the fallout, wonder of wonders, it found that there was no chance it would affect American troops, a finding the Pentagon years later reluctantly acknowledged was false when veterans stepped forward with videotapes of what happened at Khamisiyah on 4 March 1991.

Bush threatened Iraq that if they used chemical weapons, we would nuke Baghdad. Did Bush also know there was no way the world would let him unleash nuclear holocaust after the Cold War was over? He must have known about the downwind hazard to the troops, since we now know the Pentagon and the CIA knew about it in advance. Is the cover up an attempt to preserve our macho image in the face of Bush's obviously empty threat?

Why can't we believe that Saddam Hussein would employ chemical and biological weapons in such a way as to cause long-term illnesses instead of huge body counts on the battlefield? Why can't we believe our own veterans *when they tell us, by the thousands, that their illnesses are combat related? Have the same men and women this country glorified when we went into battle been magically transformed into lazy malingerers out for an easy buck, especially when that buck is far from easy to wrest from the tight fists clenching it?*

Is the DOD justifying the cover up because they think it's a national defense issue? That if we find out what really happened, it will reveal a fatal weakness in our military?

And why did it take six years for the DOD to acknowledge that a soldier who rubbed against mustard gas in an Iraqi bunker, a soldier whose wounds were clearly the result of such an exposure, was indeed exposed to mustard gas during the war?

Will we uncover some top secret experiment or operation or weapon they were testing? Was it the United States who used the chemical and biological weapons? Did they backfire and affect us? Was the military testing experimental vaccines on us?

Where is the patriotism now? Where are the cheering throngs? Where is the media? Why does no one seem to care what is happening to us?

Questions, I have so many questions. Answers I have none.

Bandits, Twelve O'Clock

March 1997

I get a call one day from Congressman Shays' office.

"Major Donnelly?" the voice asks. "I believe you're aware that we are conducting hearings on Gulf War illnesses? On the Pentagon's handling of the investigation of this matter?"

"Yes," I answer. "I am."

"Congressman Shays would like you to testify before the Subcommittee on Government Reform and Oversight at the end of April."

I have to think how to answer. It's not that I don't want to have the chance to speak my piece. I know that would be good for me. But it's much more complicated than that.

I have to think whether I really want to travel to Washington, D.C. to testify against the very people I dedicated my life to serving, to tell the world that my superior officers are lying. Everything I've always believed in has been turned inside out, stripped bare, hung out to dry. Do I really want to make my loss public? Do I really want to advertise their treachery in Washington? Can I risk it?

"Can I get back to you?" I ask. "I need some time to think about this."

"Absolutely," the aide says. "Can you give me a call next week? Oh, and keep in mind we'll reimburse you for expenses. Airfare, or mileage if you drive. Hotel and food. Here's my number," he adds. "Why don't you give me a call, say, next Wednesday?"

I have until Wednesday, then, to decide if by testifying I will betray some kind of trust or something sacred, if I will open myself up to criticism from people I respected and admired. More frighteningly, if I might in some way jeopardize the retirement and medical benefits for which I fought so hard and feel I deserve. I fear the VA will find some loophole that will allow them to yank my medical coverage and leave me stranded with this illness and no insurance. I lie awake at nights worrying the DOD will discover some obscure regulation entitling them to stop paying my pension and leave me and my family destitute.

I have to make a decision. If I don't go, will I regret it to the end of my days? I feel a duty to those veterans who cannot speak for themselves. I'm still an officer, after all, still a man who was trained to lead. And what I learned about leadership little resembles what I've seen from my superiors thus far. Maybe I misunderstood, but I thought leadership had to do with making difficult choices, with taking the heat for your fellow soldiers, with being the first to brave enemy fire.

I also know this is literally my last chance to speak out. Soon, I will no longer be able to speak. As it is, I worry I will be unintelligible, although Dad assures me I'm fine.

It is a Hobson's choice, one I would prefer never to have to make.

Finally, Tuesday night, lying awake, the answer comes to me.

This is too important, I decide. This is something that needs to be said. And I have to be one of the few who speaks the truth. I have to be one of those who says that the Pentagon, the CIA, the Air Force are the ones betraying me, not the other way around. If they had held true to their promise of justice and integrity, I would not be in this position.

I decide I want to show them that what I learned about leadership in my Air Force career was to lead the troops, not abandon them.

I decide I will lead. I will take the risk. I will testify.

This time I will be on the right side. I will be on the side of truth. I am not a liar and I cannot abide lies. I thought justice was what we were supposed to be about. I feel a fool for having believed all that crap now. But I will not be made a fool by those who managed to lull me into that stupor of trust. I am awake now, and I will speak.

There are so many veterans who have nothing. I know them and their stories. Many have no benefits because they became ill after they were discharged. Since they cannot prove any connection between service and the various and horrific illnesses that plague them, the military feels no obligation to provide them with any medical benefits or disability income. These are men and women suffering and dying from cancer, from heart conditions, from neurological diseases so bizarre I would not believe them unless I knew them to be true.

It's not that the Pentagon has been idle. Back in 1994, after three years of complaints from Gulf War veterans and their legally elected representatives, they set up the Gulf War Registry. Veterans were encouraged to call and enlist, to undergo a special physical. We were allowed to self-select ourselves into their database, so that we could be told, nine times out of ten, that we suffered from somatoform disorder and PTSD.

In other words, soldier, it's all in your head.

Like the kid with all the marbles who gets to make the rules, the Pentagon started its own investigation into its own investigation. And to no one's surprise, their studies corroborated their earlier conclusions, their investigations turned up no evidence of any wrongdoing on their part.

Then Clinton set up his own special commission in response to congressional pressure. The President's Advisory Commission toured the country to solicit and listen to veterans' testimony.

When one renegade commission member, Dr. Jonathan Tucker, expressed his willingness to believe that there was some pattern here indicating that we might indeed have been exposed to chemical and biological weapons, he was summarily dismissed—with one hour's notice. So much for freedom of speech and an independent authority.

We learn about the latest developments online, through sites on the World Wide Web, sites with names like Gulfweb, or Desert Storm Justice Foundation. We trade stories in chat rooms, send one another encouraging e-mails, wonder to ourselves and each other how we ended up disenfranchised, disenchanted, disbelieving, when only a few years ago we were heroes.

Most of us haven't really taken it in. We are in shock. We truly thought this time was different. That we were different.

I have never liked bullies.

I will show them that they can betray me. They can abandon me. They can shit on everything I believe in. But they can't shut me up.

On Wednesday morning at 0900 hours I call Shays' office. I tell Bob Newman to count on me.

For weeks I work on my statement. I feel a lot of pressure, because there is so much riding on this. I want it to be perfect. I want it to be meaningful, real, my story and the story of every other Gulf War veteran.

I struggle with the words. I write and rewrite. And then I lose my file. Some kind of weird virus affects the disk so that I can't open the file with my testimony on it. And only that file. I can open all the other files on that disk, but that one is locked tighter than the vault at Fort Knox. If I weren't so sane, I'd think the CIA had broken into my house and corrupted just that file. Or maybe they didn't need to break into the house, I think. Maybe they just came through a back door in Windows, found the file and killed it?

Naw, I think. That's nuts. They must have better things to do than worry about a sick man's testimony to a congressional subcommittee.

I start over. It takes me another week, but eventually I re-create the entire statement.

We decide that Dad will make the trip with Sue and me. We need Dad to do the driving, and I need Sue to dress and care for me. And anyway, I want them both to be there. I have a feeling I'm going to need them.

Early on Tuesday, 23 April, the day before I am to testify, we pack the van, send the kids over to Sue's parents and hit the road.

This time we check into the Marriott. Since I'm scheduled to testify the next morning, we have the evening to recover from the trip. I will have to get up very early so Sue will have time to dress herself and then get me into my uniform.

I sleep just fine.

Next morning, we head over to the Capitol at about 0830 hours. Dad drops us off in front of the Rayburn House Office Building, and Sue and I go inside to wait in the cafeteria while he parks the van.

We are eating our shredded wheat and banana when a woman approaches me.

"Aren't you Major Michael Donnelly?" she asks.

The word is out already? Jeesh, maybe it was the CIA.

"I'm Denise Nichols," she says. "I've spoken with your parents just about every week for the last year." A nurse who served in the Gulf, she's one of the activists. She also has her own strange illness to contend with. My parents have called her for emotional support and for information. Denise is often one of the first to learn of the latest medical theories relating to Gulf War illnesses.

She has also come to attend the hearing, she says, and when she saw an Air Force major in a wheelchair, well, she put the pieces together. She knows all about me. It is a little disconcerting, but at the same time reassuring to run into someone familiar with my story.

Dad finds us and after breakfast, we make our way upstairs about 15 minutes early.

I am surprised at the enormity of the room where I am to testify, the elegance. We enter through two huge oak doors that extend all the way up to the 30-foot ceiling. Inside, a chandelier hangs suspended from one of those architectural reliefs I've only ever seen in French castles.

Up front, the committee members sit facing a long table crowded with microphones. Rich oak paneling gleams on the walls, and a deep navy blue carpet patterned with yellow stars cushions the wheels as I roll toward the front. An American flag stands in the corner.

We take seats in the spectator section. Dad parks me on the end, partly in the aisle. I'm not feeling very talkative. I sit reviewing my statement, wondering how in the hell I ended up in this situation.

Suddenly, I am very, very nervous. The jitters are making my breath come in abbreviated little bursts as I try to calm my nerves, so I use my old trick. They're not shooting at me, I tell myself.

Ever since the war, I've found that only live ammunition aimed in my direction gets my heart really pumping. Except maybe talking about my illness and this insane circumstance I find myself in. As far as I know, no one here will break out a gun and start shooting during the hearing.

Trouble is, my trick doesn't work as well as usual. They are shooting at me. They're just not using bullets.

I am determined to have a say, though, to make some kind of impact. But if I had a choice, I would much rather be flying jets. Testifying against the Air Force, against the Pentagon, against my country is not exactly the way I thought my life would go. I would give almost anything to trade my place now with a seat in a fighter jet, my health restored.

But I am here to testify, and I will speak.

Slowly, my nerves steady. I review my opening sentence, over and over.

When they announce that the hearing will begin, an aide comes to tell Dad where to place me. Dad wheels me up, and pushes my legs up under the table. I place the sheets of my written testimony in front of me. Dad adjusts the microphone so that it points at my mouth. To my right sit two other individuals, also here to tell their stories.

Congressman Shays bangs the gavel and opens the hearing. He makes a short statement, and then Congressman Sanders of Vermont speaks. Then every committee member is given the chance to also make a brief opening statement. This is Washington, after all.

"We're going to hear first from Major Michael Donnelly," Shays announces, and the cameras turn on me. "Major Donnelly is a former F-16 pilot who flew 44 combat missions during the Persian Gulf War. He is a highly decorated Air Force veteran with 15 years of dedicated service. Major Donnelly, we are honored by your presence here today and very anxious to hear what you have to say. Please begin when you're ready."

Whereas moments ago I was all calmness, a rush of anxiety sweeps over me and I begin to sweat. I try to look only at the congressmen up at the front table.

"Congressman Shays," I begin. "Members of this committee."

My voice is wobbly. I think I sound teary. I am worried because I know it's hard to understand me. I will my tongue to behave, but it feels like a wet wad of inert muscle in my mouth.

Before I can begin, though, Shays interrupts me.

"Is his microphone on?" he asks no one in particular. An aide comes rushing up to adjust my mike. Moves it closer to my mouth. I cannot grab the stand to hold it close, so I must lean forward, stiffly.

"I apologize, Major Donnelly," Shays says. "Please forgive the interruption."

"That's kind of the way things have been going for me lately," I say. They laugh. Suddenly, I feel much better. Less tense, anyway.

"Don't feel bad," Shays says. "I lost five bucks on the way over here today." We laugh again.

"Please begin when you're ready, sir. And I apologize again."

I start again.

"Congressman Shays and members of this committee," I say, concentrating on my tongue, my jaw, on getting them to move. I am doing my best to enunciate, to put volume behind each word. I want them to hear me, to hear what I have come to say.

"I want to thank you for giving me the opportunity to testify before you today," I continue. "My name is Major Michael Donnelly," I say.

I look at them, every one of them, individually.

"I am not the enemy," I say. And then I begin to weep.

But I recover and I continue. The room is silent. I have the feeling it isn't often this quiet in here.

"Never during any of my missions during the war," I tell them, "was I warned of the threat of exposure to any chemical or biological weapons. Although we expected and trained for that eventuality, we never employed any of the procedures we learned because we were never told that there was any threat of exposure.

"Had we been warned," I tell them, "there were steps we could have and would have taken to protect ourselves."

I am feeling stronger and as I speak, I realize that I am doing the right thing.

I continue.

"Evidence now shows," I say, "that the chemical and biological munitions storage areas and production facilities that we bombed released clouds of fallout that drifted over our troops through the air—and that's where I was, in the air. While I don't remember a specific event that might have led to my illness, I do know of other pilots who do remember a specific incident that caused them later to become ill."

The cameras are all around me. I am glad. I hope my commanding officers are watching. I hope they're watching at the Pentagon. I hope they're hearing every word, loud and clear.

"I come before you today to tell you that I am yet another veteran from the Gulf War with a chronic illness."

I tell them the whole story. The strange symptoms. The fogging truck. The denial on the part of Air Force doctors. The initial offer of 50% disability and temporary retirement.

"To this day," I tell them, "no one from the DOD or VA has contacted me personally to involve me in any tests or studies. I myself have found more than nine other Gulf War veterans, some who have already come before you, who are also suffering from ALS.

"Why is there no special emergency study of this outbreak? Why is no one worried about what is obviously a frightening cluster of a terrible neurological illness among such a young and healthy population?

"One thing I can tell you: this is *not* stress.

"Why aren't the DOD and the VA warning everyone else who served in the Gulf War that they should avoid exposure to pesticides? How many more people are out there waiting for that one exposure that will put them over the top? Why is no one putting the word out? A warning could save the lives and health of many individuals, could save them from going through what I am now going through.

"I'll tell you why. Because the DOD is not interested in saving lives. The DOD is concerned that warning veterans and their families of that danger would be tantamount to admitting that something happened in the Gulf War that's making people sick.

"You've heard about all the recent bizarre air crashes lately. I wonder, how many of the air accidents and mishaps that have occurred since the end of the war have involved Gulf War veterans? Those numbers shouldn't be hard to find: the military keeps records on all of that. In fact, I wager that someone out there already knows the answer to that question and hasn't shared it, either because of a direct order not to or because the right person has yet to ask."

I know that Dad and Sue are still back there, listening to me speak. But I don't want to think about them now. This is my moment and I want to make the best of it.

"How many other pilots are still out there—flying—who are not quite feeling right? Just as I flew for four years after I returned from the Gulf, how many other pilots fear for their livelihood and the repercussions they know they would encounter if they were to speak up? They know what they'll hear: There's no conclusive evidence that there's any link between service in the Gulf and any illness.

"Imagine my dismay when the DOD announces $12 million (a drop in the bucket) to study Gulf War illnesses and four of those studies are centered around the effects of stress or post-traumatic stress disorder.

"You would think that the DOD and the VA would have an in-depth knowledge of the effects of stress after all the wars this country has fought. Most of them were a lot more 'stressful' than the Gulf War. Why aren't they taking our illnesses seriously?

"I'll tell you why, because that would take admitting that something happened in the Gulf War that's making people sick."

It's going well, I think, but my voice is starting to give. I push on.

"Part of the ongoing cover up has been to trivialize the illnesses that Gulf War veterans are suffering from. In the press and from the VA, you hear about skin rashes and joint aches, about insomnia and fatigue. There is no doubt that these are real symptoms and are debilitating in and of themselves. But what you don't hear about is the high incidence of rare cancers, neurological illnesses such as ALS, and immune-system disorders that are totally debilitating. And terminal.

"I say again, this is not stress. This is life and death.

"Why is it impossible to get accurate numbers from DOD and the VA about how many veterans are sick or have sought treatment? Why is it more important to protect certain high-placed government officials than to care for veterans who are sick? When it comes time to fund the military, budget concerns are usually set aside in the interest of national defense and the public good. Well, the national defense issue now is that it's public knowledge that the DOD mistreats people who serve.

"They don't want this story to get out because then America will have no one to fight its wars.

"Despite all that has happened, the primary goal now is not to find out whose fault all of this is. Someday, someone will need to investigate what happened and why. The people responsible for this tragedy should be found out and punished.

"The top priority now for all of us is to help veterans and their families get their health and their lives back. Or at least that should be the goal. That should be your goal.

"All I want is what I brought to the Air Force: my health.

"I'm not interested in hearing how surprised Generals Powell and Schwarzkopf are about how we were all exposed to chemical weapons, or that the CIA really did know Hussein had these weapons, or that the CIA alerted the DOD to this fact. It's obvious now that there's been a cover up going on all this time as more and more information gets released or discovered. It's time for those people who know something—and they do exist—to come forward. Maybe we can save some lives.

"During and after the war, we proclaimed to ourselves and to the world how we learned the lessons of Vietnam and fixed the military. We told ourselves that we had learned the lessons of Vietnam. That we had got it right this time.

"Last week, General Powell stated that we suffered only 149 casualties in the Gulf War.

"Well, I am here to tell you that the casualty count is still rising. Just like in Vietnam with Agent Orange, it appears that we didn't learn *all* the lessons. We still mistreat veterans. This country has again turned its back on the people who fight its wars, the individuals to whom it owes the most."

I am near the end, and I am glad. I cannot do much more of this. My mouth aches, my lungs are weary from pushing the air up behind each word.

"I want to thank you for what you are doing for the veterans who went to war for this country. Many of whom were squeezed out of the military right after the war and now find themselves out on the street, fighting the very institution they fought to defend.

"In the military, we have a tradition called the salute. It's used to show admiration and respect for an individual who has earned it. I salute you for what you are doing here. You go a long way in restoring this soldier's waning faith in a country that could so willingly desert its own."

At last I am finished. I have done it. I have spoken my piece. No matter what happens next, I feel I have done the right thing. I have not allowed this illness or the Pentagon's deceit to silence me.

"Remember," I tell them. "I am not the enemy."

Get me out of here, I think. I want to go home.

After the other two individuals sitting at the table testify, Dad turns me around and who looms before me but Bernard Rotsker, lately appointed special assistant for Gulf War illnesses. He is up next.

Mr. Rotsker has been chosen to succeed Dr. Steven Joseph, who was hounded from his position as undersecretary of medical affairs because of his unspeakable arrogance in dealing with veterans. Not because he lied. But because he lied so arrogantly, and the press caught him at it. Mr. Rotsker was hired to come in and tell the veterans, hey guys, I'm on your side. Let's find out what's happening here. He is an oily individual, oozing insincerity. A Ph.D. in economics from Syracuse University, he affects a misleading "Doctor." Dad calls him bullet-head, for the point at the crown of his shiny bald pate.

I look Mr. Bernard Rotsker right in the eye and I say, "I'm Major Mike Donnelly."

"Dr. Bernard Rotsker," he says blankly.

I don't know what I expected to see, but what I see is nothing much. His are not the eyes of empathy, of understanding, of concern. They are the eyes of a man who has an agenda, who lives his life by protocol and objective, in a world devoid of emotion. In a glance I can see that he is a man in control. Nothing out of the ordinary ever happens in Mr. Bernard Rotsker's world, nothing unpredictable, nothing that breaches the regulatory boundaries by which he has clearly fashioned his career.

My father says nothing to the man responsible for holding the truth hostage. My father wheels me past Mr. Bernard Rotsker.

"That man will rot in hell, sure as shit," Dad says over my shoulder once we get out of range. I can hear that he is crying, struggling to control his voice so I won't know.

"Goddamned bastard," he mutters. "May he rot in hell."

"Yeah," I nod. "May he rot in hell. At least he won't be lonely, what with all the friends who will join him there."

We stay and listen to Mr. Bernard Rotsker testify. He tells them there are only 9 to 11 cases of ALS—only!—which he claims, under oath, is well within the norm. We learn nine months later that I was not among the nine he counted. Nine months later, I am still not in their data bank, and there I was, under his nose, waving my arms.

If they haven't counted me, who else is not included in their data? I wonder. Have they even bothered to collect any real data? Who will ever know, since they don't allow any independent corroboration?

What country is this in which I find myself heir?

On our way out, after the hearing adjourns, Bernie Sanders approaches me, his eyes streaming. He reaches down and very gently kisses my cheek.

"I thought I knew courage," he says. "I was wrong. I never knew courage—until now."

We look for me on the news later that night, the next day, but find nothing. No one covers Major Michael Donnelly's testimony before the House Subcommittee on Government Reform and Oversight. Instead, the papers and television news shows cover other events: as I was testifying, Congress was approving a chemical weapons ban. At the same time, a terrorist group was calling in a sarin gas attack threat to the B'nai B'rith, located directly across the street from our hotel. As we pull up, the bomb squad is just leaving.

*   *   *

We follow winter up I-95, and arrive home late Friday night. I am exhausted by the exertion of traveling, of testifying. I have hoarded my strength for weeks to get through this ordeal, and now I must rest. I am glad to be home where spring is still a rumor and the promise of summer a faint whisper I can pretend I don't yet hear. I am grateful to travel backwards up the seasons a little, bargain a bit more time.

The kids are in bed when we get home, and Sue's mom is in the living room, watching television. We try to keep it down, but we wake Erin and Sean up, or more likely they have been waiting. They tumble down the stairs in their pajamas, rubbing their eyes in pleasure and relief.

"Daddy! Mommy!" they screech in sleepy voices.

"How was your trip?" Erin asks me. I wonder if she understands where we have been.

I haven't told them where we were going or why. I have tried so hard to protect them from this nightmare. Only lately have I begun to realize that when liars rule, there are no hiding places, even for children.

"It was good, honey," I say.

She places herself carefully on my lap. My hands lie mute beneath her weight. I am unable to move them, unable to lift them to embrace her. She leans back against my chest, her head under my chin, arms around my neck.

"Daddy!" Sean shouts. "Want to see my new karate move! I learned number twelve!"

"Go ahead, Bub," I answer. "Show me number twelve."

He leaps into the air, punches the sky with his right fist, then lands on his bare feet. He punches left, his imaginary enemy vanquished.

"Hai!" he shouts. "Hai!"

Part V

Fallen Angels

For by your words will you be acquitted,
by your words will you be condemned.

Matthew 12:37

He will judge between the nations
and will settle disputes for many peoples.
They will beat their swords into ploughshares
and their spears into pruning hooks.
Nation will not take up sword against nation,
nor will they train for war anymore.

Isaiah 1:4

This illness is a vagrant, and it has made my body its home. It is an invading army, and I am the occupied zone. It is a parasite on my health, and I its unwilling host.

This illness is all of these things and none of them. Mostly, this illness is an artist of the grotesque, and my flesh is its raw material. It has sculpted my muscles so that I no longer recognize myself. A few months ago I accidentally caught my own reflection in the mirror. I now prefer not to look in mirrors, because I don't want to see that face, carved to sinew and bone by the chisel of disease. I don't need a mirror, though, to see that the web of flesh that joins thumb to hand is wasted, that my toes curl inward.

I have become a local news regular, and I am most shocked when I see myself on television. Who is that? I wonder, for the split second before I realize that the stunned face looking back at me is my own. Oh, I think, and the face and I share a disastrous moment of recognition. We know one another, but not well.

In my mind, I am still and always the same. I am still and always Michael, named for the archangel. I am still and always Michael, pilot, athlete, hunter, father, husband, son. Michael, patriot. American.

It's just that my body has become an inert weight suspended like a pendulum from the firmament of my mind, that pendulum ticking out the minutes of my life, and time is no longer a generous, infinite resource.

I live so much in my thoughts now that the collision of external and internal is a shock. How am I to know for certain which is real? The external is more solid, more cumbersome, a burden I must carry. Does that make it more real? I know that self I see on television is not me. But is the self who inhabits the photographs on my study wall me? This I cannot know for certain. My internal world, where I stride effortlessly across tarmacs, climb into cockpits, finger buttons on the throttle, the stick of some jet, that world is vivid, compelling, weightless. Is that reality?

Almost two years ago this illness gave birth to fasciculations in my legs, quivers of disaster telegraphing their message of doom up my nerve endings, corroding my muscles as they traveled. Now they have bred and multiplied, these tremors, and their offspring beat in my shoulders, my cheeks.

I think of them as thousands of birds, trapped beneath my skin, flinging themselves against the prison of my flesh, frantically flapping their wings for release. Gladly would I grant them their freedom. Gladly would I pierce my skin to liberate them, slice the thin membrane that imprisons them and watch them soar, triumphant, exuberant, into the sun. But they insist on the warm, known comfort of incarceration, these traitors, each the alate despot of its own red island of tyranny. In the end, like all parasites, even they will be betrayed by their omnivorous persistence, their gluttony rendering all of us victims to a treachery we could never have invented on our own.

Nordo

November 1997

We didn't yet have the new modified van when I went to the South Windsor Rotary Club to accept my service award the other night, so we had to use the minivan. Getting in and out, what's known in the trade as "transferring," has become difficult. I used to be able to hook my hands into the window opening, haul my body up, slowly twist around and then fall backwards into my seat. Now, though, my arms are stiffer, and I have almost no strength left in my legs. I just can't help much with the transfer. Especially when I'm wearing dress shoes that don't have any traction.

We make it into the banquet hall, despite the difficulties, and Sue feeds me antipasto, baked ziti, and filet mignon so rare I worry it might bleed to death on my plate. When award time comes, I begin to get nervous about making my acceptance speech. I've always been pretty good at public speaking, and in fact have suffered unfairly from a reputation of being something of a jokester. This time is different, though. It's not jokes that are on my mind.

I've been planning this speech for weeks, ever since I learned about the award. Not just what I'm going to say. That's the easy part. I am worried more about how I will manage with the microphone, if anyone will understand me. If I will keep my composure and not let the frustration I have come to live with well up and drown my words.

As for speech, it has become harder not just because of my uncooperative muscles, but because I can tell people are not understanding me. I can see them trying to hide their confusion, trying to pretend they understand as they intently watch my lips. I repeat my words to try to make them clearer. Mostly, I'm nordo these days: I'm flying no radio, and while I can still receive messages, I can't transmit my situation, my position.

In conversation, I sometimes find it easier to say nothing at all. The frustration never diminishes, but I am learning to let the little things go unsaid, undone. No longer a participant, I sit in my chair and observe life from a distance. In my head, I interject an occasional witty remark and even catch myself smiling at the imagined appreciation of my humor.

"And finally," the moderator announces, "we would like to recognize Major Michael Donnelly as a Rotary Club Paul Harris Fellow." I am trying not to blush. The other award recipients all have 30 years of service to the community and here I am, just under 40, insinuating myself into their ranks.

The moderator detaches the microphone and draws it up to my place at the head table. Sue stands beside me, holding my plaque, smiling proudly out at the audience, who have all gotten to their feet to honor me, which has the opposite effect of what they intend, however, because only I remain seated. This has become a familiar perspective of late, and one I have needed time to come to accept. Actually, I still don't accept it, but here I sit.

Altitude used to be my ally. When I wasn't airborne, riding the sky in the cockpit of a jet, I saw the world from a height of six feet two, and my horizon was mostly composed of the tops of other people's heads. Now I often find myself looking up to make eye contact, like I've lost something down here and need to keep looking skyward for the clues. My perspective of the world may have changed, but in my mind, I am still a giant of a man, still six feet two, and when they call my name, I hold my head up high, like a tall man looking out over a crowd.

The microphone is in front of my lips now, and I peer down at it as if it were alive, as if it might tell me what to do. Time has slowed in that way it has of magnifying moments you wish would pass. And while I am a prisoner of this chair, at the same time I seem to see the whole room as if I were suspended from the ceiling, watching like a disinterested observer, or a movie director setting a scene in a melodramatic movie. The hero speaks slowly into the mike, his eyes watery with effort. The crowd stands rapt, hands on hearts or clasped over breasts.

I speak. I do not look around me because I do not want to see their faces. I must just assume they understand me. In my head, my words are perfectly formed. But in my ear, I can't tell if I am intelligible or not. Like a musician with a head injury, I've lost my perfect pitch and can no longer hear if the sounds I make are rhapsodic or dissonant.

I must concentrate now to force the muscles in my mouth and throat to do what they used to do so effortlessly. My lung capacity has diminished as the muscles surrounding them have become flaccid and diseased. I have to concentrate on trying to take a deeper breath and forcing the air up and out with my diaphragm. Otherwise, there's no volume behind the words.

My dialogue with the world is interior now. It's not that I don't have re-actions or don't want to contribute to conversations. It's just that I have discovered that speech inhabits its own dimension. It travels at its own speed and has no patience for me to slowly puff out my words. Speech travels at the speed of sound, and I, who used to travel faster than sound, now find myself locked in some other dimension, one where time is both accelerated and slowed, where the mind lives an isolated life, where so-liloquy is the only dialogue.

I talk to myself these days, silently, and the constant inner monologue that we all have running through our heads has now become not the background music but the very script of my life. I have internalized all that was once external, I who lived so much in the world. Only occasion-ally does the outside distract me from this version of my life, a life that has become very intimate, so personal that I cannot share it with anyone com-pletely. It would seem too foreign, too strange.

In the outside world, people are applauding.

Thank you, I tell the Rotary Club. I am honored, I say. I don't know what they hear.

I finish, bow my head to the applause and try to keep the tears of frus-tration from running out of my eyes and onto my cheeks. I wait for the audience to find another victim so I can snuff up my snot and have Sue blow my nose.

Finally we are done. They take photos, the recipients together, my fam-ily around me, and then they release us to the night. We wheel out to the van, load me up and head home in the wet autumn darkness. I really am honored to receive their award, but also a little ashamed. I feel like an im-postor. When I was living the life they honored, I never thought of myself as placing service above self interest. I just loved what I did and wanted to keep doing it.

The plaque hangs on my wall of fame now, above my computer, with my diplomas, the photos of me in my cockpit, my medals and other awards. I have integrated my new award into the script in my head.

*   *   *

Yesterday, Sue took me to an appointment at the University of Con-necticut ALS clinic, where I've been a regular since we moved back out here. I didn't want to rely on the VA alone for care, not that they haven't treated me well. The people at the VA center in Newington have done all they could for me. I just wanted to get private care, too. My distrust became too powerful to ignore, and I wanted to be doubly sure my treatment was the most current available.

Dr. Will North is one of the kindest physicians I have ever met. How he manages to stay so compassionate given what he deals with every day, I have no idea. But he always finds the time to return our calls, no matter how often we bother him or what new theory we want to check with him. Never once have I felt I am a bother. I have found a doctor, like Dr. Brown and Dr. Nathan, who understands what it is like to be living this disease.

I have an inkling of what this appointment is about. I know what's happening in my body better than anyone, and I know I'm losing ground. I also know what comes next. Dr. Tolland in Washington made sure of that. So I've already given some thought to the ventilator and feeding tube question before we arrive. I don't think Sue has any idea.

Dr. North seats us in his office, offers us water, coffee. We decline. He looks weary, very sad. I feel sorry for him. This can't be easy. He knows how hard I have fought.

"Michael, Susan," he says, sighing, "there comes a time with this illness when we have to discuss some very painful things, decisions that you have to make." Dr. North speaks quietly, and he is not at all condescending. I get the feeling that he knows we are each of us equally vulnerable to fate.

He is trying hard to be gentle, but I sense Sue wilting next to me. She, too, has fought hard. But lately she has softened, and I have felt us coming around again, through the pain and anger, back to love.

"I wish we didn't have to have this discussion," he continues. "I hope you both know that. I wish there was something else I could offer you. Some treatment, some way to buy more time."

Now Sue is weeping, and she never cries. I think this may be the first time she has cried about this in front of anyone else. It is a soft weeping, not angry.

"I am so very sorry, Susan," Dr. North says. "But it is important for Michael—and for you—to discuss these things and make a conscious choice while Michael is still able. We've found that most people suffering from fatal illnesses have very strong feelings about whether they wish to be put on a ventilator, when the time comes—and I'm not saying it has—and whether they want a feeding tube."

He is looking at me, and I at him. Even now, there is a part of me that disbelieves. That thinks we are maybe talking about some other poor slob out in the hall. But the poor slob is me, and I have already made my decision. I start to try to speak.

With Sue acting as interpreter—she understands my speech better than anyone—Dr. North lets me tell him that I've already made my decision.

"I do reserve the right to change my mind," I add. He laughs, tenderly.

"I think I've gotten to know you pretty well this last year, Mike," Dr. North says, "and I have the feeling I know what you're going to say." He pauses, considers. "And it *is* your choice, no matter what. But before you make a final decision, Mike, let me offer some advice. Don't rush it. Take a look at these two videos. They tell you exactly what to expect. It's always best to have all the facts before you act, don't you think?" He smiles, looks from me to Sue and back again.

Outside it is a brown November day, brown leaves flying through the air, brown grass, brown trees. I catch myself losing track of what he is saying. I follow instead the oak leaves as they ride the stiff wind, flutter across the wide expanse of winter lawn.

Sue cannot raise her eyes to meet Dr. North's. She rests her hand on my arm, and I turn my attention back into the room.

"How much time, doctor?" Sue finally asks, her voice thick.

"I wish I could say. Maybe six months, maybe three. Maybe a year. We just don't know," he concludes, and I can tell that he sees this as a personal failure on his part.

"I'm sorry," he adds. I believe him.

Sue cries the whole way home, silently. I look out the window at the November afternoon. I watch the cars pass us on the highway, lock eyes once or twice with their passengers, a young girl, maybe thirteen, a man in his 30s. Their faces speak to me, mutely, through the glass. What other stories travel these roads this afternoon, I wonder. Who else just got a final time sheet and was shown the clock?

The kids are already home from school when we get back to the house. We have no time to recover, compose ourselves. Maybe it's better like this. Maybe not. Anyway, it doesn't matter. This is just how it is.

*   *   *

It snowed last night, an early snow, wet and heavy. The kids were up before dawn, digging through boxes in the attic looking for their snow things. Now it is twilight, a steel blue November twilight, and the trees are stalks of black lace against the darkening winter sky.

Erin and Bubba have been outside all day with their new friends. They must be freezing, I think. But they are at that age where they don't notice how cold they are. I remember that age. It seems like yesterday when I was sledding down a hill behind the school long after the sun had set.

They are having too much fun to freeze. I have positioned my wheelchair at an angle before the far window in the living room, and from here I watch them as they slide down the neighbor's hill, crash to a stop in the sidewalk gully. There is no way they can see me from here, even if I had the light on, which I don't. Inside, my computer glows in the darkness, occasionally beeps at me, reminding me of its pulsing presence.

In my mind, I am sledding with my children, sitting upright on a Flexible Flyer, Erin in front, my knees encircling her, Sean grabbing hold of my shoulders from his perch in the back, where he stands. We shriek as we plummet down the incline, the wind polishing our cheeks, the insides of our mouths.

It is this that sustains me now, the solace of memories and dreams. Sometimes I get confused about what is real, what I am living now or what is in my mind. Or about what has actually happened, whether my fantasies are only that, fantasies. Did I really fly F-16s? Was I ever healthy and whole? I still resist when I can, but mostly I live the interior life of a man set on a path that seems to lead in only one direction, and I allow myself the comfort of those reveries.

In them I am again a tall, vigorous man. I carry Sean on my shoulders, swing Erin in circles, her whirling feet arcs of light that encircle us. I fly my F-16, surf the treetops, skim the shining earth. I am smiling, powerful, unheedful of my hands as they work the throttle, the stick.

And when I am not flying, not playing with my children, I am wondering what I will say when the time comes for me to stand before my maker and explain myself. I believe we are each accountable for our actions, I will say. I believe everything happens for a reason.

I will have to explain why I dropped bombs, why I killed people, some of them no doubt innocent, if there is any such thing as a human being who is not innocent, who deserves to have a bomb fall on his home, her head. I am working on my explanation. I'm not sure how it will play.

I pity those others, those who pushed us over the edge of Eden into hell, those who will have a much more perverse story to recount, who will have to explain the crooked path of their treachery, explain why they betrayed their comrades in arms, why they stood by and watched their fellow countrymen and warriors get sick. Why they let us die, when all the while they knew exactly what it was that poisoned us, and no doubt, what would have saved our lives.

All the while they harbored their secrets in the locked filing cabinets of complacency, chose complicity over justice, deceit over truth. It is the boring, unchanging story of "humanity" I suppose, and I suppose I was naïve to think I would never find it happening in my own country, never find myself and my family on the wrong end of that equation.

They committed acts of murder, those traitors; I committed acts of war and called myself a patriot. Is there a difference, I wonder?

I would have preferred to remain a warrior and a patriot. I would have preferred to avoid this education in the sad detours of the human mind. I would have preferred a different ending to this story. But this is the ending I have met.

Reluctantly have I beaten my sword into a ploughshare and sown this field of pages with my words. Perhaps I may lose the battle, perhaps not. But I will win the war, because now you know my story.

You tell me: what is false, and what is true?

Epilogue

The Gulf War changed forever the nature of warfare. By establishing early air superiority, and by relying on a vast and sophisticated system of satellites in outer space, the United States was able to bring the war to the enemy before the enemy ever had a chance to launch an offensive. It was a war for the information age, in which information truly became a weapon. To this day, the Pentagon continues to flaunt its successes, calling it the first-ever clinically perfect war. Trouble is, today the clinics are full of that war's casualties, and many of them are without health insurance, destitute, unable to work and waiting to die.

But it was not just the nature of warfare that changed during Desert Storm. The nature of casualties and fatalities also changed. This was a war where information was not the only invisible weapon. Time will eventually reveal the truth, as it did decades after the Pentagon denied that Agent Orange caused cancer, birth defects and early deaths for thousands of Vietnam vets and their families.

We are the victims of a perversely modern form of friendly fire. Many of us have been poisoned, perhaps all of us, and some of that poison was allegedly manufactured in that most American of states, Texas.

Just as the war relied upon the wizardry of computers, so has our battle for the truth. Thousands of us converse daily on the Internet, through Gulf War veterans' mailing lists, on webpages of our own design. We tell one another our stories, we locate the comfort of truth and camaraderie in this most democratic of media. Daily we thwart the efforts of the world's most powerful, wealthiest aggressor with the click of a mouse.

The long-term effects of the perfect war, a war that lasted only 36 days, are yet to be tallied, and the fatalities and casualties continue to mount. While the Pentagon has ensured that you will not see us dying in your living room every night, every sick Gulf War veteran has a story to tell, a story that may never be known to the millions of Americans who supported the men and women who fought that neat but deadly war.

We salute these courageous men and women, heroes all, so that their suffering may not go unacknowledged, their sacrifice not have been in vain.

A Fighter Pilot's Glossary of Terms

More than most professions perhaps, fighter pilots have their own language. They travel faster than the speed of sound, members of an elite fraternity of men and women who have endured incredible physical and mental tests to achieve their position. Because they soar above life's mundane realities every day, because every day could be their last, because they live a life different from most, and they speak in code.

When you're moving at 800 or 1000 feet per second, 300 feet above the ground, or when you're going face to face with an enemy at 1200 miles an hour, seconds can be a lifetime and mean the difference between life and death. Your own, that is, or your comrade's. For these reasons, brevity is key. A pilot packs as much information into the fewest words in the quickest way possible.

Naturally, pilot talk gets adapted to everyday life, too. We often found ourselves speaking pilot on the ground, at home, in K-Mart, at the pizza place. And especially at the bar.

Some of the terms you see in this glossary are used in this book. Others are included as a way of sharing a sense of the unique dimension in which I traveled.

AAA—Anti-aircraft artillery. What ground forces shoot at enemy aircraft. Also known as flak and triple A.

Bandit—A definite enemy aircraft, identification confirmed.

Bandits, twelve o'clock—Bad guys, dead ahead.

Bingo—Refers to a preset fuel level which requires the pilot to return home. The pilot otherwise risks running out of fuel.

Blind—The opposite of visual. The pilot does not have visual contact with a friendly aircraft.

Bogey—A possible enemy aircraft that is as yet unconfirmed.

Burners—Refers to the afterburner of a jet engine, an area located in the rear of the engine, where the highly compressed air exits the engine. Raw fuel is dumped into this area through spray bars and then ignited when a pilot moves the throttle to a certain position, usually all the way forward. This augments the thrust and accelerates the aircraft at a high rate. A pilot will reserve use of the burners to an absolutely necessary situation due to the high rate of fuel consumed. Also known as A/B, blowers, or the wick, as in "Let's light the wick and get the hell out of here."

CBU—Cluster bomb unit.

Check six—Pilot talk for "look behind you." Aviators speak in terms of a clock, with themselves at the center: 12 o'clock high means "dead ahead and above."

Engaged offensive—Used by one pilot to tell his wingman that he is engaged in an air-to-air dogfight and that he has the advantage.

FAC—Forward air controller, who spots targets and adjusts fire for artillery and/or airstrikes. FACs liase between the infantry and air or artillery.

Flares—When someone calls "Flares! Flares!" he is telling the other pilot to punch a button in the jet that ejects flares out of the back of the aircraft which are designed to lure a heat-seeking missile away from the aircraft.

G-suit—Special inflatable trousers fighter pilots wear, the G-suit (gravity suit) helps minimize the effect of G forces. The trousers have a stomach bladder, two thigh bladders and two calf bladders. The bladders inflate automatically when the pilot pulls Gs. Their purpose is to give the pilot something to tense his muscles and push against in order to keep the blood from pooling in the lower extremities under high Gs.

Hot pit—Like a pit stop in auto racing, a previously designated point to which a pilot taxis, then stays in the cockpit while crews swarm all over the jet to refuel and re-arm it.

HUD—Heads-up display. A combining glass mounted directly in front of the canopy upon which all or most of the aircraft data is projected so that the pilot can continue to fly while looking forward through the canopy. A combining glass is a transparent glass plate.

IFF—Identification friend or foe. Each plane is equipped with a radar transponder—known as a "parrot," ergo "squawk"—that broadcasts a distinctive picture, so that friendly radar operators can tell whether an aircraft is friend or foe. In addition, each transponder is programmed to produce multiple frequencies, so that each plane produces a particular blip on the radar screen, enabling the radar operator to identify the specific aircraft.

IMC—Instrument meteorological condition. The opposite of VMC—visual meteorological condition—IMC requires the pilot to fly on instruments only because visibility is so poor.

Lat-longs—Latitude and longitude of a given location.

MIG—Soviet-built fighter aircraft. It's a general term assigned to a wide variety of aircraft. MIG is short for Migregorian, a Soviet aircraft designer.

No joy—The pilot does not have visual contact with a bogey, bandit, target or other object.

Nordo—A pilot who is flying nordo is flying without a transmitter. While he may be able to hear messages, he is mute. He cannot communicate his position or situation.

Pickle button—Refers to the button on the stick which releases the bomb or missile which the pilot has selected in his weapons system.

Pipper—The aiming dot displayed in the HUD which the pilot uses to determine where his bombs or missiles will fall.

Randolph—A point on the ground that can be either a steer point or any other fixed, prearranged location. In the case of Psycho Andrews' downing, Randolph was just the name the other pilots gave to the particular steer point they were using to try to locate him. They could have assigned any name to the steer point.

Recce—Reconnaissance flights.

RWR—Radar warning receiver. A screen or audible device whose purpose is to warn the pilot when enemy radar and/or missiles are looking at him or being fired at him.

SA—Situational awareness. It's what every pilot needs to stay alive. SA refers to a pilot's ability to be aware of his total environment, the events occurring around him, what is happening inside the jet, where he is headed (up, down), altitude, the location of the horizon in relation to the jet.

SAM—Surface-to-air missile. Any missile or rocket whose purpose is to shoot down aircraft. There are both radar-guided and heat-seeking SAMs.

Sortie—One flight for one aircraft, a sortie can refer to any flight, including combat missions. Pronounced sor-tee, as opposed to the CNN buffoon who started to call them sor-ti, with the French pronunciation. This induced a spate of French-accented exchanges among the pilots, who asked one another, "How was your sor-ti today, mon ami?" and "Going on ze sor-ti aujordhui?" or "Mon Dieu, you would not believe my sor-ti today!"

Steer point—A predesignated point on the ground associated with a specific latitude and longitude which the pilot loads into his inertial navigation system. It allows pilots to refer to specific points on the ground without revealing their location.

Tally ho—This means the pilot has visual contact with a bogey, bandit or target.

Visual—Refers to a pilot's ability to see a specific aircraft.

VMC—Visual meteorological condition. When a pilot is flying in clear air where he can reference the horizon in order to maintain control of the aircraft attitude.

Zulu time—There are 26 time zones on the globe and Zulu time, also known as Greenwich Mean Time (GMT), is the letter assigned to the time zone in which GMT falls. GMT became the Royal Navy's standard when the British navy ruled the world. Using Zulu gives everyone the same starting point so that no matter what time zone you're in, you know what time it is.

Congressional Report— House of Representatives

105th Congress, *1st Session*   Union Calendar No. 228, Report 105–388

GULF WAR VETERANS' ILLNESSES: VA, DOD CONTINUE TO RESIST STRONG EVIDENCE LINKING TOXIC CAUSES TO CHRONIC HEALTH EFFECTS

November 7, 1997.—Committed to the Committee of the Whole House on the State of the Union and ordered to be printed.

Mr. Burton of Indiana, from the Committee on Government Reform and Oversight, submitted the following

SECOND REPORT

On October 31, 1997, the Committee on Government Reform and Oversight approved and adopted a report entitled "Gulf War Veterans' Illnesses: VA, DOD Continue to Resist Strong Evidence Linking Toxic Causes to Chronic Health Effect." The chairman was directed to transmit a copy to the Speaker of the House.

I. Summary

Responding to requests by veterans, the subcommittee in March 1996 initiated a far-reaching oversight investigation into the status of efforts to understand the clusters of symptoms and debilitating maladies known collectively as "Gulf War Syndrome." We sought to ensure sick Gulf War veterans were being diagnosed accurately, treated effectively and compensated fairly for service-connected disabilities, despite official denials and scientific uncertainty regarding the exact cause of their ailments. We also sought to determine whether the Gulf War research agenda was properly focused on the most likely, not just the most convenient, hypotheses to explain Gulf War veterans' illnesses.

After 19 months of investigation and hearings, the subcommittee finds the status of efforts on Gulf War issues by the Department of Veterans Affairs (VA), the Department of Defense (DOD), the Central Intelligence Agency (CIA) and the Food and Drug Administration (FDA) to be irreparably flawed. We find those efforts hobbled by institutional inertia that mistakes motion for progress. We find those efforts plagued by arrogant incuriosity and a pervasive myopia that sees a lack of evidence as proof. As a result, we find current approaches to research, diagnosis and treatment unlikely to yield answers to veterans' life-or-death questions in the foreseeable, or even far distant, future.

We do not come to these conclusions lightly. Nor do we discount all that has been done to care for, cure and compensate Gulf War veterans. But lives have been lost, and many more lives are at stake.

Six years and hundreds of millions of dollars have been spent in the effort to determine the causes of the illnesses besetting Gulf War veterans. Yet, when asked what progress has been made healing sick Gulf War veterans, VA and DOD can't say where they've been and concede they may never get where they're going. The CIA continues to resist broader declassification of Gulf War records. The FDA meekly chastises the DOD for the failure to observe agreed-upon rules for the humane use of experimental drugs.

Sadly, when it comes to diagnosis, treatment and research for Gulf War veterans, we find the federal government too often has a tin ear, a cold heart and a closed mind.

Our hearings convinced us the journey from cause to cure for Gulf War veterans runs through the pools, clouds and plumes of toxins in which they lived and fought. It is a journey VA and DOD might never have taken but for persistent pressure from this subcommittee, and other House and Senate panels, that forced the Pentagon to acknowledge a "watershed event"—the probable exposure of United States troops to chemical weapons fallout at Khamisiyah, Iraq.

With that first admission, the three pillars of government denial—no credible detections, no exposures, no health effects—began to crumble. As the number of US troops presumed exposed grew from 400 to almost 100,000, as the credibility of the other chemical detections was sustained, and as private research probed the parallels between Gulf War illnesses and the known symptoms of chemical poisoning, some significant role for toxins in causing, triggering or amplifying neurological damage and chronic symptoms could no longer be denied.

Those denials and delays are symptomatic of a system content to presume the Gulf War produced no delayed casualties, and determined to shift the burden of proof onto sick veterans to overcome that presumption. That task has been made difficult, if not impossible, because most of the medical records needed to prove toxic causation are missing or destroyed. Nevertheless, VA and DOD insist upon reaping the benefit of any doubts created by the absence of those records.

The subcommittee believes the current presumptions about neurotoxic causes and effects should be reversed and the benefit of any doubt should inure to the sick veteran.

Finally, we reluctantly conclude that responsibility for Gulf War illnesses, especially the research agenda, must be placed in a more responsive agency, independent of the DOD and the VA.

The battle to cure Gulf War illnesses must be fought at the cellular, molecular and genetic levels if we hope to heal the delayed wounds of that war and protect future warriors. Absent precise exposure data which can never be recaptured, the best evidence linking toxic causes to chronic effects lies within the bodies and minds of Gulf War veterans. That evidence has been too long ignored.

NOTE: On June 4, 1998, a bill proposing that responsibility for the investigation of Gulf War illnesses be taken away from the Pentagon and the VA and be given to an independent GAO agency met with resistance in committee. The compromise bill to be reported out of committee leaves responsibility for treatment and investigation in the hands of the same agencies and individuals who have ensured that we will never know what happened to our soldiers in Desert Storm—the Pentagon and the VA.

About the Authors

MAJOR MICHAEL DONNELLY retired from the U.S. Air Force in October 1996 after 15 years of active duty. At the time of his retirement, Major Donnelly was the Divisional Chief of Standardization and Evaluation of the world's largest flying training wing instructor force attached to the 80th Flying Training Wing at Sheppard Air Force Base in Wichita Falls, Texas. An accomplished F-16 pilot, he flew 44 successful combat sorties during the Persian Gulf War with the 10th Tactical Fighter Squadron, 363 Tactical Fighter Wing. Major Donnelly's awards include the Meritorious Service Medal; the Air Medal with three Oak Leaf Clusters; the Air Force Commendation Medal with four Oak Leaf Clusters; the Aerial Achievement Medal and the Air Force Achievement Medal. Among his other achievements are a Top Gun award and Pilot of the Quarter Award. Major Donnelly has also been recognized by the International Rotary Club as a Paul Harris Fellow. In addition to testifying before the House of Representatives, Major Donnelly serves on Connecticut's Persian Gulf Veterans' Information Commission, formed at the order of the legislature to assist Desert Storm veterans in receiving the benefits and support they earned. He lives with his wife Susan and their two young children in South Windsor, Connecticut.

DENISE DONNELLY, a professional writer and the sister of Major Donnelly, has been a fiction editor at the *Missouri Review* and has taught English and creative writing at Tufts University and the University of Missouri. She lives in Rockport, Massachusetts.